AF729836

Praise for *Big Time Off*

"In our work-obsessed culture, grabbing even a few days off is hard—let alone taking a real sabbatical. But it can be done, and it might be the most important career move you ever make. Read this book to see why—and how to do it."

—Arthur C. Brooks, Harvard professor and
#1 *New York Times* bestselling author

"Sabbaticals of various types have played a major role in my life. So, I was thrilled to read DJ DiDonna's compelling and nuanced take on this often overlooked yet undeniably powerful strategy."

—Cal Newport, *New York Times* bestselling author
of *Slow Productivity* and *Deep Work*

"This book is a long-overdue challenge to the way we've been taught to think about work. Backed by original research and compelling stories, DJ DiDonna elegantly makes the case that stepping away from your job could be the most important thing you can do for your success and your happiness. A practical yet empowering guide, this book is essential reading for reclaiming your direction and your life."

—Laurie Santos, professor of psychology at Yale University
and host of *The Happiness Lab* podcast

"Could our best life be the one we step back from? An insightful and convincing call to take the time to live the examined life."

—Daniel Gilbert, Edgar Pierce Professor of Psychology at
Harvard University and *New York Times* bestselling
author of *Stumbling on Happiness*

"I read DJ DiDonna's beautifully written book with admiration—and, admittedly, a touch of envy. *Big Time Off* is filled with compelling stories that reveal the surprising power of taking extended time away from work to rediscover meaning and vitality. And if you anticipate thinking, 'That sounds wonderful, but there's no way I could do it,' don't worry—DiDonna offers a thoughtful, practical guide to help you make big time off possible in your own life."

—Amy C. Edmondson, Novartis Professor of Leadership and Management at Harvard Business School and author of *Right Kind of Wrong*

"The clearest and most persuasive case I've seen for why stepping away from work can change a life. DiDonna shows that sabbaticals aren't indulgences—they're powerful engines of renewal, creativity, and reinvention. If you've ever wondered whether time off could really matter, read this book."

—Herminia Ibarra, Charles Handy Professor of Organisational Behaviour at London Business School and author of *Working Identity*

"DiDonna shares groundbreaking work on sabbaticals with expertise and vulnerability. I riddled my copy with notes, highlights, and exclamation marks as I considered his challenge that we carve out time to be fully human. This practical guide is both an existential call to action and a life-affirming offering of hope."

—Dolly Chugh, professor of management at NYU Stern School of Business and author of *The Person You Mean to Be*

"Many of us secretly sense that our lives are moving faster than our souls can follow. This book names that truth and offers something rare: permission. DJ DiDonna shows that the modern quest for a sabbatical is really a rediscovery of the ancient human need for a Sabbath—a rhythm of stepping away in order to return whole. This is not a book about escaping your life; it's about reentering it more fully, with clarity, intention, and heart."

—Jerry Colonna, CEO and cofounder of Reboot.io and author of *Reboot* and *Reunion*

big time off

The Transformative Power of Sabbaticals and How to Take One

DJ DiDonna

Simon Acumen
New York Amsterdam/Antwerp London
Toronto Sydney/Melbourne New Delhi

SIMON
ACUMEN

An Imprint of Simon & Schuster, LLC
1230 Avenue of the Americas
New York, NY 10020

First Simon Acumen hardcover edition July 2026

SIMON ACUMEN and colophon are registered trademarks of Simon & Schuster, LLC

INTERIOR DESIGN BY KARLA SCHWEER

Manufactured in the United States of America

10 9 8 7 6 5 4 3 2 1

Library of Congress Control Number: 2026934439

ISBN 978-1-6680-6089-6
ISBN 978-1-6680-6091-9 (ebook)

Certain names and identifying details have been changed.

To: KCU, BUD, and NED

CONTENTS

big time off

Introduction

I grew up terrified of having a midlife crisis. The whole scenario was seared into my imagination from a young age: a guy in a red convertible flying down a coastal highway, tie flapping in the wind with reckless abandon.

I absorbed this story about midlife through osmosis, from the countless movies, TV shows, and books that warned of the possibility of burning out or, worse, spending a life heading down the wrong path. When it came time to choose my own career, I was determined to avoid this fate, and I knew exactly how I'd do it. Unlike my red-convertible-driving protagonist, who I assumed was some corporate drone, I'd pursue work with Meaning and Purpose. I was going to figure out what was authentic to me at an early age and grab it by the horns.

It all seemed so obvious: you can't have a midlife crisis if your life is crafted intentionally, if it's authentically yours.

You can't burn out from your dream job.

Or so I thought.

Twenty years later, I felt I'd escaped my fate. Together with two academics, I cofounded a company called EFL Global that created a new, more inclusive credit score that helped entrepreneurs in emerging markets grow their small businesses. The product impacted millions of lives and created jobs all over the world. Plus, it was fun work. We had a great company culture comprising talented employees and good humans. My life was exciting. I traveled to dozens of countries and spent weekends exploring fascinating corners of the world, all while doing something that helped people. I was thirty-three years old, and professional life was as much of an adventure as my childhood self could've hoped for.

One late fall day, I had just left the recording studio at WGBH, NPR's Boston chapter, where I'd been interviewed for a segment. It was the latest in a string of public-facing victories, and while the thrill of being on NPR was enough to boost my mood that afternoon, like so many other accolades, after it was over, I returned to what had become my new normal: all-consuming dissatisfaction.

Despite all the marquee news on the job front, my personal life was in shambles. I felt chronically disengaged, was increasingly snappy with my colleagues, and presided over an unfortunate and wispy beard. Our company spanned more than a dozen countries, and the travel had taken a toll on my sleeping habits. My most promising romantic relationship in five years had failed. My lifestyle was great for grand gestures and vacations to far-flung places, but it was incompatible with the rhythms of a healthy relationship. That same fall, my parents had worked up the courage to tell me I'd become increasingly unreliable. They'd given up casually reaching out to me, intimidated by time zone math and worried they'd catch me in a bad mood. The culmination of this dynamic hit when a last-minute acquisition deal pulled me from a dinner table in New Hampshire celebrating my father's seventieth birthday to a boardroom in South Africa. The company had gotten my time and attention, while my family got short shrift.

It made no sense. The gap between how I felt and how I was doing on paper felt vast. Which inevitably led me to wonder: If all this doesn't satisfy me, what will?

Something—maybe everything—had to change.

Calling this realization a product of burnout and overwork alone doesn't fully do justice to my motivations at the time. I wasn't just feeling burdened by the work I had to do, though the voice telling me to ramp down was increasingly difficult to ignore. There was also a growing sense welling up in me that there were some things I'd like to do in my life that would never fit neatly inside the bounds of my allotted vacation days. I wanted to spend time developing my spiritual side, immersing myself in nature, and investigating the hobbies and curiosities that always seemed to get overlooked on the list of life priorities. In other words, I wanted to spend more time on the important things in life instead of just the urgent ones.

In a middle seat on my flight back from Johannesburg, I began to hatch a plan while most of the cabin was asleep. I started by looking back at the past seven years of my life since graduation: What had I accomplished, what was I proudest of, and what were my regrets? I then tried to channel my older self: What would I regret not doing before I turned forty? What life would I want to tell my grandkids I'd lived? While I had a lot of ideas for my future, the prompts mostly served to underline the reality of the situation. There were so many things I wanted to do that would require me to set down my current life, at least for a while, to explore.

Before the plane touched down in Boston, I'd decided to give it a shot. I didn't have much of a plan, only an invitation to join a two-week tour around New Zealand with a small group of friends in a few months. But it was enough activation energy to get me unstuck. I also knew of a Buddhist pilgrimage in Japan that would give me ample time for spiritual exploration. Between these two activities, I figured a few months would be sufficient.

After some logistical conversations with my leadership team, I announced my departure to the team and our investors. I'd be back in four months, I told everyone. I sublet my apartment, spent entirely too much time researching the latest lightweight backpacking gear, and bought a one-way ticket to New Zealand.

Changing Views on Time Off

When people hear that I took extended leave from my job, they think of it as a luxury, something only a rare few can afford to do. Most people don't have easy access to a long break. I know that. But in my journey to write this book, I was surprised to find many more examples of sabbatical takers of varying means, from teachers to journalists to nonprofit employees and students. Some people could take only six weeks off, others a year. They were able to make it work either due to an employer offering the benefit, through advance planning, or because they simply had no other choice.

Increasingly, extended leave is no longer a privilege reserved for the lucky few. More and more companies, individuals, and societies take sabbaticals as a matter of course. Intel, for example, has had a sabbatical policy in place for more than thirty years. Even McDonald's has been offering managers a paid sabbatical since 1977. Blue-chip companies and unicorns like Adobe, Automattic, and Genentech have used sabbaticals to attract talent for decades. And a rotating cast of tech giants and even staid Wall Street banks such as Citigroup have rolled out multi-month paid leave in recent years. Swedish citizens are entitled to six months' leave to work on an entrepreneurial project, while, by law, all Australian civil servants receive long service leave after seven to ten years of employment. Sabbaticals not only exist but are standard issue in many unexpected places already, available to more than just those who can afford to quit their jobs.

But Americans are notoriously bad at taking time off, even when it's given: we habitually leave a third of our paid vacation days unused.[1] In the early twentieth century, economist John Maynard Keynes predicted that advancements in technology would shrink the workweek to fifteen hours.[2] Instead, the highest-paid Americans work more than ever, and significantly more than their peers in other advanced countries.[3]

It's hard not to feel that most everything has been centered around productivity, as if we've lost the plot around how to measure our lives with any other yardstick. Call it the Protestant work ethic, as German sociologist Max Weber did, or Workism, as journalist Derek Thompson has.[4] Either way, productivity is often framed in opposition to leisure, as opposed to time off enabling and enriching our work. If you've ever felt guilty for not checking your work email on a hard-earned vacation, you know what I'm talking about.

But if you look past the headlines where our society lionizes CEOs who sleep under their desks and run multiple companies, a vastly different story explains the early success and creation of companies like Apple, Salesforce, and Impossible Foods, one where leaders used retreat and recovery to spur innovation and regain energy to excel on the next leg of their journey.

Attitudes around the cost of working so hard have been undergoing a seismic shift. The youngest generation of workers are willing to forgo raises for time off, flexibility, and meaning at work.[5] Employers are beginning to realize that competing for the best talent means rewarding employees with something other than money—for example, continuing education stipends or flexibility. There's evidence this employer-led shift is underway around sabbaticals too, as organizations offering corporate sabbatical policies have nearly doubled between 2019 and 2024.[6]

Stepping Away

In the decade since my moment of surrender, everything has shifted for me. And all because I stepped away from work for a few months.

While my marquee accomplishment on sabbatical was walking nine hundred miles through Japan on pilgrimage, a much more important transformation occurred in mundane environments but required something even more foreign: time. I spent weeks back at home with my mother, cooking her meals as she recovered from a serious illness. I helped my cousin rebuild a three-story deck, remodeled my kitchen, and learned how to cut tile with my dad. I sat with a close friend in the waiting room of the children's hospital as he fielded devastating news about his newborn daughter.

Much to the surprise of everyone watching from afar, my time off was also difficult. As my sabbatical unfolded, I came to understand that I could not return to my own company. I was doubt-ridden, lonely, and scared of the prospect of an uncertain future. Did this mean I failed to achieve something, or that I'd chosen the wrong path in the first place? But as my time off progressed, I grew more confident. I got stronger—physically, mentally, spiritually. I also felt lighter, more creative, less anxious. I wrote songs, journaled prodigiously, took photos. My mindset shifted from scarcity and fear to abundance and joy. Looking back, it was the most memory-dense period of my life, but also somehow only 121 days. It would alter how I viewed myself forever.

In the wake of my sabbatical, I exchanged a public-facing version of success for one that felt more authentic to me and who I wanted to become. I decided to give my time away through the end of the year as I contemplated my next steps by volunteering at my alma mater in Indiana to help lead a poverty lab. Doing so took the pressure off of finding the next thing right away and gave me the space and perspective to imagine a new path for myself. My sabbatical had reenergized me with the personal resources to make a change. And it gave me the courage and permission to quit the life that no longer fulfilled me and set out on an unknown journey to understand what had happened to me, and so many others, on sabbatical.

In a strange way, the timing of my search couldn't have been better. Work and life ground to a halt just a few years later, in early 2020. Uncertainty reigned. With surprisingly few exceptions, work was severed from the workplace. But it still got done. A year later we saw the highest quit rates in more than twenty years, a trend economists called the Great Resignation.[7] Faced with the prospect of returning to work as it had always been, employees demanded more flexibility and benefits than ever before, and people chose to take a beat or two outside of work, for themselves and their families. And for the first time on record, more people were quitting en masse *without* concrete plans for their next jobs.

The pandemic didn't create workplace dissatisfaction, but when our work and home lives collided, it enabled a unique moment to reevaluate the appropriate role each should play going forward. Something had shifted in our work culture. Not some incremental change in work-life balance but a drastic departure in how we take time off and view our lives. How would we choose to spend our time if we fully reckoned with both its fragility and its value? As I dug into the practice of people leaving their jobs for uncertain shores, I realized there was more to the story. Sabbaticals were part of a larger pattern over decades, perhaps even on the precipice of a movement instead of an aberration.

Finding a Path Forward

With this as background, I started delving deeply into the benefits of sabbaticals for both individuals and companies. On the surface, sabbaticals look just like really long vacations, so of course they'd feel a bit better than your most recent week or two off from work. We've all taken a vacation, but it's the sabbatical takers who insist there's something incredibly distinct and powerful about Big Time Off. (We'll talk about what constitutes a sabbatical in chapter 2.)

After returning from my sabbatical, I began interviewing people about these profound experiences in their lives. Having spent much of my career with two organizations based on academic research—my credit scoring company and the nonprofit I co-led during my sabbatical, the University of Notre Dame's Lab for Economic Opportunities—I was surprised that there was no rigorous research on sabbaticals outside of academia. So I partnered with academics to launch the first study of sabbaticals for the rest of us.

Our research was groundbreaking and clear. The study participants consistently described their sabbaticals as "peak life experiences"—that is, moments of euphoria and self-understanding that remain instructive for your entire life. Sabbatical alums considered their time off to have been as significant as the birth of their child or their wedding day. We found that taking a few months off from work addresses burnout, increases creativity, improves relationships, and helps folks reinvent themselves.[8] People return from their sabbatical with improved confidence to make changes in their lives, and fresh ideas for what to do next, either at their existing job or a new one.

The positive outcomes for people who take sabbaticals are nearly universal. Access, unfortunately, is not. That's why this book is more than a practical guide. It is a call to action. It goes beyond surveying the sabbatical ecosystem to offer a vision of a better world—one in which access to time away is not dictated by income or job type, and where its costs are understood in proportion to a lifetime of work. After all, what is six months off over the course of a forty-year career?

Those of you who are feeling stuck in your life, called to explore the world, or simply wondering if there's another way to structure your working life have landed in the right place. The stories and strategies in this book will show you how others have navigated this path—and how you might find your own way forward. What you'll discover here is that taking a sabbatical isn't about having all the answers before you begin; it's about creating enough time and space to ask the right questions.

ooo

But before we proceed, I'd like to recalibrate. I've been intentionally appealing to the rational, practical side of your brain. That's the part of you I need to work hardest to convince in order to entertain the idea of a sabbatical.

The other part of you relished the long summers of your childhood and never feels satisfied with your allotted vacation days. It lusts over the travel section of the newspaper or an unwritten bucket list. It's the inner child who wants to experiment, and play, and throw caution to the wind and get the fuck out of Dodge. This side of you doesn't need convincing. It just needs help cajoling the other part of you, the one that holds the checkbook, monitors your reputation, and metes out permission.

I've spent almost a decade working with people looking to take a sabbatical, as well as those coming back from one. There's a convincing case to be made around productivity increases and health improvements and career enhancements, for sure. You'll come away from this book with all the relevant research and case studies to support this conclusion. But the strongest case for sabbaticals lies in one of the most common phrases in my research: feeling human again. Not like a machine whose habits and schedule revolve around work but a living, loving, sensitive individual seeking meaning, fulfillment, and joy in the day-to-day.

There's obviously intrinsic value in feeling this way, but it's hard to put a statistic on it, let alone write about it in a way that doesn't scare off those wearing the armor of their practical self. If we can't be open to the possibility of returning to something essential in ourselves, to pursue our dreams for a little while . . . what is it that we're all doing here?

How to Use This Book

This book is arranged in two parts. The first part aims to equip you with inspiration and permission for taking a sabbatical. We'll define a sabbatical and explore a textbook example. The heart of the book follows some of my favorite sabbatical takers on journeys. These stories illustrate the possibilities and evidence for sabbaticals, as well as the best practices, common difficulties, and anticipated outcomes from a successful sabbatical.

Don't worry—you're not just trailing someone on their vacation. Interwoven with alumni stories is research from academic fields like psychology, as well as examples from companies, cultures, and religions that consider extended leave essential to a good life.

In the second part of the book, I share my blueprint for taking a sabbatical—what I call the Field Guide. Here, you'll put the learnings into practice. First, I'll scold you for immediately flipping to the end of the book (only partly kidding). Then, I'll walk you through the most important considerations for the three phases of your sabbatical: planning, execution, and integration. After that, I'll help you think about a sabbatical for your work self and for your company. Finally, we'll explore returning to normal life and prepare you for the tough parts of sabbaticals—mismatched expectations, loneliness, and fear of what's on the other side. This isn't a vacation we're talking about—it's much more important.

We all know deep down that many things worth doing are difficult. But sabbaticals pose a different challenge than a hard project at work. A sabbatical isn't a specific or tangible thing; it's the *lack* of a task to accomplish or a specific level to attain. It's an empty space for you to experiment with the wishes, dreams, and aspirations for your life, whether or not they are "productive." It prompts you to consider who you are when you're not working, and, once you're there, to ask if this is still who you want to become. Taking off is a subversive act in our society that requires the moral courage to prioritize your personal growth. It also asks us to transcend from inward-focused self-care to identifying and nurturing how our gifts can be used in service to others.

I am confident that your sabbatical will be one of the most significant periods of time in your life. The highest-order purpose of this book is to give you license to view time off not as an optional luxury but rather as an investment in a life well lived. To do so, I must equip you with the inspiration, the permission, and a blueprint to get there. Our first story illustrates some of the best practices, common difficulties, and anticipated outcomes from a successful sabbatical.

Now let's get to work, so to speak.

1

Setting a Good Example

What will be the good of the conquest of leisure and health if no one remembers how to use them?

—Bertrand Russell, *Education and the Good Life*

There was no dramatic moment at work that pushed Winston Chen over the edge from a comfortable life in Boston to an island above the Arctic Circle. No heated meeting with management, no threat of the business going under. It was less a tsunami from the outside than a rising tide from within, a culmination of things he and his wife, Kristin, wanted to do with their lives and a growing awareness that the window for acting on them as a family was closing.

Winston had worked in tech for both decades of his career, but he felt a clear difference in how he worked in his thirties compared to his twenties. Fresh out of college, he had capitalized on the tech boom to create a flexible life as an independent tech-consultant-for-hire. He got paid well enough, but to him, the real reward was the flexibility it offered. Winston traveled so frequently that he kept no permanent address and took long periods off between projects. The life of a nomad had its perks: Winston met Kristin on a backpacking trip in her native Norway. After the two were married, Winston settled into a more stable and traditional role in management, working for a major tech company in Boston.

A decade in, the company's prospects had plateaued, and somewhere along the line, Winston's career became progressively more stressful. Like the proverbial frog in the pot, Winston had only a passing realization that something was wrong on the way toward boiling. At the same time, life on the home front was pleasant and stable. The couple had two children and a great community. They loved their house, which was biking distance to Winston's office. They had a routine that worked. Nothing was *wrong*.

Winston's story is about finding inspiration to take a sabbatical. It also illustrates how to navigate the inevitable vacuum left behind when we step away from work, and the unexpected role of play in getting ourselves back into it. Like all the stories in this book, Winston and Kristin's sabbatical experience provides a case study to help you envision your own sabbatical and structure your time off. But what makes Winston's story particularly important in the exploration of sabbaticals is precisely that it wasn't precipitated by some emergency or irrepressible desire to transform his life. To quote Michael Pollan's examination of psychedelics, it should be enough to use sabbaticals just for the "betterment of well people." An act to deepen and enrich your future, and the sign of a healthy life instead of one in dire need of a change.

Finding Permission to Take the Leap

One day at work, a friend sent Winston a trending TED Talk about taking a sabbatical called "The Power of Time Off." In the talk, Austrian-born designer Stefan Sagmeister outlines his decision to shut down his eponymous New York–based design firm for a full twelve months, once every seven years. Not just for him but for his entire staff. His core message is this: What if we borrowed a few years from retirement and sprinkled them across our working life?

Sagmeister retreated to Bali on sabbatical to heal from a decade of hard-charging work and find inspiration by creating art for art's sake. At least, that's what he assumed he was doing. But after returning to work, he was surprised how many design ideas his seemingly frivolous experiments on sabbatical had given him. For example, spending months living next to Ubud's famed monkey forest inspired Sagmeister to create a campaign using bananas at various stages of ripeness to spell out a client's advertising slogan. Sagmeister claims that the contracts derived from his ideas in Bali more than recouped the money spent paying staff to *not* work for a year.

Winston's heart raced at the idea, but his blood pressure also rose at the practicalities of a year off. How could his family afford it? What would his colleagues, investors, and peers think? He wasn't in his twenties anymore, after all. The stakes of leaving his job as chief technology officer at a venture-backed company weren't only financial—Winston had dedicated years of his career to building his reputation. It was a big part of who he was and not something he could easily discard. His work identity felt at times like an anchor preventing him from moving freely, but it was also undeniably a ballast supporting his family and a broader life he cherished.

Completely ejecting from his routine life seemed drastic for sure, but it wasn't completely out of character for his and Kristin's relationship. After meeting on Winston's backpacking trip to Norway, the two adventured across multiple continents in their young relationship before Kristin followed Winston back to the States.

While Winston weighed the trade-offs of taking a sabbatical, Kristin was hatching her own return from a long career break from teaching. Five years into being a full-time primary caretaker to their two children, she worried that her professional skills as an educator were atrophying. She'd relished being able to be there for her kids at a young age but felt a bit restless, overeducated, and underutilized. With their kids finally at school during the day, life had developed a *Groundhog Day* feel.

In a moment of synchronicity, one of Kristin's friends had recently recommended a reality show called *Heavenly Blue*, where a couple relocates to a small island in arctic Norway to take over the local bed-and-breakfast. The show follows the family trading their urban lifestyle for a completely new existence. Not normally one for daytime TV, let alone *reality TV*, Kristin nonetheless felt like the show spoke to her. A change of scenery, an adventure in her childhood country, and, yes, even hard work sounded tremendously appealing.

Describing the urge to a friend from home, Kristin learned about another island in the Norwegian sea, Rødøy, which reminded her of where she used to spend summers growing up. The coastal municipality on the Arctic Circle was big enough to have its own school and checked a lot of boxes on her wish list: she could get back into teaching, at a salary they could get by on, while at the same time immersing their children in her native culture and language. Moreover, she and Winston could spend quality time as a family, without the work travel and constant logistics that were consuming their lives back home. Kristin picked up the phone and called the principal. He had an opening for the upcoming school year and expected her application by Monday.

The Power of Examples

Both Winston and Kristin had found inspiration from the stories of complete strangers whose lives bore absolutely no resemblance to their own. It might seem incredible that Winston decided to uproot his entire life by watching a seventeen-minute video. Especially since he and Sagmeister, who's famous enough to be on the TED mainstage, design album covers for the Rolling Stones, and run his own design firm, have almost nothing in common. But that's how powerful these examples can be. I've found versions of these stories throughout my interviews on sabbatical takers. Witnessing someone living out their dreams helps you muster the courage to alter the trajectory of your own life.

This phenomenon is not unique to sabbaticals and has been studied extensively. University of North Carolina researchers Dale Schunk and Maria DiBenedetto have explored the crucial role so-called exemplars play in helping people change their lives. According to their work, by observing and comparing the successful actions of others, we can feel empowered and motivated.[1] We seek psychological permission to undertake something that's not currently part of our existing story. Especially something that appears to run at odds with the norm of success in society. And as the popularity of Sagmeister's TED Talk makes clear, we don't even have to know the people we are comparing ourselves to. But the effect is even more powerful for those we perceive as similar to us. A couple with kids is more likely to be inspired by how another couple with kids took a sabbatical, rather than how an unencumbered traveler found the time and resources to do so.

In our research, exemplars came in all shapes and sizes. The most common examples, tragically, were negative exemplars: People seeing their parents work themselves to the bone to save for a retirement that they never reached, due to poor health, the death of a partner, or some other exogenous event that clipped their dreams. Or people seeing someone their own age, long before retirement, become ill—or worse.

In addition to showing the power of examples, Winston and Kristin's story also illustrates how the negative pressures of social norms make it incredibly hard to take a sabbatical. For most people, taking a sabbatical is fraught with risk. That's mostly because it's so out of the norm in our society, at least not normal the way that the weekend or vacations are. While not *everybody* takes weekends off, at least we all agree that there is a workweek and a weekend. We know when the weekend starts and when it ends. For salaried workers, it's generally understood that you're not in the office on the weekend. And for the most part, you know your job awaits you when you come back to the office on Monday. The same goes for vacations and, increasingly, parental leave. Speed of adoption within these movements can vary widely. For example, the concept of the weekend is relatively recent—hardly a century old.

As you know, sabbaticals are still far from the norm in the workplace. While the number of employers who offer official sabbatical leave is growing, the supermajority of those who embark on a sabbatical do so on their own dime, and between jobs. On top of this uncertainty, taking a sabbatical can introduce real negative consequences for those who take them. Some research suggests that taking time off, even if *technically* allowed by an employer, can negatively impact both future salary and promotions.[2] This so-called work devotion bias especially impacts mothers like Kristin, whom extended leave can hit hard, often preventing them from reentering the workforce at their prior salary and position.[3]

Even in a country with progressive policies regarding time off, like Norway, fewer than 3 percent of fathers used their parental leave until it was required to be taken by both parents, instead of shared between the two.[4] Now more than 70 percent of Norwegian fathers take the leave, although they're more likely to take their mandated leave if their bosses already have.

In the case of sabbaticals, there are pockets of corporate America where it's totally normalized—for example, journalism. NPR's policy gives its reporters up to a year of unpaid leave to pursue personal projects that advance their work. One of our interviewees whose story you'll encounter later, Aarti, credits this policy with enabling her to imagine taking a break. In the absence of this institutional permission, we need something—or someone—to prove that the risk is worth taking. Which is how a person like Stefan Sagmeister, or a reality TV show, comes to share an outsized role in the stories of complete strangers making one of the most risky-seeming decisions of their lives.

Stories can open the aperture for what we believe is possible. When you see someone who appears to successfully do something that everyone says isn't possible, it gives you the courage to do it yourself.

The Process of Unwinding

Aflame with permission from a TED Talk and a TV show about a bed-and-breakfast in a lighthouse, Winston and Kristin decided to strike out in pursuit of a year to remember: a full twelve months away from their routine lives. Winston gave notice at his work, and they listed their house on a website called SabbaticalHomes.com, which matches (mostly) academics with people looking to swap or rent out their homes for the school year. The rent they earned would more than cover their mortgage over the course of their sabbatical. Within three months of making the decision, they boarded a plane to Kristin's homeland, flush with bags and bursting with excitement.

The island of Rødøy is about three miles long by one and a half at its widest. The longest—and only—road on the island is a little over a mile long. There are about 150 year-round inhabitants, employed mostly in the local fishery. The island has one church and one school, which teaches kindergarten through ninth grade, and employs two teachers. Kristin would take over homeroom for one-third of the students. With their kids now attending the school, the size of the student body increased by 10 percent.

Their life on the island was simple, if sparse. The community was tight-knit and self-contained. Far from the American way of having overscheduled kids enrolled in various afterschool activities, the local children had little to do after school let out at 2:30. Kristin and Winston's house became the de facto after-school youth club on the island.

Once they'd settled into some semblance of a routine, Winston set about making the most of his time off. He divided his days into the same three buckets he'd allotted for his sabbatical as a whole: time for himself, time for his family, and time investigating his work. On a typical day, Winston helped his family get off to school before heading off for a long hike to clear his mind. He would then spend hours on a collection of long-neglected hobbies, tinkering with art projects or learning the ukulele. He set aside an afternoon each week to spend one-on-one time with each of his kids, a tradition that they termed "daddy days." He read books that had long festered on his shelf and dove into academic research on things that caught his imagination, like how vocal cords work, something his father had once studied.

But one of the chief appeals of island life for Winston was something completely unrelated to any sort of "productive" sabbatical whatsoever: fishing. A lifelong angler, he was excited to catch fish; learn how to smoke, dry, and salt fish; and, of course, cook and eat fish. Luckily for Winston, the nearby waters were so fertile that catching enough for dinner for the family during a thirty-minute fishing session with an unbaited jig was virtually guaranteed. Winston caught cod, haddock, some halibut, and his favorite, mackerel. Kristin says that "it got to the point where it was less of a concern that Winston would actually catch something for dinner, and more like choosing from a menu. If you wanted halibut, you went to this fishing spot. Mackerel? Over there."

Within the span of a few months, almost every aspect of Winston's life had completely changed. Whereas his prior existence was incredibly busy, his new life was the inverse. For the first time in more than a decade, he had huge, unstructured blocks of time open during the day to be alone with his thoughts. Winston relished this at first. Having just left an industry, city, and even country where busyness is a currency, he experienced having nothing to do but play around with hobbies as an antidote to his prior life.

But as the novelty of his life on the island began to wear off, Winston noticed that boredom began to creep in, alongside a low-grade anxiety. Was he spending his time in the best way possible? He found this feeling profoundly unsettling. The un-hustle didn't feel just like a benign absence of something to do; it felt more like a vacuum, pulling his attention toward a problem to be solved. When he wasn't concentrating on fishing or enmeshed in creative projects with his kids, doubts about the future (What would people think? Would he be forced to take an even worse job than he'd left?) emerged. When people from his prior life reached out to ask about his sabbatical, on balance he found that he wasn't yet sure he and Kristin had made the right decision to uproot their lives and leave. It had been so long since he'd had so much uncertainty about the future; he longed for some reassurance that he'd turn into something better, not worse, for having left his former life.

Occupying the In-Between

Unbeknownst to Winston, the funk he found himself in is so routine that I've come to think of it as an essential part of the sabbatical process. This letdown goes by many names, but William Bridges, one of the leading voices on midlife transitions, calls it "fertile emptiness." Bridges explored this feeling during his own rocky departure from academia in his book *Transitions: Making Sense of Life's Changes*, which applied research in adult development to those undergoing big changes in their lives.

As unpleasant as it is, Bridges found emptiness a necessary ingredient for identity growth and creative expression. In the same way a muscle must be exercised to the point of breaking down in order to reform and grow, the "chaos, loss, and doubt" of uncertainty in a transition helps people build up the courage and perseverance to chart their own unique path for themselves.[5] Academics call this in-between time liminal space, from the Latin term meaning "threshold." Crossing the threshold is a key concept in human stories across time and traditions, and once you're attuned to it, you'll find it omnipresent in modern literature and movies—from Elizabeth Gilbert getting on the plane to Italy to eat to Luke Skywalker crossing the galaxy to train with Yoda.

In early tribal cultures, liminal space was a crucial component of the rituals that marked a member's passage from one role in society to another. For example, the transitions associated with a child becoming an adult. Early twentieth-century French anthropologist Arnold Van Gennep was the first to coin the phrase describing these practices as "rites of passage" and study how they supported important transitions in people's lives.[6] Though novel to the person going through them, the rituals had been designed by the leaders with very specific plans in mind for the initiates. Typically, they'd suspend the novice's role by sending them away from the village, often alone at night, for a finite amount of time, to experience a physical and psychological trial of some sort. Upon their return, elders would help the initiates process what had happened and explain their new role in society. People in the tribe understood that, upon returning, you had a new role in the community, and in that way, the coming-of-age process was "institutionalized" in their society. Once you'd progressed to a new stage, there was no going back.

We lack most of these rituals and rites of passage in modern times, especially outside of religious traditions. Sure, we throw parties for graduation and withhold driving, voting, and drinking responsibilities until certain ages. But there's little training or preparation for what to expect in adulthood. In most modern cultures, entering the workforce more resembles being pushed out of the nest than guided through an apprenticeship. I suspect this is behind the explosion of structured gap year programs over the past fifty years, which we'll address in chapter 7.

Counterintuitively, when transitions lack institutional support, the wisest move is often to resist the urge to rush ahead, even when waiting feels wrong.[7] Some academics believe that it simply takes more time than we give ourselves to try on possibilities for ourselves and our lives. Otherwise, we risk thrusting ourselves into a major, a school, or a job that we have to unwind down the road when it's harder to realize that some of the ways we've been living are outdated and overdue for a change. Even after leaving a job, if you want to switch careers completely, it's much easier to get a job in the same industry, calling on your former coworkers or bosses to connect you with people in their network.

Other academics believe the struggle itself, associated with the intense emotions of liminal space, is an essential ingredient to the most authentic changes.[8] Existing in liminality spurs creativity and innovation due to the introduction to a diversity of ideas and influences and the freedom to experiment with new possibilities.[9] In the words of the Stoics, if personal transformation is what you're looking for, "the obstacle is the way."

Embracing Play

For the first few months, when Rødøy was bathed in sunlight, Winston's day-to-day outdoor routines were enough to keep him fully engaged. But as the light (and temperatures) started to recede, Winston felt his excitement around not working wane. Getting outdoors and learning to fish had been fun and mentally enriching, but he missed working on more challenging and sustained projects.

Winston began to shift his focus—not toward his next job but back to his old obsession with software coding. Despite his having worked in tech for almost two decades, Winston's role at work had become far removed from the nuts and bolts of the programmers he supervised. He missed the creative aspect of technology, but being a manager was a necessary evil for many ambitious and talented programmers. It was 2010 and the mobile revolution was underway, and he'd spent too many years away from the coding front line. For Winston, not feeling capable of playing with the latest building blocks of technology made him feel older than, say, having two kids or at least as many gray hairs.

At Rødøy's latitude, the daylight shrank from almost twenty-two hours per day to just over two. With the Arctic Circle's famed darkness rapidly encroaching, Winston decided to dive in and learn mobile application development. He spent more and more of his day indoors, wrapping his mind around new languages and learning to ask for help on the same forums his former employees referenced. His curiosity was piqued. And his work ethic shifted from learning the ins and outs of fishing to a more practical exploration of how to create within his area of expertise.

Winston decided to build a text-to-speech app to occupy his time and to allow him to listen to articles while fishing and walking around the island. It would be a capstone project for his sabbatical, like a master's thesis. From a learning perspective, it would allow him to see his product across the entire technology life cycle: from an idea in his head to a working tool in someone's pocket. Winston's family's schedule helped keep his work hours in check. But he reveled in a new joy; for the first time in more than a decade, he woke up with a childlike giddiness to get to work.

The only person developing an iPhone app on the island, Winston found camaraderie and feedback on forums with coders working through similar bugs and hurdles. Three months later, Winston put the finishing touches on his app, which he called Voice Dream. It was simple, but he was proud of it. It worked, and it could actually serve a real need in the vision-impaired community by transforming any digital text into audio. Eager for feedback, he submitted the app to a popular developer forum to publish the back-end code for scrutiny. At dinner that night, he and Kristin toasted with some local aquavit, a traditional Norwegian potato-based spirit, and called it a night.

To Winston's surprise, he woke up to a rejection from the site's moderator. Not because anything was wrong but because it was so . . . good: "Are you sure you want to submit this here? Once it goes live on this forum, you'll be banned from ever submitting it to the app store. If I were you, I'd submit it as is to Apple and see what happens."

Winston was pretty happy with himself—the moderator's response validated what he'd set out to do. But he felt reservations about going fully public with Voice Dream. Once he started having real users on the app, Winston worried it would cross the lines from playful hobby to job, even though in all likelihood no one would even notice the app. On the plus side, real users would mean real feedback, instead of nerds debating the best way to code. He'd charge two bucks a download and vowed to shut it down if it stopped being fun. He decided to submit.

How Play Helps Us Construct a New Identity

Unbeknownst to Winston, his approach up to this point—toying around with learning a new skill, as opposed to aiming for a specific outcome—was well supported by research about how we play. As you can imagine, most of the research on play revolves around childhood development. In this context, play is driven by enjoyment and discovery rather than goals and objectives.[10] When kids are relieved of the constraints of output, reward, and punishment, they inhabit a safe space that encourages them to experiment with different versions of who they want to become. As it turns out, play can also be an impactful approach for adults navigating changes in their identity—who they are both at work and outside it.

Approaching identity change indirectly through play has several advantages.[11] First, it takes the pressure off finding a "solution" to who you want to be or what you want to do with your life. As a child, you don't play astronaut to pad your résumé for a job at NASA. You do it because it's fun to float in zero gravity.* Because play is something we typically do in private, it gives us the opportunity to experiment, fail, and try things that will never "work"—at least not in the sense that we could actually change careers or be able to support ourselves financially by doing them back in our real life.

But at the same time, when else do you give yourself permission to spend hours, days, and weeks on end fiddling with a creative hobby or testing your limits physically or whatever it is you dream of doing? You certainly won't know what will result from it if you don't try it. This is why I recommend *not* telling people what you're up to on sabbatical. The moment others can see what you're doing, the stakes change. It's no longer your private sandbox to play in but an aquarium where you're subject to the judgment, opinions, and constraints of those back in routine life.

Successfully creating enough distance and privacy around your identity play enables you to collect internal feedback (how does it *feel* to mess around with programming apps?) *before* you expose your provisional identity to people whose opinions can materially impact your life (will future investors think my app is a joke when I try to start my next business?). For Winston, this was geeking out about a new technology. For others in Sabbatical Land, it can be recording and writing a biography of an elderly grandparent or trying their green thumb by gardening for one planting season. I've met sabbatical alums who interned at nonprofits they had no intention of joining full-time or got their pilot's license just for fun. As long as it's an experiment instead of an expectation, you're playing with a provisional identity.

Identity work takes time, especially when we suspect a big change is in order. It's not as simple as switching jobs or declaring that you'd like to be someone else for a while. Perhaps you've experienced this yourself when you first take on a new job, especially at a higher level

* And you get to eat space ice cream from a toothpaste tube.

or in a different industry. It can be hard not to feel imposter syndrome until you experience a certain level of competence, often derived from an external party.

This is precisely why a long vacation differs from a sabbatical. There's simply not enough time to get into the good stuff, like progressing toward who you want to become or restoring your health. For Winston, the months spent fishing and afternoons spent having daddy days one-on-one with his kids helped him heal and rekindle his creative energy. Taking a playful approach—the scenic route toward accomplishment—facilitates self-expression, discovery, and creativity.[12] Equipped with this renewed creative energy, Winston delved into his playful coding project and began his identity shift into becoming an entrepreneur.[13]

Beginning Again

At the end of their sabbatical year, Winston and Kristin returned to Boston facing considerable career uncertainty. If the prior twelve months was to imagine a new life, their next year back in Boston was to build it. Armed with confidence and a track record on her résumé, Kristin was determined to parlay her teaching experience into a fulfilling full-time job in Boston.

But the timing couldn't have been worse—recruiting season for the fall semester had ended by the time they returned. She could substitute-teach her way into consideration for the following year, but that meant that either Winston would need to return to a full-time job commensurate to the one he quit before their sabbatical or they'd be forced to substantially dip into their savings. With a mortgage and all the other expenses associated with living in Boston back on their plate, they had a costly decision to make.

But Winston and Kristin were confident that the life they'd glimpsed in Rødøy—with its flexibility, family time, and lower intensity—was worth manifesting back home, even if it meant compromise. Financially, Winston and Kristin felt forever altered by their experience in Rødøy. They knew they could live happily with less, especially if it afforded them a chance to run headlong toward their dreams. Once you've lived out a version of your life where you're both fulfilled at work and at home, with plenty of time for creative projects outside your job and family time to boot, it's hard to give that up without a fight.

At the same time, Voice Dream continued its modest but steady growth. Winston had raised prices, and at ten dollars per member and growing at one hundred new users a week, he figured it could replenish their Norwegian salary in a year or so. Financially it would be tight, but both Winston and Kristin were clear-eyed about their goals and much less willing to trade a higher income for a diminished version of the quality of life they'd experienced firsthand in Rødøy.

Sure enough, by the next school year Kristin had a full-time dream role teaching, and Winston was busy hiring people to help manage Voice Dream's growth.

ooo

For the past seven years, since Rødøy, the family has traveled for two months each summer, thanks to the flexibility Winston built into his company. Pulling this off required him to design his company in a way that could withstand his absence. It also undoubtedly meant he was sacrificing some financial upside to make his company work with his and Kristin's life. But on his sabbatical, Winston had had a realization: his motivation to get rich had always been about buying time—time with himself and his family. If he could build his business to provide that time directly, why chase a high-risk exit that might never materialize? He could channel Rødøy and treat the next chunk of his work life like a playful experiment instead of another job.

In other words, Winston took what Stefan Sagmeister introduced into his life fifteen years ago and innovated on it; instead of borrowing a year of retirement to sprinkle into his career every seven years, Winston has crafted a career that utilizes breaks in smaller but more regular doses. Winston and Kristin still aspire to take another yearlong sojourn, but that can wait until their children are off at college. And even during the year, traditions from Rødøy, like daddy days, persist. Prominently featured on their kitchen wall is Winston and his son's custom countdown display based on the arrival times of public buses to the stop nearest their home. Next year, his son will take his gap year in Norway, where he'll live in a dormitory among students from across the country looking to experience life a bit differently before university.

Winston's sabbatical story has little in common with Sagmeister's, but like him, he and Kristin have become exemplars themselves. NPR's *Morning Edition* covered their sabbatical above the Arctic Circle, and the app's Norwegian creation story is prominently featured on Voice Dream's website. Winston and Kristin's story gives inspiration to families, women reentering the workforce, and aspiring techies looking for a sustainable relationship between work and life.

Their experience hits many of the notes of an ideal sabbatical: enough time off, properly disconnected, with a healthy dose of work and play. They were able to navigate their existing responsibilities (children in school, a job, a mortgage), which could feel like impossible hurdles and foment unexpected change in their lives. We can—and should—use extended leave for enriching our lives through joy and connection instead of as a last-ditch effort to change our lives at a precipice. But leading up to every successful sabbatical is a series of decisions that have the potential to enrich or derail your hard-fought time off. To better understand the components of a successful sabbatical, let's start by defining one.

2

What Is a Sabbatical?

Six days a week we wrestle with the world,
wringing profit from the earth;
on the Sabbath we especially care
for the seed of eternity planted in the soul.

—Deuteronomy 4:10

For such a popular term, "sabbatical" is surprisingly difficult to define. It means something very specific for university professors: a year without teaching duties. But as the term has crossed the Rubicon into mainstream jobs, the meaning and parameters have become a bit fuzzy. While you're free to define it as you'd like, when we agree on its necessary components, I believe we increase our chances of embarking on a *successful* sabbatical.

My definition of sabbatical is *intentional extended leave from your job*. This chapter will explore the components of this definition and delve into the history of extended leave to help you feel emboldened to embark on one.

But first, a perhaps surprising confession: I don't love the term "sabbatical." In fact, I'd go so far as to say that the goal of the sabbatical movement should be to eradicate the need for the label altogether.

In an ideal world, we wouldn't need a fancy word to attend to those aspects of our lives that aren't devoted to our careers. But we don't live in an ideal world, so we borrow the term "sabbatical" to dress up—or downright disguise—our reasons for taking time off. Sure, it lends a hint of prestige to an act that may sound frivolous or even irresponsible. But I believe that we primarily use the term "sabbatical" out of fear. Fear of what the world thinks about us for stepping away from our careers, and fear that talking about time away sounds like we're bragging or, worse, blind to the circumstances of those who can't afford such an experience.

My reason for calling my break a sabbatical is the same as many folks'—it sounds cleaner and more distinguished than some variation of "I'm X years old, in a job/relationship/identity crisis, and I have no idea where to go from here."

The few who don't call their break a sabbatical are likely to have taken a long break previously or come from a culture in which this sort of action is common. Israelis, for example, famous for their year of travel after mandatory military service, don't require labels or permission to take time off. It's a cultural hallmark, an almost universally shared and loved experience that has become part of the identity of that country in the same way that a devotion to work is part of ours.*

The Fundamentals

The first sabbatical policy was created at Harvard in 1879 for the purpose of "health, rest, study, *or* the prosecution of original work in literature or science [emphasis mine]."[1] Prior to formalizing this policy, the

---

* Israel has one of the highest GDPs per capita, and its entrepreneurs command more venture capital dollars per capita than do American company founders.

university had experimented with shorter stints away, as well as with partial-year and unpaid versions of extended leave, before landing on a full paid year off, which remains the norm almost 150 years later.

Other universities quickly followed suit. Within forty years, fifty top academic institutions offered sabbatical policies to their faculty. Their justification wasn't just out of the kindness of their hearts. Columbia University's Trustee Report described the need for the sabbatical as "an intellectual and practical necessity . . . for the good of university education. . . . The teaching body," it said, "requires a periodic refurbishing of its equipment."[2] Feelings about considering human beings to be machines aside, the primary reason American professors needed a year off from teaching on top of their summer breaks was because their European counterparts took their summers seriously.

The report continues: "Contact with other institutions, with specialists of other countries, with methods of acquiring and imparting knowledge in vogue elsewhere, cannot be obtained during the summer vacation, as this is a period of rest practically everywhere."[3] This is a theme you'll see throughout this book: once a behavior is normalized, whether it's rest or overwork, it can have long-lasting effects on how we live.

There's no agreed-upon definition of a sabbatical outside academia.[4] That's where the territory can get quite tricky. Folks love to debate the edge cases:

"So, are you saying maternity leave is a sabbatical?"

(No. Time off to care for a newborn child is almost never a sabbatical.)

"At our company, we get a week of sabbatical each year on top of our vacation after four years in the job."

(The term alone doth not a sabbatical make.)

"What if I work remotely or quit my full-time role to start freelancing?"

(Sorry, no.)

"Does that mean I can't do *any* work on my sabbatical?"

(Actually, no. But with a caveat.)

There are three components for a proper sabbatical: *duration*, *intention*, and *disconnection*.

Duration

"What's the *minimum* amount of time I can spend on sabbatical?" is the most frustrating question I get. It's a dead giveaway that someone both needs a sabbatical and is unlikely to carve out sufficient time to take one. As one sabbatical alumnus said, "That's like asking someone the least amount of time you can spend in Paris. I can suggest an answer, but the fact that you're asking the question makes me think you need much more time in Paris."

Sabbaticals should be aged in months, not weeks. There is no such thing as a weekend sabbatical, and you can't extract the benefits of one from an app.

Most sabbatical takers recommend between three months and a year. The majority feel like it took up to six to eight weeks—much longer than they'd expected—to even *begin* to feel like themselves again.[5] Remember, you're shedding not only your meeting schedule but years and layers of the work (and identity) that has defined your life. Your experience can vary widely based on the conditions that brought you to your sabbatical, as well as what awaits you on the other side. Obviously, it's a lot easier to fall into a relaxed state of bliss and playful experimentation when you're on paid leave from work, with your job guaranteed upon return. It's trickier and more time-consuming if you're sputtering into your sabbatical burned out and emotionally raw.

If you're willing—and able—to set aside enough time to really sink back into yourself outside of work again, a completely new experience awaits. A former attorney who spent her sabbatical hiking and volunteering in Latin America told me, "I was surprised by how long it took to melt away into my time off, but once I did, I kind of forgot the fact that I was a lawyer for work, which is normally an all-consuming part of me. It was so unlike anything else I'd experienced before. It just all fell away."

Examples of an ideal sabbatical include time off between graduate school and a job, or between leaving a job and starting a job you've already landed. This way you're free from needing to think about what's next. The gold standard is, of course, a company-sponsored sabbatical in which you retain full pay and benefits, and they've blocked your access to work email. This enables you to sink into your time off without an internal countdown clock to add anxiety about your future. But these opportunities are hard to come by; very much still the exception, rather than the rule, which we'll explore together.

Intention

A proper sabbatical must also have intention. As used here, intentionality doesn't mean your time off needs to be planned in advance. The truth is, most sabbatical takers in my interviews—more than two-thirds—did *not* intend to take time off. That is to say, instead of taking a sabbatical, a sabbatical took them.

We usually capitulate to extended leave only in an emergency brought on by a health, job, or relationship crisis instead of the more difficult and intentional process of planning, saving up, and making space for it in advance. Too often, our relationship to time off is like waiting until we need a root canal to visit the dentist instead of undergoing regular checkups throughout our life.

Used here, intention just means that once you're off, you stay that way. It's not easy. We're wired to think of our job as something we must always have. Inevitably, over the course of our careers, we'll leave our positions, either of our own accord or not. At that point we're acculturated to believe that our immediate, primary job is to find other employment. Sure, there are legitimate and practical reasons for this, like health insurance, childcare, and mortgages. But even people who don't have a pressing financial burden feel many other pressures to move to the next thing—it's an automatic reflex.

A proper sabbatical suspends that reflex. Your only job when you're on sabbatical is to be free of one. This requires resolve to make space for your time off instead of viewing it as a problem to be solved. A sabbatical may not pay well, but you must view the cost as an investment instead of a penalty.

Intentionality requires focus and will not be rushed. We need sufficient time off to explore who we are and what we want before committing to a new direction. But because this "between" time is so uncomfortable, many people quickly pivot to the next thing without exploration, a process developmental psychologist James Marcia calls "identity foreclosure."[6] Identity foreclosure means settling for the familiar past version of yourself instead of the authentic version you could become. We saw this in our research as well: the people who skipped exploration during their sabbatical were more likely to return to their old ways of working. Whereas the sabbatical takers who explored and also tried some new ways of living on for size were most likely to experience a positive transformation in their lives.

But to transform, we must create and protect our chance to do so.

Disconnection

A proper sabbatical requires sufficient disconnection. Ideally, we disconnect by physically getting away, going out of town, out of the country, for as long as is feasible. Countless interviewees cited the journey itself as symbolic of a new beginning. For Mary, who took a sabbatical from her stressful work life in Boston, flying to the other side of the planet made her work feel like "such a tiny piece of the world." Dropping herself in a foreign land reminded Mary that there were so many other ways of living, and so many more pressing needs for the majority of the world than the things that felt so urgent back home.

The importance of physical separation for transformation is a central theme in human storytelling, stretching back in time and across cultures. So much so that literature professor and mythology expert Joseph Campbell described it as the common denominator to personal transformation across societies in his book *The Hero with a Thousand Faces*. According to Campbell, until you've left your life behind, you cannot truly change; you're stuck with a foot in the old world. If you're going to take a journey, commit.

But even outside of the geographic sense of separation is the importance of psychological disconnection. Maintaining ties with their past working life is one of the biggest regrets among sabbatical alumni. The trade-off for headspace and freedom is not worth it. The damage caused by staying on with your old company part-time or taking on some hours of related consulting projects isn't limited to missing out on a few additional hours of fun here or there. You're preventing yourself from fully embarking on your journey altogether. Frodo from *The Lord of the Rings* couldn't have completed his quest if he needed to return to the Shire each weekend to water the lawn.

Obviously, geographic separation is not feasible across all seasons of life. It's much easier to cast off ropes for a gap year before college than in midlife. Responsibilities deepen and increase over time. But don't let your constraints deter you from doing the best you can to escape—while you may not experience the full sabbatical benefits, less comprehensive breaks can still catalyze significant change. We'll cover what to do when faced with the prospect of a more modest sabbatical in chapter 11.

Issues disconnecting come up in other forms too. Increasingly, even those of us who can escape geographically remain technologically attached to our routine lives. This can deflate our sabbatical mindset and transport us back to our routine life instantaneously, no matter where we are in the world. A hard-won extended trip abroad is more susceptible than ever to this fate. Our only defenses are uninstalling apps and establishing strict expectations for how people can reach us in an emergency. Most of us overestimate the importance of *continuous* connectivity. Trust me, you're infinitely more likely to return to text messages like "It feels like you just left yesterday!" than "We couldn't survive without you!" Your world will carry on without you plugged into it.

The Sacred Gift of Time Off

Sabbatical comes from the old Hebrew *šabbat*, or Sabbath, meaning to cease or rest, a practice deeply ingrained in Judaism.[7] (Perhaps one reason why sabbaticals are so common in Israel.) The most common way Jews observe the Sabbath is through the tradition of shabbat, which entails "resting from work activities"—and I love this adjective—"with great rigor, and engaging in restful activities to honor the day."[8]

The concept of Sabbath also applied on a larger timescale, requiring farmers to let their fields lie fallow for one year out of every seven. According to the Torah, it's technically a matter of life and death: "The man who profanes [the Sabbath] shall be put to death; whoever does any work on that day shall be outlawed from his people" (Exodus 31:14). Jews are forbidden from working during the Sabbath, but are encouraged to spend time resting, reflecting, and eating with family and community.

Even the most secular among us have benefited directly from religious groups advocating for rest: before Jewish millworkers in New England lobbied for a weekly rest from work on their Sabbath day in 1908, there was no regular weekend. (You can thank their Christian coworkers for winning the right to take off Sunday as well.)[9]

A beautiful way to envision the roots of rest can be found in *The Sabbath* by Abraham Heschel. Heschel argues that one of Judaism's greatest gifts is the art of sanctifying lengths of time from the "magnificent stream of a year."[10] Time is, of course, intangible and irreplaceable, the most precious resource we have. We can't pause or possess time, but we can choose how we spend it. By regularly setting aside time to focus on the most important aspects in our lives—family, friends, God, or simply recreation and leisure—we create a "cathedral in time," according to Heschel. It's a retreat from our hectic routine and an opportunity to be fully present with whatever is most important to us.

For Heschel, holding time sacred allowed the Jews to create "a shrine that neither the Romans nor the Germans were able to burn."[11] For the rest of us, carving out enough for a sabbatical helps us build something equally enduring—the most important memories of our lives.

For Jews, rest and the Sabbath are interwoven into the fabric of a society that spans countries, cultures, and a few millennia. But our secular, overworked, productivity-focused society also has its own sacred, unassailable cathedral in time, and it's down the road from now. Something I typically refer to as the "Capital R" sabbatical: Retirement.

No matter how hard we work, or how few breaks we take during our lives, most everyone looks forward to retiring. And we all assume we'll get there. The story of retirement comes up often in discussing sabbaticals. Some people frame their sabbaticals as borrowing time from their future retirement, spreading it out more evenly along the course of their lives instead of holding it in reserve to experience all in one chunk. As noted, many others were motivated to take a sabbatical by witnessing their parents deferring their dreams until retirement, only to see them left unfulfilled, beset by a health crisis or other tragedy. To state the obvious, making it to retirement is not guaranteed: only about half of couples who are fifty today can expect both partners to be mentally and physically able to travel extensively by the time they reach retirement age.[12]

We all believe we deserve to retire. At some point, we will stop working for the remainder of our lives. The call to take a sabbatical asks us to reexamine that assumption—haven't we already done enough to deserve a chance to enjoy some of the fruits of our labors before it's too late?

A Growing Movement

Despite my reservations about the word "sabbatical," it's a unifying description that serves an important purpose. Taking a sabbatical can be a very isolating undertaking. You're retreating from society to live out a personal dream that's often at odds with the predominant story of how work is supposed to be performed over the course of our lives: all gas, no brakes. Knowing that there are others also detaching from their routine lives helps us set out on our own unique path with confidence.

As you journey through this book, I encourage you to think about yourself as part of a larger collective, something bigger than your own journey of self-discovery. Your fellow travelers, people of all ages, jobs, countries, and even across history, have also embarked on something very personal, uncomfortable, and unknowable—that experience we have agreed to call a sabbatical.

So feel free to use the word. It's not perfect, but it is useful. As permission, or armor, or to make something you've always wanted to do feel tangible and possible for your life. As a sabbatical fellowship, together we embody a shared identity that protects us from outside expectations and inner voices. When doing something hard, it always helps to have company. My hope is that this book, and the Sabbatical Project movement, can serve as a convening ground, a base camp from which you can set off on your journey, no matter where it starts.

3

Working on Time Off

If you bring forth what is within you,
what you bring forth will save you.
If you do not bring forth what is within you,
what you do not bring forth will destroy you.

—The Gospel of Thomas

Growing up the daughter of undocumented immigrants, Aarti Shahani was taught three things about work: it was necessary, it was mostly difficult, and it was life. It wasn't that complicated, really. *What* you did for work wasn't all that important. It was just how you earned a living.

Though Aarti's father, Namdev, was educated and skilled in the professional class in his native India, in America he scraped by running a little electronics shop with his brother. The two men worked long hours, competing against a gaggle of similar stores on the block. Aarti saw the hard work her father put in to support his family and, for much of her youth, focused on outrunning her parents' precarious life. Same work ethic, but different, more prestigious work, she thought.

But her father's work—and life—would nonetheless end up playing a motivating role for the next twenty years of her career, culminating in how she spent her sabbatical at age forty.

After Aarti went off to college, her father was wrongfully detained in the shadow of 9/11. Tensions were high, legal mandates were sweeping, and civil rights were murky at best. Given his citizenship status, Namdev was almost certainly set for deportation; it was just a matter of when. While not a lawyer, Aarti still felt that she could aid her father and decided to take a year off from school to help orchestrate his legal defense.

As she publicly fought conviction by the government, Aarti's voice began reaching other families across the country. In the overwhelming response she saw an opportunity to champion a larger movement and decided to start a nonprofit, Families for Freedom, to provide legal and social services for immigrant families involved in the deportation process. While her work ultimately failed to prevent her father's deportation, Aarti discovered a passion for uncovering the truth and empowering those around her to act on it. Graduate school and journalism seemed a natural next step.

Over the next seven years Aarti rose to the top of her new field, ultimately becoming NPR's Silicon Valley correspondent. It was a coveted position interviewing some of the most powerful figures in tech. In her words, "I had a stable job with great benefits, a home of my own, and, most important to my immigrant roots, a great credit score." She continued, "I had a lot of stability in my life, more stability than ever. And no one in my family was in need of help."

Beneath the surface, however, something was stirring.

It wasn't boredom, malaise, or burnout but something completely unrelated to her day-to-day work: the story of her prior life, how she was impelled to recast her career in service to justice for her father, was bubbling up to the surface. The stable façade of her identity as a journalist reporting other people's news was beginning to feel like someone else's life. The more she reported on others, the louder the untold history of her father's deportation became in her mind. Aarti remembers waking up one day with absolute certainty: "This story has been inside me for too long—I need to write this book to be able to keep living."

Life as a journalist was nonstop; there was no way Aarti could find the time and energy to write her memoir on nights and weekends (which themselves were often taken over by work). But NPR offered its employees unpaid leave for up to a year. Aarti requested nine months, referring to it among friends symbolically as her "book-baby leave." She wasn't even thinking about whether she'd return, only that it was time to go plumb the depths of herself.

ooo

Working during your sabbatical can seem like a betrayal of the act of taking off itself. What's the point of taking off from your job if you're just going to turn around and clock into another office of your own making? But "Can I work on sabbatical?" is one of the most commonly asked questions I get. It makes sense. Most of us have something we've always wanted to do—not because we should but because it calls to some authentic part of ourselves. It might be teaching English abroad, researching our family history, or that remodeling project we've put off for too long. These projects can represent unexpressed facets of our identity or creative impulses that get crowded out by the demands of our regular work. That doesn't mean we don't also want to have fun. But making progress on something we've wanted to get done, even if it looks a bit like a job to others, gives us a sense of personal accomplishment.

Using your sabbatical for achievement, if done well, can do more than provide you with a sense of accomplishment, it can help you explore and express your evolving identity. Experimenting with work-like tasks lets you try out your dreams to prevent living with regret and, perhaps counterintuitively, helps you rest and recover before returning to your job.

Identity and Sensemaking Through Work

For something we so often complain about, work is surprisingly hard to put down, even temporarily. Our work plays a huge role in who we are, so it's no wonder we struggle to give it a rest during our sabbatical. You never think you'll miss the constant hum of work until you're on sabbatical, compulsively wondering if things are okay at the office.

Work helps us create meaning, and we use it in many positive ways. We rely on work to help figure out who we are, to test our assumptions, and to find belonging among others. Feedback on the job helps us mark progress as we acquire skills and grow as a human being, which is one reason why lines between ourselves at work and who we are outside it are understandably blurred.

It's also scary to move from one identity to another. Sabbaticals can expedite a process of identity change, which is key to progressing toward a more authentic self. As we saw with Winston in chapter 1, one way we can do this is through aimless play. Aarti illustrates another way: through hard work toward a deeply personal goal.

In Aarti's case, her work identity morphed many times throughout her life. Before college, she'd wanted to be a lawyer, because she thought it was a prestigious and important career. Not that she knew any attorneys, but from the catalog of job options she saw on television, lawyers seemed among the smartest, best dressed, and most empowered. Becoming a lawyer would be a way to excel and escape her family's financial precariousness.

But her experience working in the legal system gave Aarti the evidence to reconsider. Then she became a community organizer and discovered her love for enacting change and helping people. Eventually, however, Aarti saw her whole life up until age thirty as defined by her family's needs instead of her own. That's when she picked up stakes and went to grad school to explore a role that felt more suited to her.

Arizona State University professor Dr. Blake Ashforth calls this evolution "enacting identity"—the gradual process of first feeling out, then behaving like, and ultimately thinking and believing a new identity.[1] According to Dr. Ashforth, we make our identities by first recognizing an inclination toward something, then identifying and naming it, and then, ultimately, acting it out.

Once we take on a new identity (a job, say, or a relationship), we're either intentionally or subconsciously taking stock of how it feels and whether or not it fits. This is one of the most important tools we have to figure out who we are and who we are becoming: trying it out ourselves. Living out our dreams when on sabbatical—whether as a scuba diver, an artist, a fisherman, a yogi, or a writer—gives us the space to see if our idea of doing something lives up to our hopes for it—that is, the difference between expectation and reality. It's one of the many unique benefits of a sabbatical: an opportunity to do an internship, working on yourself.

Sabbaticals can expedite a process of moving from one identity to another, which is key to progressing toward a more authentic self. This is because sabbaticals offer the chance to undergo experiential lessons without the commitment and potential messiness of starting and stopping jobs. It's a way to live out and feel the consequences of a decision rather than just imagining what they would be like. You're time-rich on sabbatical, giving you enough space to try something on in this unique manner. For me, I craved a deeper investigation of my spiritual side. Walking for six weeks on pilgrimage, with few inputs and essentially in silence (due to my lack of Japanese), disabused me of this notion. It wasn't that I hated it, but I realized that while it was an interesting existence to get a peek into, it was not a good fit for my personality.

This process of making sense of who we are in the context of others and society is quite literally called "sensemaking," and it's crucial to our personal development and self-esteem. We have a desire to feel that how we live makes sense, both in the present and along some sort of coherent trajectory for the future. Of course, the past plays a part in this too. You can think of it like archaeology, digging under layers of identities and roles you've taken on to find the "real you."

The "you" that you're seeking during sensemaking isn't a static concept. It's a constantly evolving sense of our identity that incorporates all the disparate experiences and the many roles we play throughout our lives. We instinctively seek out our "true self"—the most authentic and comprehensive version of ourselves at any given moment in our lives, including our strengths and weaknesses, trials and errors.[2] Having the time to find and be their truest self gives people the capacity to actualize their fullest and most preferred self.[3] It's empowering to realize that finding yourself is a healthy, recurring practice, not an indication that you've somehow lost your way.

Whatever the strategy, there's an inherent tension at play: we crave coherence among all our internal parts, yet we're also a chorus of disparate identities rather than one unified self.[4] Too much internal dissonance can hinder our ability to move forward in one direction at all. So we must provide space and time to make room for a newer, more coherent, and truer-to-self primary identity.

Seven years into her journalism career, Aarti wrestled with multiple voices about what to do. Part of her wanted to relish her newfound security—e.g., the credit score—and hard-won victories as a journalist. Whereas another part—the part seeking to write her memoir—was "bubbling up" and threatening this stability.

In her book *Working Identity*, Dr. Herminia Ibarra recommends "acting your way into a new way of being" instead of trying to discover yourself through introspection. (This in itself could serve as a thesis statement for sabbaticals. Still, it's easier said than done.) According to Ibarra, we can picture a collection of possible selves within us, engaged in a "Darwinian struggle" to become the primary self that we embody.[5]

In Aarti's case, her desire to write her memoir tamed all her other identities into submission, for the time being. But the problem with spending your sabbatical wrestling with all this identity work is . . . that it's hard work. The prospect of spending your long-sought time off sprinting through personal development and returning to the office completely gassed is understandably not very attractive. However, our research revealed the surprisingly positive role that work like this—distinct enough from your job—plays in our recovery.

Active Rest

After a few weeks back in New York City, where she interviewed key figures in her father's story, Aarti hunkered down and wrote. She isolated herself geographically, holing up in a meditation retreat center and in a cabin on a New Hampshire lake. She cooked and ate alone, talked to no one, and wrote, on average, three thousand words (approximately twenty pages, herculean by the standards of mortal writers) per day. As she recalls, "I was one thousand percent immersed in something I believed in, and there was no other way I would rather have spent my time."

Instead of rewarding herself at the end of the writing process with a multi-week vacation to contemplate her next steps, she found herself back in the office, as though she'd stepped from the finish line of a marathon to the starting line of another. But surprisingly, she felt much less exhausted than when the sabbatical began. In fact, she felt reenergized.

Aarti's experience highlighted a crucial aspect of our research: we found that even achievement-focused sabbatical takers emerge from their time off feeling significantly better and less burned out than before they left. The current understanding of recovery from work is that you must completely disengage from work to do "low-effort" activities that "reduce demands on personal resources."[6] Low-effort work being what people assume you're up to on sabbatical: bingeing Netflix or sipping from a coconut on a beach.

This is what we expect from vacations. Vacations, along with other so-called micro breaks, are almost always intended to be respites. You put down work for a week to relax, but while you're away, work piles up at the same pace, so you end up checking email anyway. The cognitive load of thinking about returning to the office saps your enjoyment of your time off and reduces your motivation when you return.[7]

Sabbaticals are different. Though not oriented entirely around respite like vacations, they actually offer *greater* respite than vacations. Sabbaticals are long enough that the work *must* get done in your absence, which means that it's not piling up on your desk (or in the back of your head) while you're gone. In this way, a sabbatical is more like parental leave—the company can't afford to wait until you're back; it needs to figure out how to get the work done in your absence. This makes the quality of your time off that much better.

This freedom from professional obligations creates space to engage very differently with job-like tasks. When you choose to work on something during your sabbatical—writing a book, building a deck, taking a class for fun—you are operating by your own rules. There is no boss evaluating your performance, no company politics to navigate. Your work is self-directed and intrinsically motivated.

This is likely why sabbatical takers find that high-effort work, even the kind that could be someone else's job, can also be invigorating and restorative. What's key here is that while this may be someone else's job, it's not yours. You can set it down at any time; it doesn't directly affect your salary or your ego. And in this way, work becomes more like play. This is why Aarti was able to push herself as hard, if not harder, than she would at work during her time off and still emerge feeling more powerful and energetic than before. Routine work feels heavy, while finishing something of your choosing feels like getting a weight off your chest.

When we dedicate significant chunks of time to accomplishing something important to us, the work transforms from a job to what Stephen Cope would call "the great work of our lives."[8] It's *identity work*, and the results pave the way for a more intentional, coherent, and fulfilling future. Doing work that helps us self-actualize is fulfilling not only in the short term but also in the long term, because it serves to stave off regret for having not lived the life you always wanted.

Regret Insurance

I teach a class about entrepreneurial failure, and we have a very specific definition of the term: we deem a start-up to be a failure if it can't return at least as much money as its investors put in. It's not so easy to pin down a definition of personal failure or personal success.

This is no small feat, but one definition of a life well lived that I use in class is one with as few regrets as possible. When we choose to act, we might not like how something turns out, but we won't regret having given it a shot. Otherwise, we'll always wonder what would've happened had we moved across the country after college or asked our dream person out on a date. Knowing what doesn't work, or who you aren't, is helpful in ultimately finding what does work and who you are.

In the academic literature, this is called alternative selves or counterfactuals—basically exploring "what might have been" in any given scenario. We all have these alternate versions of ourselves that we wonder about. While it's impossible to know exactly what would have happened if we'd made different choices, experimenting with possible selves gives a pretty close approximation. Sabbaticals offer enough time and freedom to try on other versions of ourselves. Aarti, for example, had a pretty good idea of what it felt like to be a journalist, but she didn't know how it would feel to be an author of an entire book, or to excavate her personal story, until she did it herself.

In the beginning stages of my research, I had a conversation with a close family friend, Connie, whose husband, John, had been a career trial lawyer. It was core to his identity, how everyone knew him in their town. Turns out that he'd always wanted to be a novelist.

One year, while in the prime of his career, and with two young daughters at home, John decided he was going to quit his lucrative position to chase his dream. In his new life as a writer, instead of putting on a suit and driving to the office, he'd have breakfast with his family, grab his coffee, and walk out to his outdoor-shed-turned-writing-workshop and get to work. In the evenings, he'd pick his girls up from school—it was rare to even have him home for dinner normally—and hang out with the family until everyone went to sleep. Then he'd go back out to write.

He hated it.

About two months into his new life, John tore up his manuscript and tossed it into the trash. He never let anyone read it, not even his wife. The next Monday he resumed his life as a trial attorney as if nothing had changed. But something important inside him had shifted. You might expect him to look back at the time as a waste, or with bitterness that his dream couldn't be realized. Exactly the opposite: John marked that time as the turning point and a way to extinguish his lingering regret over not having tried on the writer's life. His sabbatical enabled him to see in high definition that a life spent in a shed, plumbing the depths of his imagination and interacting with nobody save his inner demons, wasn't for him. He loved being around other people. He had a huge personality and savored the impact he was making in his community. Time spent living out a counterfactual creates meaning and heightens self-understanding.[9] For John, a few months trying on another life for size quenched his aspirations and quelled his doubts.

John's sabbatical represented a pattern I was coming to recognize in my research. He inspired his family by his actions, not by his regrets. No wonder Connie's perception of her husband changed after his sabbatical. She saw him as not just a lifelong careerist in a competitive workaholic field but also as a softer creative: "Pre-sabbatical and post-sabbatical John were subtly different people. After tearing up his manuscript—which, I admit, I thought about trying to piece together and read myself—he was just lighter. I know it sounds corny to think about the book as something that was hanging over his head, but it was true. He enjoyed his work more and gave himself more permission to take time off to be a bigger part of the girls' lives. I think he even enjoyed reading more. And importantly for the rest of the family, he stopped bitching about never having written the Great American Novel."

Aarti's Next Steps

I caught up with Aarti five years after her sabbatical ended and her memoir was released. We'd huffed up to the top of Rocky Outcrop Park, which towers over San Francisco's western Sunset District and offers both ocean and Golden Gate Bridge views. It was windy but warm, and we'd worked up a considerable sweat mounting the park's hundred-plus steps. Almost every aspect of Aarti's life had changed since we last spoke. Her memoir, *Here We Are: American Dreams and Nightmares*, became a bestseller and was being optioned to become a movie. She left her reporting job at NPR and, armed with the economic proof of her creative powers, launched an enormously successful podcast, interviewing the likes of Barack Obama, Stacey Abrams, and Ezra Klein over the course of two seasons. She then returned to NPR on her own terms, in a limited role cohosting a national news segment, while she worked on her first novel.

Aarti looks back on her sabbatical as a revolutionary inflection point in her life. It allowed her to wrest herself from playing a role in her family's and her editor's stories and to begin to write her own future. She has a few regrets—mostly around not taking more time off to enjoy herself before jumping back into the newsroom—but cannot imagine having written the book without the extended leave. "I just needed time to lose myself in the creative process. This wasn't the same as churning out a story for my job; it was all-consuming, messy, and self-guided," Aarti told me.

Writing the book also helped Aarti grow closer to her family. It gave her a chance to embody the lives and perspectives of people like her mom and brother, and a better understanding of what was really going on during a fast and frantic era. As for her new novel, Aarti believes that the only way she was able to get to the finish line—which took more than three times as long as her first book, with everything that comes with being a new mother—was because of the confidence she found by completing her memoir.

"I felt like a badass being able to write a book that I was proud of. It's an objectively hard thing to do," she reflected, "and it raised the ceiling for what I felt I could do in the future."

Out of all the research participants in our sabbatical study, Aarti's path stood out to me as a model example of what we can aim for as a society integrating time away from work into our careers. It wasn't that Aarti was burned out. It was more like she had something she really wanted to do in her life that wasn't a part of her routine job. She needed space to do work that was important to her, regardless of whether it would turn into anything more.

After getting the freedom from her job to do so, she returned refreshed and empowered. Psychologically armed, Aarti could have an honest conversation with her manager about her role and figure out another way to use her more self-actualized talents to still benefit the company more broadly (her podcast was produced and distributed by another NPR affiliate, and she's now employed by the national organization).

Work is not the enemy, nor is it the antithesis of sabbaticals. Our jobs give us purpose and camaraderie. Working enables the many things that give us meaning outside business hours. Recall the definition of sabbaticals from chapter 2: as long as we choose our work wisely, by setting strict boundaries and making sure it's very distinct from our routine job, work can be an important and helpful part of our sabbatical. A sabbatical requires stepping back from our job, but it doesn't require the absence of work. Neither idle time nor a vacation, a sabbatical is an opportunity to create a beautiful gift to the many versions of yourself. It gives "future you" a life with fewer regrets and "current you" an opportunity to grow, change, and live out the dream you've always imagined.

Aarti's path wasn't easy, but it was relatively straightforward. She knew what she wanted to accomplish, and her employer enabled her to pursue it. But there are many ways to enter Sabbatical Land and, once there, many ways to proceed. Next, we'll explore these entry points in depth.

4

Catalysts, Archetypes, and Barriers

What is the meaning of life?
The world is asking you, and it's your
job to answer with your actions.

—Victor Frankl, *Man's Search for Meaning*

While every sabbatical is unique, there are patterns that connect even the most disparate breaks. Understanding these themes can help us plan our sabbaticals in advance, take advantage of our strengths, and avoid getting foiled by our weaknesses while we're gone. I call these the sabbatical catalysts, archetypes, and barriers.

The Three Catalysts

Broadly speaking, I've observed three types of catalysts for sabbaticals: positive, negative, and neutral. A positive catalyst requires something unexpected and out of the ordinary to give you the financial or logistical freedom to take off. Maybe you receive severance from a job, sell your company, or inherit money when a long-lost great-uncle dies. (Okay, not so positive for your uncle, but a windfall for you.) Negative catalysts are unwelcome and often sudden. A crisis occurs in one of the vectors of your life: a professional setback, a relationship ending, or a health crisis (yours or that of someone close to you). A neutral entry isn't a surprise, and it doesn't come about as the result of a major event, windfall, or tragedy; like vacations or retirement, it's something we come to expect as part of our life.

The Positive Catalyst

Of course, everyone hopes for a positive beginning to their sabbatical, something akin to a big win—what I call the "windfall start." Basically, a victory lap arising from some success. The windfall enables you psychologically (if not financially) to take the break of your dreams. In addition to relieving the financial pressure of a sabbatical, a windfall also quiets the voice that says you don't deserve it. We're okay with treating ourselves after a big win, whereas we're less comfortable doing so when things aren't going well.

But few in this privileged position ultimately take time off—not because of any concrete barrier but because the idea is so psychologically foreign and intimidating. All too often, people who have had a big win rush off to the next thing, high on the fumes of their success, cocksure that the quickest way to their next triumph is a straight path forward. Our internal programming—that we must work in one uninterrupted sprint for our entire adult lives—runs counter to the idea of savoring the win with a break.

Most of us think of retirement as our windfall, when we'll *finally* have the opportunity to check all those items off our bucket lists, to live the lives we've been postponing. Unfortunately, the opposite happens far too often: my interviews are littered with stories about parents or grandparents saving up for their entire lives only to be thwarted later. Most fear that financial limitations will be their retirement burglars (delaying retirement age is a worldwide trend), but more often physical or psychological incapacity, whether ours or that of our partner, rob us of our long-awaited dreams.

For those who make it to retirement age with the ability to pursue their dreams intact, their internal wiring might still prevent them from enjoying it. Our jobs take up the majority of our waking hours. When we step back from our place of work, we leave not only the mundane work tasks behind but also our relationships, ongoing learning and growth, and the harder-to-pin-down feeling of *usefulness* to others. If you've spent your life focused on productivity—and so many of us have—the vacuum left after work vanishes can be devastating.[1] All the more reason to claim a life outside work sooner rather than later, and as soon as possible.

The Negative Catalyst

It's no accident that many of the chapters in this book feature someone who was forced into a sabbatical by a situation outside their control. You'll meet, for example, a consultant who was forced into caregiving mode for himself and his father in chapter 6. Approximately two-thirds of sabbaticals fall into this camp, which I refer to as the "time bomb." The classic time bomb is fomented by an unexpected negative personal or professional event. For example, an end to a relationship or an unexpected illness or death of a loved one—usually a parent, but more unexpectedly a spouse, child, or friend close in age. Or the sudden loss of a job, or burnout in one you haven't left.

An emergency is no way to start one of the most highly anticipated experiences of your life. Negative sabbaticals are more expensive because they're often sudden and unplannable. Gone is the ability to decrease costs by arranging things ahead of time, such as subletting your place or choosing a shoulder season during which to travel. Negative sabbaticals are also less self-directed because an external event has snatched away your agency. You lose control of the narrative of your time off, as well as your emotional state and, many times, your geographic location. As Mike Tyson once said, "Everyone has a plan until they get punched in the mouth."[2]

Finally, negative sabbaticals also require more time off than the average to be successful. You can't expect to launch directly into a transformative period of self-discovery if you're completely worn down or in shock. First, you must recover, which takes time. As one company leader put it, "I came to think of my time leading my organization as collecting various small injuries. Over time, the little things on the personal and professional fronts add up to overwhelm and take you down altogether, ultimately requiring significant time to heal and get back to baseline."

Humans are afraid of change. We're much more comfortable staying the course than leaving our familiar habits and patterns, no matter how counterproductive they've become.[3] We'd rather be in a bad spot that we're comfortable with than risk striking out anew. Anyone who has stayed in a bad relationship—personal or business—understands this sad reality. When it comes to leaving your job, it's often not until you've left that you realize the negative impact of the work at all.

It can take an enormous amount of effort and energy to pull off a sabbatical, especially as responsibilities and constraints increase over the course of your life. Waiting until something goes wrong to catalyze your sabbatical won't preclude you from the many benefits of doing so, but it will require more time and money and give you less control over its contents. All the more reason to schedule your break far in advance.

The Neutral Catalyst

Imagine a world in which taking a sabbatical is the same as taking any other break from work. After all, you don't have to convince yourself to leave the office over the weekend or go through all the additional logistics to execute your child's summer break. Aarti's sabbatical was catalyzed by a neutral event: the policy was there, and when the time was right for her, she simply took it. No need to worry about her job security or benefits, though because her sabbatical was unpaid she did have to save up to afford to take off.

Think of a neutral catalyst the way you treat owning a car (maybe even your red convertible). Car ownership requires periodic maintenance like oil changes and annual inspections. We perform these regular checks not because of any perceptible change in our car's performance but because no matter how inconvenient or costly these things are, it's much more inconvenient and expensive to perform major emergency repairs. An auto emergency is completely disruptive, so we're willing to trust the mechanic and put aside the time and money on a regular basis to prevent an unexpected crisis.

In an ideal world, our employers would provide us with both the time and resources for an extended, paid leave. In some parts of the world, governments have already taken this on as a part of the social contract.* Until we get there, we must treat a sabbatical as something we make time and space for in our lives and on our calendars. Expecting to take a sabbatical doesn't necessarily make the sabbatical process easy. But having this foresight takes a couple of psychological barriers out of the equation, like how much you've stored up in savings or whether it's exactly the right time to take off. Otherwise, like a neglected car, if you wait too long to take a sabbatical, a sabbatical will take you out of service unexpectedly, and at great cost.

The Three Archetypes

The type of sabbatical you choose depends on your life stage, job status, and a variety of other factors, such as personal responsibilities and desires. A forty-five-year-old father of three will not have the same

* See: France (*congé sabbatique*), Belgium, Sweden, Austria, or Australia, among others.

considerations—or priorities—as a thirtysomething who just sold her company or a twenty-six-year-old between jobs. That being said, a sabbatical doesn't have to map perfectly with your age or the expectations of others. A gap year, for example, can make as much sense at fifty-five as it does at eighteen.

On top of what you're able to pull off logistically, it's important to consider your intentions for your time off in the context of who you are and what you really need. Which part of you is planning your sabbatical—is it your exhausted work self, your internal productivity monster, or the creative version of you from deep down? Understanding your tendencies doesn't just give you a lens to help choose the most suitable sabbatical, it also provides a mirror to help you see the life that warrants reexamination. Ultimately, understanding the various types of sabbatical intentions will help you align your sabbatical to what you need and to return with greater self-understanding.

Over the course of my work, I have come across three archetypes among sabbatical takers: Seeker, Achiever, and Explorer. Recognizing yourself in these archetypes can help you make the best of your hard-earned break from routine. (You will likely identify with more than one of these archetypes, and that's completely normal. In fact, many folks experience all three during their time off.)

Understanding what each archetype hopes to gain and into which traps they're likely to fall will also allow you to take advantage of the experiences of many alumni who have gone before you. You'll be better equipped to know when your work-obsessed self may be taking over. For example, sometimes you can redirect a competitive, work-obsessed mindset into a beneficial sabbatical activity, like volunteering your time for others or whipping yourself back into shape with gusto. Other times, you may realize that it's this mindset itself, not your chosen activities, that you need some time away from.

The Achiever

The first and most common archetype is the achiever. Achievers view their sabbatical first and foremost as an opportunity to get things done.

Achievers are easy to recognize. They're looking to make up for lost time by trying to squeeze years of life goals into a few months. They're primed to view their sabbatical from the perspective of what they got done instead of how it made them feel. Don't judge—most people initially conceive their sabbatical this way. Because we so rarely have freedom over large swaths of our life, it can be hard *not* to think about a sabbatical as a prime opportunity for productivity on the personal front. As we saw with Aarti, personal achievement (in moderation) can be a great thing.

The achiever approaches their sabbatical with an accomplishment mindset. They often use external benchmarks—like fluency in a foreign language or completing a long hike—to determine whether they're making progress. Or they attack private goals, like writing a book or organizing a community garden. This way, the achiever comes away from their sabbatical having *accomplished* something. Whether the product is applicable to their post-sabbatical life is beside the point. The achiever's biggest fear is feeling like they wasted the opportunity to make some sort of tangible impact. They'll use easily explainable milestones to guard themselves from looking or feeling unproductive.

An achiever can turn anything into an achievement. Type-A yogis are a textbook example. Instead of using their time off to simply do more yoga or attend a yoga retreat in a more exotic location, achievers devote their sabbaticals to becoming certified yoga instructors. It doesn't matter that most of them don't ever intend to teach yoga; the structure, magnitude, and mere fact of the accomplishment offer proof that they've "done something" on their time off. And that *certified* proof is irresistible.

Ironically, almost everyone I've spoken to who took this achievement-oriented approach to yoga regretted not taking the time to simply practice, learn, and play. What's more, many of them found that the experience was almost anti-yoga. When you find yourself trying this hard to do something with your time off that's supposed to be fun, the achiever mindset might be taking a little too much control over your sabbatical.

If you see yourself in this archetype, you'd be wise to force yourself to schedule a period of rest and healing at the start of your sabbatical. This is the time when many overachievers finally realize that their relationship to work has tangible negative effects on their bodies and minds. From ulcers to trigger fingers to insomnia and worse, stories of unexpectedly rapid healing from achievers who tend to themselves first when taking a sabbatical abound.

Second, I challenge you to consider how you think about your sabbatical wish list. Deconstruct the list of things you want to accomplish on sabbatical, paying attention to which goals have meaning for you personally versus ones that satisfy your accomplishment mindset. Does becoming a certified scuba instructor simply make a better post-sabbatical story than telling people your most treasured moments were playful days with your children? It's almost inevitable that you will try to stuff your days and weeks on sabbatical with planned activities and aspirations, but for most, the real magic lies in serendipity and discovery, through play and experimentation.

The Seeker

The seeker also wants to accomplish something, but it's less about reaching a destination than embarking on the journey. Seekers have questions, as much about themselves as the world outside them. The type of project a seeker pursues rarely feels *urgent* among the chaos and routine of normal life but remains *important* across large swaths of their life. Seekers are drawn to pilgrimages or road trips to reconnect with friends, family, people, and places from their past.

Seekers are like personal archaeologists. They're likely to engage in activities they used to love, trying to pick up on the scent of joy and engagement from the past. The external journey is a metaphor for the seeker's ongoing internal search. They are deeply engaged in identity work, sensemaking on a path from uncertainty to certainty. A sabbatical beckons them to answer questions that have been bubbling up about the world and how they relate to it. Aspiring career switchers, or just folks looking to discern between garden-variety burnout and a strong signal to switch jobs, fit into this bucket.

I embarked on my sabbatical as a seeker. I had an overriding feeling that I'd ignored some core parts of myself for a long time. Primarily, that I'd neglected to make progress on deep questions within me about spirituality. I sensed that this project was important to me and required a lot more time and effort than I'd given it so far. I needed a more active approach if I wanted to make progress.

Seekers are prone to unrealistic expectations, which can put them at high risk of disappointment when they return from a sabbatical. The fact that they've finally made the time and space for something incredibly important and long overdue adds pressure to find the *perfect* next steps upon return. The kind of "good enough" steps that follow most sabbaticals—like staying at your old job for a bit longer or changing things up slightly before you make a big career move—are unlikely to satisfy seekers. In short, the quest for perfection becomes the enemy of success, spurring a more protracted sabbatical that becomes increasingly expensive and anxiety-inducing.

Seekers should consider two strategies to avoid this vicious cycle. First, restrict the amount of time you allow yourself to seek. Seeking is a lifelong pursuit, not something you're likely to knock out in several months. Instead of expecting to find your dream job (or state of being) by the end of your sabbatical, consider it a success to identify the next tangible step toward what your dream could be. You can control the process of the search, not the results. For example, have twenty coffee chats about career possibilities with people you admire. Your first sabbatical won't be your last. To avoid burning out or spinning your wheels, it's far better to end your sabbatical a bit closer to your ideal self than to flounder in the liminal state between the last thing and the next.

Second, seekers should prioritize others during their sabbatical. Seekers can easily lose track of time peering deep down into their personal rabbit hole. But sometimes the best way to learn about yourself is by setting your concerns aside entirely. Our research interviewees consistently recalled the time they spent with others as their most treasured moments. This finding emphasizes what the happiness literature has found over and over—that supporting other important people in your life and nurturing your relationships are instrumental to self-fulfillment.[4]

The Explorer

Explorers have an appetite to see what's out there in the world. They're less concerned about how or if it will apply to their lives at the other end.

You don't have to travel across the world to qualify as an explorer—I've met plenty of folks who, during their sabbaticals, spent time closer to home. They volunteered in their communities, experimented with new hobbies, and took shorter regional trips. All these detours took them out of their routine and cracked open their shells. Even going through a stack of books on your reading list can trigger awe. It can widen the aperture on what's possible.

It's rare to encounter a sabbatical that doesn't incorporate a segment of pure exploration. Setting off on a journey is the most natural way to break free from routine life and to celebrate what's next.

For those who can afford to explore someplace far away, a sabbatical enables them to both get off the beaten path and to sufficiently sink in once they get there. As a burned-out marketing executive from our study put it, "I was having a very difficult time disengaging from my work for a couple of weeks after my sabbatical started, checking my personal email constantly and reflexively looking at my calendar. But as soon as my plane's wheels left the runway en route to Bali—laptop behind—my work concerns evaporated completely." Challenge yourself to get as far away from your routine experience of life as possible.

Exploration introduces uncertainty into our lives. In our world of limited vacation, we simply can't afford to go off track and get lost. We can't miss work, we can't fly on weekdays, and we can't risk traveling during shoulder seasons to save money. On sabbatical, you become time wealthy. Mistakes and inconveniences transform from vacation-ruiners to serendipitous encounters. Exploring on our sabbaticals asks us instead to leave some important things to chance for a change. Living in the present and traveling flexibly leads to higher reported satisfaction among travelers and is correlated with greater psychological resilience.[5]

While traveling far away may be the surest way to get out of your comfort zone, explorers who take an exotic, far-flung sabbatical often miss the beautiful things nearby, alienate themselves from their community, and set impossible standards for what quenches their sense of adventure. As a dyed-in-the-wool explorer, I know how difficult it is to go from a jet-setting expat to living a more sustainable life. But a well-balanced sabbatical (and life) requires also finding beauty in the mundane, closer to home. My advice to explorers is to spend a significant portion of your sabbatical as a tourist in your own land. If you're able to travel to far-flung places, do that first to completely disconnect and satisfy your more traditional sense of adventure. But then return to your routine surroundings and try to inhabit the energy that newcomers to a city have: sign up for a special interest club, like a pottery or dance class. Volunteer locally or go to a city council meeting. It's a totally normal mistake to treat your home turf as unworthy of the same attention and awe as some exotic locale. No matter how far afield your sabbatical takes you, the point isn't to leave forever but to return home better off.

The Two Barriers

In the world of sabbaticals, there are two types of barriers to taking time off: responsibilities and perceptions. Responsibilities are real and represent a tangible commitment you must work around. Perceptions can certainly feel real, but they're intangible and contextual, shifting over time. Learning about the barriers and differentiating between them helps strengthen your resolve and ability to navigate around them.

Perception

Perception is how we think about taking time off, as well as how we believe others will judge us for doing so. As much as we like to complain about our jobs, work provides plenty of meaning, positive self-worth, and fulfillment.[6] When we're unemployed, our self-esteem takes a hit, a common experience I hear from sabbatical takers who've left their job without concrete work plans.[7]

Even if you're able to get over your own perception about what it means to *not* work for an extended period of time, you may fear others' perceptions of you. Unfortunately, research validates this fear. There's even a name for it—the work devotion norm.[8] This unspoken expectation celebrates people for staying late at the office, staying available on vacations, and generally prioritizing work over personal life. Even if vacation is technically allowed, certain office cultures reward us for not taking it. The paradox of unlimited vacation illustrates this perfectly: in companies (usually start-ups) where vacation days are uncapped, people are more likely to take fewer days than if it's prescribed.[9]

The pull to conform to the image of an ideal worker is so strong that it can even compel some to forgo their rights by law to avoid standing out. For example, research on paternity leave in Sweden uncovered that new fathers were significantly more likely to reduce or even skip their parental leave altogether if their bosses also did so, despite Sweden having one of the most generous parental leave policies in the world.[10]

While the work devotion norm still presides in today's workplaces, there is—reassuringly—steadily growing evidence that the ideal worker norm is reversing. Hiring managers are beginning to view time off as a healthy choice, a positive sign of a thriving inner life, and a desire for healing and self-renewal.[11] The number of American employees who are on sabbatical has tripled in the past five years.[12] People are increasingly listing their sabbaticals as part of their résumés. In 2022, LinkedIn introduced a career break job title, which more than a million people have integrated into their online CV.[13] Sabbaticals are even more common among younger workers, who are twice as likely to take a sabbatical as their older colleagues. In other words, work culture has begun to view sabbaticals as courageous acts rather than thinly veiled excuses for failing, burning out, or not being able to "cut it." A superpower instead of kryptonite.

If your employer isn't providing one of these opportunities on paper, I still recommend having a conversation with a manager, ombudsperson, or HR representative about your desire for extended leave. Approach the conversation with an awareness that there may be challenges, but know that many people who've successfully taken sabbaticals found that having an honest discussion opened up informal opportunities they didn't know existed. I'm reminded of a conversation with a partner at a prestigious consulting firm who told me that, while they didn't have an official paid sabbatical policy, he'd helped many of his employees take advantage of their generous disability leave policy and offered to connect them with a doctor who recognized the rehabilitative effects of extended leave among their patients.

If a potential employer passes you over for a job because of a break from work, consider it an early warning sign that you should look for another employer.

Responsibility

Broadly speaking, there are two types of responsibilities at play: logistical concerns around your everyday life commitments and financial concerns around the tangible costs of taking time off. They are often a bit intertwined, as many of our ongoing responsibilities are financial. You have a mortgage to pay, or a whole host of recurring living costs that persist whether or not you're working. But outside of financial obligations, there are likely other high logistical barriers to leaving your routine life behind for a while. A partner who can't take off work, say, or the logistics associated with your children's schooling that may prevent you from taking leave.

In terms of financial concerns, you have both current and future costs to cover. Sabbaticals can be expensive relative to normal life, often involving foreign travel, eating out in restaurants, and many other situations that would be the exception, rather than the norm, in routine life. The key to overcoming both logistical and financial hurdles is to remember that advance planning is your friend. When we talk about taking a sabbatical, we're not asking ourselves if we can take time off immediately. Of course that's out of reach, including for the most privileged among us. The financial impact of suddenly pulling the plug from your life can magnify financial hardship that could be bridged with some thoughtful planning, saving, and foresight. For example, subletting your apartment, putting large expenses on hold, and cutting off unnecessary recurring costs.

Some of my favorite sabbatical stories come from people who overcame financial constraints with determination, long-term preparation, and commitment to enact their dream. They couldn't afford to wait for their lives to blow up before considering taking time off, so they prioritized bringing their dreams to life on a feasible timeline. One teacher and her husband saved up for a decade so that they could share the vagabond lifestyle with their children once they were old enough. Together, they crammed four people into a fifty-year-old Land Rover and drove from Arizona to the tip of Argentina on the cheap. The trip had such a big impact on the father that he quit his teaching job to start a small business restoring old Land Rovers. But that's another story altogether.

In an ideal world, sabbaticals are in the same bucket as parental leave: typically paid, with benefits, and a guaranteed slot upon return. Until then, the clearest path for those without much financial cushion requires long-term planning and years of saving up for one's sabbatical. It's important to acknowledge that even with careful planning, taking a sabbatical requires a level of financial stability and job security that isn't accessible to everyone. The ability to step away from income—even temporarily—is itself a form of privilege. A sabbatical doesn't need glitz and glamour, but it does require you to be away from work, company policy or not. My hope is that this book can help shift the Overton window toward more inclusive sabbatical policies. Sabbaticals should be recognized as a broader right rather than a luxury available only to a few. In the meantime, this book can provide sufficient justification for those who currently have the means to save up and embark on their own.

Privilege

The elephant in the room when we talk about sabbaticals is accessibility. At this moment, sabbaticals are an immense privilege reserved for the very elite few, with little exception. As a white American guy who went to some pretty fancy schools that lend a career safety net—and who also happens to be writing a book about sabbaticals—I recognize my responsibility to address that. In fact, we *need* to address it, because, like any barrier, in order to dismantle it, we must first identify it and confront it.

Most of the examples in this book come from a relatively privileged segment of people who have more financial and psychological security. Taking a sabbatical was within the realm of possibility for them. The reality is that taking extended leave from work can cost significantly more money than normal life, and requires either a generous and forward-thinking employer or quitting your job and taking a chance on the future labor market. Stocking the book with an even ratio of "sabbaticals are for everyone" stories would have been disingenuous. The question is: Can we use this privilege to expand access and make sabbaticals more broadly available?

The best predictor of someone's likelihood to take a sabbatical is whether or not they knew someone who had taken one—an exemplar, as we saw with Winston in chapter 1. Seeing someone like you, whether demographically or career-wise, who's taken a sabbatical gives you permission to imagine it for yourself. It alleviates both the *willing* and the *able* arguments from above.

The more people taking sabbaticals, the more examples there will be for others to look up to. Importantly, the more people in positions of power who take a sabbatical, the greater chance they will support and enable their coworkers and employees to do so. Someone must be able to afford to be at the front of the movement, when it's relatively expensive and inconvenient to do so. Only then, as with so many other expensive and exclusive things, from early cell phones to electric cars and, heck, even indoor plumbing, will the costs go down and availability increase for the rest of us.

In the same way that we can't ignore the financial barriers to taking a sabbatical, the psychological component of taking a sabbatical cannot be overlooked. Many of us lack the role models to help us feel okay about not working or, at the very least, to not feel ashamed when telling our families or peer groups that we're intentionally stepping out of the workplace. Even in one of the richest countries on the planet, taking a very small chunk of time off in the context of our long careers can cause hurt or inspire resentment among the same people who want the best for us. This creates a vicious cycle wherein those with the greatest ability to take a sabbatical are unlikely to do so for fear of how it looks. And it's precisely those people that the world *needs* to take time off, in order to create inclusive policies (and set a good example) at work for everybody else.

This is the current state of extended leave. But I do not believe it's the permanent state of things.

The aspiration for this book is to accelerate the evolution of sabbaticals from a privilege to a norm in our society. Initially, the weekend was a privilege for landowners and the elite. Now, taking two days off per week is the norm. The battle for sufficient paid parental leave has followed a similar trajectory. Globally, around 40 percent of organizations offer paid leave above the minimums that more than ninety countries now require by law.[14] In the US, a dozen states have mandatory paid leave systems, with another dozen or so erecting voluntary systems en route to the same destination. At the same time, the US is still the only high-income country in the world without guaranteed *paid* parental leave, and the availability of parental leave varies significantly by income and other demographic factors. For example, one study found that "access to parental leave among high-wage workers is four times more common than in low-wage workers."[15] Compared to fifty years ago, parental leave has become a norm in the workplace, but it still remains an aspirational norm for many.

Consider summer vacation—one of my favorite examples when discussing the feasibility of a sabbatical. No matter how you slice it, summer vacation makes no sense in any practical dimension. For parents, it's enormously inconvenient and expensive. For children, it's bad for learning. Studies peg the impact of learning loss (the so-called summer slide) at up to three months' worth of academic progress.[16] But I've yet to meet someone who would take summer breaks away from their kids. Most folks trace some of their fondest memories to the summers of their childhood. When you defend the concept of summer vacation, you're subconsciously affirming that your child's summer outcomes—joy, wonder, freedom, exploration—are more important than the incremental educational benefits of year-round schooling.

Somehow, we've all agreed that the downsides of summer break are worth the intangible benefits. I invite you to use this frame of mind to evaluate the decision to take a sabbatical. Things are a privilege until they become the norm. If we value something enough, then as advocates, executives, legislators, and everyone in between, we must fight to make it work for all by making it the default.

ooo

All of this can feel intimidating. Archetypes, barriers, and privilege—wasn't the purpose of going on sabbatical to relax and enjoy yourself? Take solace in the fact that almost every person who has taken a sabbatical has done so without much guidance or preparation. The stories and frameworks in this book are meant to help you sketch the broad outlines of an uncertain journey ahead, not to prescribe your exact experience. Take what's helpful and refer back to the rest if and when needed.

In whatever capacity we desire guidance, despite our best efforts to follow the script on sabbaticals, life, left to its own devices, often dictates when and how we can take a sabbatical. But there is something that can help. Instead of letting life alone decide, we can use inflection points in our lives as opportunities to step back—or step up—to the next chapter.

5

Inflection Points

The pilgrim could step outside of all roles and just be a person, someone without responsibilities or expectations or any constraint besides continuous forward movement to a distant goal.

—Gideon Lewis-Kraus, *A Sense of Direction*

Renuka Sastri prided herself on raising capable, independent children. When her eldest daughter, Leela, declared her intention to walk the Camino de Santiago, Renuka was initially supportive of her plans. Though the five-hundred-mile Camino was originally a pilgrimage for Catholics, it wasn't a religious experience that Leela sought. She saw it as a way to detach from the stress of her senior year in high school before her next steps in the fall.

As summer approached, Leela's preparations neared completion: she'd broken in her new hiking boots and mercilessly trimmed her packing list until everything fit into a small backpack. But an unexpected snag occurred when, either by algorithm or coincidence, her mom's Facebook feed surfaced some frightening posts about a suspected murder on the Camino. The victim was a young woman who had disappeared about a month into her journey.

Suddenly, letting Leela walk alone felt like an unnecessary risk. After expressing her concern to her daughter (read: threatening to pull financial support for school), Renuka got her to agree to a compromise: Leela would walk the Camino, but not alone. Instead, she would draft a few friends and family members to join her on different segments across Spain. When one roughly two-week (two-hundred-mile) section remained unclaimed, Renuka decided she would join Leela on that stretch of the walk herself.

ooo

Renuka's decision to join Leela turned into much more than just a good vacation. It became an inflection point for her life to head in a new direction. In mathematics, an inflection point marks the exact moment a line changes direction. In our lives, these are the pivotal moments when our path fundamentally shifts course, often in ways we don't recognize until we're looking back.

The tragedy is that too many of us miss the chance to invest time and attention during the inflection points in our lives. We sense that something significant is happening, that we're at a crossroads, but instead of leaning into the change, celebrating it, or contemplating another path, we ignore the opportunity its significance presents. I'm reminded of a high-achieving law partner whose firm offered sabbatical policies. He and his son had always dreamed of hiking part of the Appalachian Trail together, but when his son graduated high school, the father was close enough to a major promotion that he skipped his sabbatical. Four years later, he'd achieved his career goals, but his son was too busy starting his first job out of college to join the hike. It wasn't an acute tragedy, but it was a pretty big missed opportunity—one of those moments you can't easily re-create once life moves on.

Stories like this are all too common, and why one of the biggest barriers to taking a sabbatical isn't about what we do while we're away—it's having the confidence to leave to begin with. What keeps us from Sabbatical Land is often our failure to recognize when we've reached an inflection point, that precise moment when the curve of our lives is ready to put us on a new path. Without an understanding of the opportunity these threshold moments present, we become overwhelmed—stuck, even—by the extra work and intrinsic uncertainty that comes with stepping away from the workforce. Like Renuka, we need a good-enough reason to step out of our comfort zone. Unfortunately, more often we wait until it's too late, and either let a great opportunity pass us by or, worse, allow a negative event to force our hand.

While some milestones offer clear cause for celebration—graduations and weddings, for example—long stretches of our lives can go by without obvious occasion to step back and take stock. But as anyone firmly rooted in midlife knows, that doesn't mean we aren't in dire need of changing the direction of our lives. This chapter explores how to use inflection points that would normally fly under our radar—like pausing for caregiving, becoming an empty nester, or experiencing a health crisis—as opportunities to step back and move forward in a different way. These opportunities often evade us due to the busyness of everyday life, sure. But we also lack established rituals to help us celebrate and sanctify moments that we'll look back upon wishing we'd paid more attention to.

The Modern Pilgrimage

Renuka's inflection point arrived during her unexpected pilgrimage. A pilgrimage is a great metaphor for a sabbatical, and it's also a near-perfect sabbatical activity. It's a long journey, often undertaken solo, in anticipation of revelation. A pilgrimage can take weeks or even months, can require you to leave work completely, and ensures your days overflow with physical and mental activity.

The term "pilgrim" derives from Latin's *peregrinus*, meaning "foreigner" or, more charitably, "traveler." The modern definition has expanded to include anyone undertaking a journey of personal significance, searching for new or expanded meaning for themselves and their place in the world. The modern pilgrim creates their own path for their own reasons, rather than adhering to some rigid religious requirement. This is likely why Elizabeth Gilbert's *Eat, Pray, Love* resonated in such a deep way. By endowing a personal quest with enough significance, it becomes sufficiently holy in even the most atheistic adventurer's books.

In Renuka's case, the pilgrimage felt much closer to normal life than she ever would have believed. It certainly wasn't the ordeal she'd imagined a two-hundred-mile walk would be. Life became surprisingly simple. The only choice she faced every morning was how far to walk.

Renuka adapted quickly to her new reality: putting one foot in front of the other, eating simple, cheap meals, sleeping, and hand-washing underwear and socks at the end of the day. It didn't hurt that Leela had had a couple of weeks on the trail to get used to the rhythm of the walk. She knew the best time to set out in the morning, whether to take a siesta after lunch or power through, and which parts of the pilgrim housing were likely to be the best for sleeping. Renuka had been somewhat anxious about the trip. (Would she be physically able to complete the task?) But once she was steeped in the daily pace of the Camino, her sense of unease died down completely.

Renuka and Leela would spend mornings and early afternoons walking together before reaching their *albergues*, the hostel-like former convents where most trekkers sleep. In between, they'd give each other space to chat with fellow pilgrims, listen to music, or get lost in their own thoughts. Often, Leela would be a kilometer or more ahead.

Renuka had never struggled to talk to her daughter, but the expanse of time and surrounding beauty deepened their conversations. She treasured the opportunity to get to know Leela's dreams and fears (and Camino crushes) as she transformed into an adult almost before her eyes. Renuka's primary goal was to make sure her daughter was safe. What she didn't realize was that her seventeen days on the Camino would set off a chain reaction that would completely alter her own life.

Renuka had needed a break from the stresses of work when she decided to join Leela—not that she admitted or realized it. Her two-decade-long career in digital strategy at a large travel insurance company with a best-in-class time-off policy had provided enough career evolution to keep her growing without intruding on her perceived work-life balance. Now that she had reached the end of her three-week segment (in what seemed like a long weekend), Renuka felt lighter. Physically she'd shed a few pounds, sure—but psychologically, the worries and realities of work had fallen off at an even faster clip. She felt like the end of this journey was the beginning of a much larger one, a catalyst for big changes to her roles at work and at home.

ooo

American cultural milestones are connected to legal and work-related indicators. We celebrate driving when we turn sixteen, becoming an adult at eighteen, and being able to drink at twenty-one. The car-renters among us rejoice at twenty-five, but that's about the last formal reminder of our adulthood until our AARP card arrives in the mail, which doesn't exactly get us jumping for joy. We throw parties for weddings, funerals, and retirement. But we're on our own for some of life's most important and difficult transitions, like becoming a parent, ending a marriage, empty nesting, or experiencing perimenopause.

Some religious traditions offer guidance through sacraments like confirmation, baptism, bat mitzvahs, and the like. Renuka possessed a framework about life changes from her Hindu upbringing in India, which gave her permission to imagine moving on to the next phase.

Hinduism presents four life stages, called *ashramas*, which we move through over the course of our lives.

The first, *Brahmacharya*, is focused on education and self-discipline. This is the time for foundational religious schooling and training up until one starts a family. Next comes the "householder" phase, *Grihastha*, which is a time of active engagement in life's responsibilities, such as supporting your family and being a productive member of society. This is where Renuka found herself leading up to her sabbatical. The third phase, *Vanaprastha*, marks the beginning of a retreat from life's day-to-day demands. Individuals in this stage begin to withdraw from service to others and instead return to their own ambitions.

Sannyasa, the final phase, prepares one for death—or, ideally for Hindus, liberation from the endless cycle of birth and rebirth. By this time in life, you've fulfilled all of society's expectations. You're free to live a simple life, devote yourself to nonviolence, and, if you're into it, go full ascetic-monastic.

Renuka's time with her daughter during Leela's transition out of the house made clear the enormity of the changes she would soon face in her own life as an empty nester. In her words: "For women in particular, as you depart from your caregiving life stage, it's really important to ask: Who am I outside of the roles I've been playing in others' lives since my twenties?"

Catalyzing a Big Change in Midlife

But as our collective religiosity wanes, so does society's ability to prepare us for, and to celebrate, important transitions in human life. Without these broadly accepted mile markers, we often wait until it's too late to make a much-needed change in our lives. Chip Conley received a wakeup call he couldn't ignore at age forty-seven, when his heart stopped multiple times over the course of ninety minutes.

Chip had worked hospitality hours as a hotelier nonstop since the age of twenty-six, when he started Joie de Vivre Hospitality. After he'd recovered from his flatline moment, returning to his old way of working took on existential overtones. Chip decided to take a sabbatical. He put his company up for sale, even though the timing wasn't ideal to step away, leaving lots of money and options on the table. But the message he'd received from his body was louder than anything his business-focused brain could muster: his former existence was no longer working, and it was playing an active role in shortening his life.

During his year away, Chip attended dozens of music and art festivals around the world, hoping to jump-start his imagination, wonder, and creativity. He remembers it as one of the most joyful and vital periods of his life. Chip estimates he met hundreds of people of all ages and from all walks of life, though the circuit tended to attract younger folks with fewer responsibilities. His interactions with people his age and older were the most telling—everyone seemed to be going through their own version of his midlife reset. Some were on a journey inspired by their own health conditions, but most had simply felt the urge to quit their lives to strike out in a new direction. Like Chip, they'd felt momentarily lost; not a great feeling at any age, but an increasingly stressful one as you get older, when you're expected to have most things figured out.

As Chip reflected on his unexpected midlife sabbatical, he realized that the popular narrative about the "midlife crisis" actually represents society's failure to recognize natural inflection points. Chip saw that while what was normally considered midlife, our forties and fifties, might technically be the middle of our lifespan, it was no longer the twilight of our careers, too late to make a big change. As the period of our productive and healthy years—our so-called healthspan—expands to what was previously thought of as our lifespan, what can we make of these additional decades?

Chip recruited academic research partners to take a closer look at the realities of midlife. Together they found that while there are many predictable, difficult situations as we advance through this stage—such as empty nesting, caregiving, and navigating retirement—very few resources exist with which we can prepare ourselves. Chip thought midlife shouldn't be a crisis but something more like a caterpillar's chrysalis—an occasion to change into our truest form. Chip wanted to create a positive catalyst for people to reexamine their lives instead of arriving at a moment of self-reflection only on their deathbed.

So, he started something new in the hospitality space: the Modern Elder Academy (MEA), a school in Baja Sur, Mexico, that hosts experts from around the world to help those navigating midlife. MEA offers weeklong programs centered around themes like catalyzing transitions and cultivating purpose in the second half of life. MEA's programming isn't designed to mimic a sabbatical but rather to act as a catalyzing event. These short retreats tend to usher in a period of significant change for participants and have spawned self-organized alumni groups across dozens of cities globally and spurred MEA's expansion to another location, in Santa Fe, New Mexico.

For Chip, it's not only the curriculum that inspires participants to make these life shifts but also the permission and inspiration given by seeing others like themselves build up the courage to make big changes. Chip describes these moments as catching the "scent of possibility" for an even more exciting and fulfilling chapter than the last. People come to MEA on the cusp of a big change in their lives, if not in the messy middle of it by the time they arrive on campus.

One of Chip's goals for the Modern Elder Academy is to bring attention to an often-overlooked occasion to reflect and transform; for much of our midlife, years can stretch by without an occasion to take stock. Another goal born from Chip's life-altering sabbatical spurred by his close call with death is to help people realize that it's never too late to take time off to take stock of their life. It's on us to mark the occasion before the choice is made for us.

On the Cusp of Big Changes

After returning home, Renuka felt restless. Many of the conversations she'd had on the Camino, both with her daughter and others along the trail, revolved around what people wanted in their lives. These conversations put the magnitude of the changes about to take place—her daughter moving on and her son heading off to college next year—into sharp relief. They were more than just future events to contemplate; they were real, existential, and accelerating life events heading right toward her. Who would she be once her kids left for school? What would she pour her excess energy into? Her short stint away had cracked something open inside her. For close to twenty years, she'd stayed at her job mostly to provide stability while her children grew up. But that stage was rapidly coming to an end.

Renuka didn't know what was next, but her relatively short time on the Camino taught her that she was capable of much more than she'd thought. So, for the first time in two decades, Renuka began working overtime on life *outside* the office: exploring what was happening in her community and building out her local network. She felt her ambitions come roaring back to life and started thinking about her career possibilities more holistically. She hired a career coach to think through her options and reconnected with a group of friends from school—all of whom were women in their forties and fifties facing similar transitions. Together they attended Reboot Partners, a weekend seminar on midlife career change, for guidance and inspiration.

After her experience on the Camino and the Reboot transition seminar, Renuka was working up the courage to leave the only job she'd had since graduation when two events pushed her over the edge. First, her son got a scholarship to college, relieving a big chunk of financial responsibility. Second, a coworker and friend retired, only to have her partner contract pneumonia and pass away suddenly. The news of the partner's passing hit Renuka particularly hard; delaying gratification until reaching an advanced age was a risk she was unwilling to take.

Finally, just as she resolved that she couldn't wait any longer, she got a text from her cousin asking simply: "Patagonia or Bhutan?"

Renuka replied, "Bhutan," and handed in her notice.

ooo

Renuka wasn't totally clear about what she wanted to do on her sabbatical, but she gave herself six months to disconnect, get healthy, and spend time with family and friends. Renuka's sabbatical had three distinct phases.

The first was the extended trip to Bhutan, where she was able to put her newfound hiking know-how (and fitness) to the test. She thought her time in Spain would have prepared her for this endurance test, but the treks in Bhutan were much more remote, requiring porters and guides, and occurring with very little oxygen due to the high altitude. But with the extra difficulty—and the effort it required—came a profound sense of achievement and renewed pride in her abilities. After Bhutan, Renuka took the long way back home to Florida, stopping in India and Europe to visit family and friends.

Renuka planned her return home around her father, who was scheduled to have surgery. Instead of the typical jockeying with her siblings about who would take care of him and when, she was able to be with him for the duration of the operation and recovery, advocating on his behalf and spending nights in the hospital sleeping by his side. Renuka felt privileged to be able to care for her parent in entirety instead of shoehorning such a powerful experience into long weekends off from work or multitasking by his bedside, computer on her lap.

In the second phase of her sabbatical, Renuka set about discovering more about herself. She'd returned from Bhutan in good spirits. The hiking had been difficult—she reckoned she was among the oldest on any of the treks—but despite sore knees, she'd conquered all the peaks. Newly inspired, she set about acquiring other skills, joining a maker space where local hobbyists could swap equipment (and expertise) and delving into pottery for the first time. She also sent an email to family and friends asking for their input on what she should do in the last phase of her sabbatical, as well as suggestions about what job might be a good fit upon return. The list of suggestions wasn't surprising—open her own consulting practice, write a book, get involved in local politics—but she noticed the size of the gulf between the things she was doing with her life and what people around her believed she could do. Knowing others hold you in high esteem and seeing it written down were completely different experiences.

Entering into the last phase of her sabbatical, Renuka surveyed the groundwork she'd laid so far, after all her accomplishments to date. She'd rebounded through exercise and nourishing time with friends and family. Her children relied on her less at home, and she'd fulfilled a familial duty to care for her father. And she'd used the skills she'd picked up at the Reboot transition seminar to better understand herself and the possible paths for her future.

Reflecting on her time away, Renuka observed that "my kids now see me as a person who's capable of doing anything she wants—not something out of fear because I'm older."

And yet, despite all she had accomplished—and the bright future she knew could be hers—Renuka couldn't help but feel alone and intimidated as she prepared herself to search for a new job for the first time in more than two decades. Fears about what lies beyond our sabbatical is enough to dissuade many from setting forth to begin with. This is particularly true for women, who leave the workforce for longer stretches of time for child-rearing and who are more likely to experience discrimination for gaps on their résumés as a result.[1] Thankfully, there are entrepreneurs like Carol Fishman Cohen who have stepped into the field of transition to help.

Relaunching After Caretaking

Carol Fishman Cohen did not realize how difficult and isolating it would be to resume her career until long after she'd left her full-time job as an investment banker to raise four children. Once they were old enough to attend school, she thought she'd reached an inflection point in her caregiving duties where she could focus on returning to work. Carol was pretty sure she wanted to return to finance but hadn't defined her career goals any further since her departure. Also, she was embarrassed that she had not even read *The Wall Street Journal* regularly over the years she had been home with her kids, let alone kept up with the developments in the high-yield debt markets.

It wasn't until she went to her fifteen-year business school reunion and reconnected with classmates, in particular one who had become a headhunter, that Carol felt things starting to move forward. Instead of focusing on what she *hadn't* been doing for the past decade, the people at the reunion remembered her for the talents they'd observed when they were in school or at work together. Being seen as a talented, in-demand worker again helped Carol begin to recover the professional confidence she'd felt increasingly distant from the longer she was on a career break.

Leveraging her classmates' willingness to help, Carol dove into an intensive study period, reviewing old deals, books, and cases and speaking with her old colleagues to catch up on the intricacies of the current financial markets. Eventually, Carol was able to relaunch her career in the high-yield debt arm of Bain Capital. At the time, it was a progressive move on Bain's part, because the job-seeking process for career returners like Carol was largely stigmatized and inefficient. Though she landed with Bain, Carol felt this stigma throughout her job search, and saw firsthand how employers overlooked valuable opportunities to hire from this under-tapped, high-caliber talent pool of professionals returning from a career break.

According to studies and data from the Bureau of Labor Statistics, Carol was far from alone in her struggles: approximately 2.1 million educated mothers of prime working age in the US were interested in returning to work.[2] Carol's challenge was convincing employers to recognize her—and more broadly, women who'd left the workforce for various reasons—as valuable contributors and additions to a team. Gender-diverse teams produce higher financial returns, increase collective intelligence, and are altogether more innovative than predominantly male ones.[3] At the same time, women are less likely than men to return immediately to the workforce after having kids. This leaves our economy with a substantial portion of its trained employees outside the workforce, and women who've taken career breaks with substantial gaps on their résumés to overcome.

Based on her return-to-work experience, Carol and her fellow business school alum Vivian Steir Rabin coauthored a comprehensive guide to relaunching careers, called *Back on the Career Track*, in 2007. Carol quit her hard-won investment job to become an entrepreneur, cofounding iRelaunch with Vivian. The goal for iRelaunch was to work with individuals seeking to reenter the workforce and organizations that recognized their potential. To do so, iRelaunch hosted Return to Work conferences to create a marketplace drawing returners together with employers interested in hiring them, and to provide returner attendees with tactics to successfully relaunch their careers. Carol found that job seekers and employers alike were gravitating to a new model that mimicked internships: 75 percent of companies hiring reentry workers were doing so through so-called returnships, where prospective full-time employees work alongside mentors and other employees in paid roles for anywhere from eight weeks to a year.

Carol summarized the approach in a successful TED Talk called "How to Get Back to Work After a Career Break" and in the *Harvard*

Business Review article "The 40-Year-Old Intern." Her message was clear: with the right perspective and strategies, a career break isn't a disadvantage but rather an opportunity to step back and reflect on whether you were on the right career path to begin with. No matter when or why you've reached an inflection point in your life, you have the power to double down and return to the career you left or to go forward in a different direction.

The iRelaunch conferences were so successful that Carol and Vivian realized it was important for companies to launch their own career reentry programs, and they developed a corporate advisory practice to do so. Since iRelaunch began in 2007, more than one-third of Fortune 50 companies have launched their own internal return-to-work programs, including JPMorganChase, Goldman Sachs, Johnson & Johnson, and Wells Fargo. Carol and Vivian's conferences blossomed to become a biannual core offering, and the iRelaunch returner community has grown to nearly 125,000 strong.[4]

ooo

Increasingly, navigating the difficulties of career reentry has become a feature of modern employment instead of an exception for those who take on full-time caretaking. We no longer expect to work in a straight line from graduation to retirement, relying on lifelong employment with one company. Instead, we're more likely to hold a dozen or more jobs across our lifetime.[5] Our careers are now entrepreneurial by necessity: we take on responsibility for everything from our 401(k)s to our professional development. This evolution from an employer managing your career to you managing your own is known as the "protean career."

Boston University professor Douglas T. Hall popularized the term, named after Proteus, the Greek god who was able to change his form at will. (Seems like there's often a Greek god behind these things.) What it means for our careers is that instead of focusing our energies on a career trajectory *within* an organization, we alone are in charge of career choices and fulfillment on a much larger and more uncertain playing field.[6] You must consider where the economy is going as a whole and figure out how to remain attractive in an uncertain future. To do that, you must jockey and prepare yourself for roles and responsibilities that have yet to be defined.

Take, for example, the product management role. Formalized in the early aughts, product managers (PMs) serve as the coordinators between what the customers want and what the engineers at a company build. Before the turn of the century, you'd have been hard-pressed to find a job description by that name; now it's the most popular route into tech.

To understand where to direct our careers, we must locate the intersection of what we have to offer with what the world needs—or *will* need. Given this new reality, navigating the career landscape becomes less about specific skill acquisition and more about perspective and self-direction. (Not to mention personal recovery and gathering energy for the next leg of our professional journey.) You're on your own to develop the professional competencies to do the work, the personal resources to execute it, and the strategic mindset to anticipate where the work is heading.

That's not an easy combination to develop, but in this rapidly changing future of work, it's vital for our survival. Acting with a protean mindset results in higher career satisfaction, engagement at work, and career planning capabilities.[7] Doing so also requires us to step out of the seeming comfort of our jobs into an uncertain landscape with little guidance about what's next. There's no way around it: doing this is intimidating, especially at first. But the true nature of the modern career suggests that staying put under the illusion of job safety is a riskier bet. Better to use a sabbatical as rehearsal—or insurance—to ensure you have the personal resources, perspective, and courage to navigate your next steps.

Learning How to Take the Next Step Again

In the seven years since her sabbatical, Renuka has had more jobs than she had over the prior twenty years—three times as many. Well, three total. When we reconnected, she was up-front about and even a little proud of this fact.

"The first job was okay, but the company ran into trouble during the pandemic. The one after that wasn't really a good fit. But I really like where I've landed now in local civil service, and the process of being unemployed, even being laid off for the first time in my life, didn't really bother me as it would have before my sabbatical," Renuka said. "I've become much more comfortable with operating within uncertainty, which has allowed me to take more risks and leave less of my life to forces outside my control."

It's something I've heard time and time again from sabbatical alums. Taking a long break for the first time in your life is undeniably scary. You feel like you're standing on the precipice of a gaping canyon, unable to see the other side. No matter how great a policy your company offers or how excited you are for the time off, uncertainty is uncomfortable. Add to that the challenging things people do during their time off—be it tackling a big physical feat or putting themselves out into the world creatively for the first time—and we find that sabbaticals require a lot of courage. In facing these things head-on, we realize that most intimidating challenges in life are, in fact, surmountable. And, almost always, not as bad as we'd feared to begin with.

In Renuka's case, the most daunting thing wasn't temporarily stepping away from a steady income. Her husband also works, and they were in no immediate financial danger. But it felt existentially scary to launch herself from a comfortable work identity into uncertainty—uncertainty about what was out there for her, how people who didn't know her would evaluate her, and how she would feel leaving behind a job that she'd called home for two decades.

Overcoming uncertainty is a required skill in life, especially in the age of the protean career where, ultimately, we are the only ones looking out for our future. As in a physical workout, we must build that skill through effort and repetition. A sabbatical can be a training gym for doing uncomfortable things like leaving a job, moving, and changing our lives completely. These occurrences may be unpleasant. They are also unavoidable. It is better to face them head-on, with confidence and experience, than to wait until they occur on their own timeline, upending our lives and sending us scrambling to put out the fires.

In this way, Carol Fishman Cohen's work at iRelaunch solves more than a onetime practical need. It's training people for a career in switching careers and changing their lives—not launching just once but doing so over and over. Similarly, Chip's Modern Elder Academy reinfuses confidence, hope, and belief that age is simply a number, wisdom is an asset, and "elder" is a compliment. Carol and Chip aren't alone. There's a growing movement around identifying milestones in the second half of our lives, from David Brooks's *The Second Mountain: The Quest for a Moral Life* to Arthur Brooks's (no relation) *From Strength to Strength: Finding Success, Happiness, and Deep Purpose in the Second Half of Life.*

Renuka didn't emerge from her sabbatical with greater clarity around her purpose per se. But she came away with something more powerful: an understanding that her current career wasn't serving her and confidence in her ability to do anything she wanted. Without the short break, her longer one wouldn't have been catalyzed. And without the purpose-filled sabbatical, she'd never have envisioned herself doing the social-impact work she does now in her public sector role for her county. It also equipped her with the courage and scar tissue to navigate an uncertain job market.

Renuka's story is more than a model for someone looking to shake things up in middle age. It's a call for all of us to intentionally consider the important inflection points in our lives and to sanctify them with our time and attention. It's all too easy to get stuck in the urgency of the day-to-day, losing sight of what's important.

My conversations with sabbatical takers have uncovered many opportunities for celebration and endowed significance lying within our normal, routine lives. For example, taking a beat between jobs instead of starting the next one right away. Or taking time off with your kids when they reach an important age or certain life stage, like elementary school or, in Renuka's case, before they leave for college. Like Renuka's Camino walk, a shorter break won't get you the full benefits of a sabbatical but it could be the catalyst you need to make the change you didn't yet realize you needed.

Renuka used the four stages of Hindu life as a guide to her transition, but you don't have to use a religious framework. Start by identifying the milestones you anticipate in the next five to ten years and ask yourself how you intend to mark them. When we identify them in advance, we bestow special meaning on them by allotting them enough time for us to savor and contemplate the occasion, milestone, or transition. If you don't know where to start, ask someone older than you—or, as Chip would say, an elder—which moments in their lives they wish they had stopped to celebrate or reflect upon. Whatever milestone you choose—whether it's a time to celebrate, mourn, or search—viewing these breaks as rest stops along the way instead of emergency detours can help you plan for them, enjoy them, and use them to inform the next phase of your life.

6

Feeling Human Again

Life doesn't pause to remind you it's running out;
it will cause no commotion to remind you of its swiftness.

—Seneca, "On the Shortness of Life"

By age thirty-five, Loren had done almost everything he had set out to do. The son of immigrants, he'd worked his way up to a coveted job as a management consultant at one of the most prestigious consulting firms in the world. He'd mastered a speech impediment, managed a childhood diagnosis of ADHD, and had (mostly) silenced his inner critic.

But his achievements didn't come without a price.

Regularly hospitalized for stomach ulcers, Loren tried to follow his doctor's orders by giving up coffee and changing his diet. But he struggled to scale back at work, and job stress continued to increase. Six years into his consulting career, work, life, and health were inextricably intertwined. His deteriorating well-being seemed like part of the career package, or an inescapable part of being an adult. It didn't ever occur to him that it was something he could control.

Loren's career was everything. Though he'd recently moved in with his girlfriend, his job still received most of his attention. In his push for the next promotion, he traveled four days a week and worked past midnight, many times until collapsing on his desk in his hotel room. Putting in time on the weekends was the norm. All of this meant that Loren was completely reliant on his girlfriend for basic life functions, from meal preparation to weekend social planning, even though she herself also had a demanding job. Not exactly the best way to nurture a budding relationship, which was made clear to him after a series of arguments and an ultimatum: Readjust your priorities or end up with one less item to prioritize.

As Loren began to examine his priorities, another painful reality hovered in the background. A few years prior, his father had been diagnosed with brain cancer. While treatments had succeeded in pushing the disease into remission, the prospect of its return loomed large. Loren and his father had always been close, and he knew visiting was important. But after traveling all week for work, the last thing he wanted to do was get back on a plane to see his father and spend even more time away from home.

Something had to give. Loren needed a pressure-release valve if he was going to turn things around. After conversations with his girlfriend, he decided on a drastic step: two months away from work. The first half would focus on personal healing, the second on a big trip together. In a moment of synchronicity, as he set about hatching plans for the summer, a friend reached out. He and his partner were going to sail across the Pacific. Would anyone care to join as a third hand?

ooo

Loren was a seeker, searching for something he couldn't quite name—a way to break free from the relentless loop of work and feel more like himself. He wasn't alone in this longing. Across hundreds of sabbatical alumni interviews, an unexpected word stood out as an overriding takeaway from their time off: feeling more "human." It's a bit of a catch-all phrase that clearly means different things to different people, like the term "sabbatical" itself. But the examples were all directionally similar: we're tired of feeling like machines whose lives are in service of work. We even frame breaks from work in relation to our jobs: weekends are about recovering from the workweek; vacations give us a chance to "recharge."

The typical two-week vacation isn't enough time to break this cycle. Only after enough time away from work—longer than our annual vacation days combined—do we feel like we're living for a more authentic purpose—a more humane objective, where we make time for family and personal health, including the difficult but incredibly meaningful moments in our lives like grieving and caring for ailing loved ones. Too often, we neglect these important moments and allow them to be overshadowed by the seemingly more urgent tasks in our life, like work.

In this chapter, we explore the roots of why we hang on so tightly to work and how taking enough time off from it can add depth to our humanity. We'll also consider what tangible gains to expect from going on a sabbatical and examine how different sectors of our economy light the way for broader workplace adoption.

Functional Workaholism

Loren was thrilled to trade in his suit and roller bag for a bucket hat and deck shoes. Just the thought of spending three weeks on a thirty-foot sailboat destined for French Polynesia was enough to lift his spirits.

That all changed when he stepped aboard the vessel. Constantly uneasy and seasick, he was miserable, uncomfortable, and often scared. He found sleeping almost impossible—not only was there constant motion but he'd also left the hatch above his bed open on his first night and water had poured in, soaking his mattress. It took ten days to dry. This was not the relaxing getaway he'd had in mind.

But after a few days getting his sea legs, Loren found that the adventure of the trip rose above the discomfort. His lack of seniority on board meant he was given the most trying shift at the helm—midnight to four a.m. He treasured the sliver of privacy from his shipmates, which gave him the chance to process what his life had become and how he wanted things to be different upon return. He even read five books in three weeks, more than he'd read in years.

In the space of several weeks Loren adapted to life at sea. He grew a beard and spearfished. He learned how to navigate the ocean at night and to sleep wedged into the ship's hull during rough seas. He was tan, with a wiry, strong physique again. It was the best he'd felt in years. His stomach issues had evaporated, and he'd lost more than a few pounds. He possessed a peace of mind and physical embodiment that he hadn't even realized he'd lost over a decade of straight work. How had he allowed himself to become so miserable?

ooo

Loren's transformation wasn't unique; it is a window into something much larger happening across the modern workforce. His sudden recovery at sea revealed how profoundly his always-connected work life had been affecting him, not just professionally but physically and mentally. What he experienced as an individual is typical of what millions of workers face daily, trapped in a cycle that's become so normalized that we barely recognize it as dysfunction.

As the boundaries between work and home disappear, both work and home suffer.[1] This state of being "always on" affects 77 percent of workers, a Deloitte study found.[2] We've termed this way of working "functional workaholism"—an ongoing state of gradually deteriorating job engagement, efficacy, and personal health. It's much more pervasive than burnout, because it's the way we work leading up to actually burning out. And it's insidious because it accumulates over time, and mirrors those around us.

Functional workaholics spend a lot of time with people like them: their colleagues at work, and spouses and friends with similar relationships to their jobs. Usually they get rewarded for their workaholism (through promotions and accolades), but still sense they aren't working hard enough. When we lack shared beliefs around boundaries and work-life balance, we enter a vicious cycle of unwittingly inflicting damage on ourselves and those around us.

Functional workaholism borrows from the concept of high-functioning alcoholism. In her book *Understanding the High-Functioning Alcoholic*, Sarah Allen Benton challenges the common stereotype that all alcoholics are fall-down drunks. In fact, many people struggling with alcohol are indistinguishable from those who aren't. The high-functioning alcoholic drinks more than is healthy while performing at a very high level. This creates a vicious cycle of positive feedback in the public-facing areas of their life, which helps them justify their self-destructive behavior. But their performance inevitably begins to slip as their consumption rises to meet their body's increasing needs. High-functioning alcoholics can keep this up for some time—decades, even. But no one can keep it up forever.

The same is true for high-functioning workaholics—they'll keep going until something forces a shift. That shift rarely comes from within. More often, it's thrust upon them.

You can't escape this way of working by "finding your passion," or aligning your interests with your work. In our research, we identified among our interviewees two groups of career-selectors: those who chose their line of work based on values ("valuers") and those who were agnostic about mission, caring mostly about achievement as a proxy for success ("strivers"). Valuers chose their trajectory based on the impact their career would allow them to have, whereas strivers worked to succeed and accrue prestige, or simply because working is what you do.

Both groups ultimately ended up in Sabbatical Land not because of *what* work they did but *how* they worked: in the same health-depleting way, with no change or end in sight. It was only once they had fully disconnected either by choice or by force that they realized the consequences of their working habits. The pivotal moment in Loren's story—where he found himself working through recurring bouts of stress-related illness—emerged frequently in our study of valuers and strivers. A former biotech marketing executive, Marielena, for example, had a long list of health issues including a trigger finger. "Every specialist I would talk to would tell me it was stress related. But I wanted to become a senior VP. So, after each visit to the doctor, I'd just think 'Whatever, I've powered through before, I'll just continue powering through.'"

Grief, Loss, and Caring

By pressing on through this slow degradation of happiness and health, we stand to miss more important, less urgent moments in our lives, all while operating under the assumption that this behavior is normal. One participant in our research described taking only one day off work to travel out of state for her brother's funeral. She had recently started a new role and "didn't want to lose a job she liked."

This way of engaging with work is rampant.

Loren's time away at sea stripped him of the ability to work in this dysfunctional way. His time was carefully allotted based on the around-the-clock shifts needed to safely operate the sailboat. Rest wasn't optional—it was mandatory in order to keep the crew safe. Plus, the physical nature of his daily tasks made it easy and attractive to rest. His new existence awakened something in him. The physical transformation was obvious—the beard, the tan, the lost weight—but the mental shift ran deeper. For the first time in years, he felt truly present in his own life.

As the boat approached French Polynesia, Loren felt a growing sense of nervous excitement. He knew that with the shore came the chance to reconnect with reality. He was eager to collaborate with his girlfriend on their impending plans now that he had only a few more days sailing between islands before flying back home. He remembered what it was like to be Loren the person and not just Loren the employee. In the span of weeks, he had rediscovered a spark of curiosity and expanded his capacity for wonder. The constant hum of anxiety that had become his baseline—the mental noise of always being "on"—had finally quieted.

But on the first phone call home, he received devastating news: his father's cancer had returned, and this time the tumor had grown too close to his brainstem. Loren had gotten in touch just in time to be a part of the medical decision moving forward. On a satellite phone, from a sailboat docked at a small island in French Polynesia, Loren helped his family decide against further radiation treatment for his father. He told his shipmates the news, received their blessing to take off early, and caught an inter-island flight to the main island of Tahiti Nui to begin the journey home.

Looking back, Loren reflected on the long, multi-stop plane ride back to the States to be with his parents: "The news about my dad's tumor was overwhelming. It opened up the floodgates, putting my newfound vigor into sharp relief. I realized that I wasn't happy at my job—and it was such a huge part of my life. Worse, I didn't see a path to happiness. I had no children, and I wasn't married. I'd spent most of my life working my ass off in a job I wasn't sure created meaning or impacted the world, at least not in the way that would justify the amount of work and effort I was putting into it."

After the trip, Loren swapped the all-encompassing job of sailor for that of caregiver. He moved in with his parents in the Oakland suburbs and found, to his surprise, that his new day-to-day routine was similar to life on the boat. Early mornings, night shifts, and a series of never-ending chores to keep the place running. He helped his father stand, get dressed, and shower. Loren prepared meals and recorded video messages from his father to be shared after his passing. Loren told his father that he planned to propose to his girlfriend and heard stories about his parents' relationship he never knew.

During that month, Loren's work shifted from consulting with some of the world's largest companies—distracted, stressed, and high-flying—to a much simpler job that he was in no way qualified for. It didn't change the world, and it made no money for anybody. The whole process took longer than his original leave from work allowed, but his job was the last thing on his mind. Seven weeks later, Loren's father passed away, with his son at his bedside.

Conserving Resources

How do you quantify the value of Loren's time—those weeks spent recovering and being present for his family during a time of crisis? The question itself feels wrong. As humans, we instinctively understand that this time has profound worth, regardless of any workplace benefits. This is what sabbatical alumni mean when they ascribe a feeling of humanity to their time off. Yet most of us still seek to translate this sense into measurable outcomes.

While this misses the point of what taking time off is all about, there is a lens from psychology that can help us understand the benefits in more tangible terms: conservation of resources theory.

Broadly speaking, there are two ways to evaluate whether a break from work is beneficial. The first asks: Were you better off during your time away? The second asks: How long did that positive effect persist upon your return?

Most of us focus entirely on the second question when justifying time off. We expect the break itself to feel good. That's a given. What we really want to know is whether we'll return as better, more effective employees. Will we be more creative? More focused? Less likely to burn out again? This is viewing time off through a productivity lens. The break is only worthwhile if it makes us better workers.

But there's another way to think about sabbaticals, and that's through an inherent value lens. This approach says that feeling fully human, something whose existence revolves around more than productivity, even temporarily, has worth in itself. The question isn't whether the experience will make you a better employee but whether it will make you a more complete person.

Consider vacations. Most people don't need convincing that a vacation has inherent value. Taking a vacation is fun, it makes you feel better, and most of us would prefer to take more of them. But we also don't expect the vacation to produce a lasting improvement in our work or life. Research supports the short-term nature of vacation benefits: taking time off increases happiness, satisfaction, and general positive affect.[3] These are most pronounced when we relax, detach from work, and have control over our activities.[4] Unfortunately, these impacts are short-lived; we return to our baseline shortly after returning to work.[5]

Underlying these studies is the conservation of resources theory, which was developed to help us understand how individuals manage stress, burnout, and recovery. We're all intrinsically motivated to acquire, retain, and protect our psychological resources.[6] Stress happens when we fall behind on replenishing them. It's that feeling of being "run down" that sleep and relaxation help restore.

Professor Oranit Davidson and her colleagues put this theory to the test in their study of more than 250 faculty members at universities in Israel, New Zealand, and the United States. They tracked professors before, during, and after their sabbatical leaves, comparing them to a control group of similar faculty who didn't go on leave.[7]

Unsurprisingly, those on sabbatical *gained* psychological resources during their time off. Compared to the control group, sabbatical takers were much happier and experienced reduced stress during their leave, and their average stress level upon return was significantly lower than before their sabbatical. Crucially, those who went abroad were even better off than their peers who stayed home on their leave. This finding has reinforced my belief that some degree of geographical separation is a critical ingredient for at least the initial breaking-free stage of your sabbatical.

But here's where it gets interesting: once they were back in the swing of their job, the researchers found that sabbatical takers' levels of energy, stress management, and other resources mostly returned to baseline. Did nothing change? As the authors dug deeper, they discovered that the energy it required to reacclimate to routine life sapped much of the additional resources they'd gained during their time away. This was especially hard on those returning from abroad, who faced stressful logistics around housing and reintegrating into normal life.

These results echo the famous concept of the "hedonic treadmill." Psychologists Philip Brickman and Donald Campbell found that we all have a happiness "set point."[8] While we can work to increase our happiness, we're ultimately likely to revert to the same general level we're wired for. If that wasn't cruel enough, Brickman and Campbell found that we end up becoming accustomed to any increases in happiness we achieve. As these gains become normalized, we don't end up *feeling* happier. And the pursuit of more continues.

A cynical observer might ask: Is all this effort worth it?

If your sabbatical is six months long, that's a substantial portion of life spent feeling significantly better. How do you quantify the value of six months of restored health, energy, sleep, and memories? After all, in the words of writer Annie Dillard: "How we spend our days is, of course, how we spend our lives."[9]

A lot can happen in six months. On sabbatical, many people go through periods of self-examination, performing demanding tasks like caregiving, and doing the hard work of getting better. But these periods of intense feelings and experiences are important. And they stick with us and inform the rest of our lives. Sabbatical alum Jeanette Mellinger reflected on the impact of this: "My sabbatical gave me the chance to question my path and to give myself permission to really think about what I can do to reprioritize things in my life. I can't imagine living thirty more years without those lessons."

Even if Jeanettes's day-to-day happiness returned to exactly where it started, she had uncovered something during her time off that she couldn't access previously. Her sabbatical gave her a new perspective that altered the way she lived going forward.

Throughout this book, we'll see many other examples where people ended up demonstrably better off—in their careers, in their health, and in their relationships—as a result of their sabbatical. While this productivity justification is important—and central to the book's argument—it shouldn't be a prerequisite for granting ourselves the gift of extended leave. We must not ignore the inherent value of time off. Pursuing self-actualization, or at least a more authentic version of ourselves, should be a birthright, not a privilege. It seems to me that the real question isn't whether time away has value but how we can build the conviction that it's as worthwhile as time on the job.

A Surprising Model for Work

When Loren asked his HR manager for two months off, it was granted almost by default. That's one of the best perks of management consulting. A notoriously demanding job with an all-encompassing lifestyle, consulting offers an extraordinary array of time-off options.

To retain talent and keep their employees happy, top firms offer a suite of innovative extended breaks to fit the personal circumstances and needs of their staff. Consultants can take an unpaid leave of absence of up to twelve months at any time. They retain health insurance, and the only restriction is that they are not allowed to work for another for-profit company during that time. There are also secondments or externships, where younger associates can work for approved for-profits, nonprofits, or even pursue secondary education, with a guaranteed job upon their return.

Finally, there's a program called Take Time, which Loren took advantage of. Introduced in 2012, Take Time lets consultants reduce their workload by 20 percent in exchange for a commensurate reduction in salary. Bolanle Asumah, one of McKinsey's regional directors of people, estimated that 40 percent of their consultants have utilized the program since its creation, compared to 10 percent who opt for unpaid leave of absence.[10] The program is particularly popular with new parents who want to continue working at a reduced level for the next phase of life, if not indefinitely.

The concept isn't new or unique. Google notoriously started a similar initiative in 2004 called the 20 Percent Program, which allowed its engineers to take one day off per week to work on whatever they wanted.* But for consultants, time-off programs operate very differently. This is because a consultant's job is divided into high-intensity customer "engagements," which are wholly self-contained chunks of work. Once you're off an engagement, there's no longer any need or requirement to be in the office. The work is done (for the time being), and consultants can generally unplug while awaiting their next assignment. It's lovingly referred to among consultants as being "on the beach" and makes it easier for consulting firms to have innovative programs like Take Time without negatively impacting their consultants' coworkers or clients.

While consulting differs from traditional business in many ways, consulting industry time-off practices also show us something impor-

---

* While it was declared a success externally—Google claims it was responsible for the invention of Gmail and Google News—internally, employees referred to it as 120 percent time. Engineers who participated in the program complained that their workload didn't decrease, they were just expected to innovate on top of their existing responsibilities.

tant about personal leave: unless it's an established norm at a company, people won't take it. A study on paternity leave usage in Sweden underlined this phenomenon. Sweden has one of the most generous parental leave policies of any country, offering each parent eight months of leave. But utilization by the non-birth parent lagged so much that to spur usage Sweden had to introduce a "father's quota," which mandated time off for both parents, in 1995. Subsequent research has found that fathers were more hesitant to take leave unless they could see their colleagues, and especially supervisors, using the benefit.[11]

There's evidence that the same business cycles that enable extended breaks among consultants are being adopted more broadly in the economy. Tech companies operate around distinct product development cycles, which are multi-month or multiyear sprints around launching a specific product or service. The bulk of tech company employee compensation comes from stock option grants that have a four-year life cycle, giving employees a reason to stay on, as well as an inflection point to jump off.

Compared to these technology companies, consulting firms' only "product" is their people, the consultants themselves. From this vantage point, it's not surprising that their HR policies prioritize human needs. They know that young employees—80 percent of people at consulting firms are under forty—are motivated by mission and experience, so externships, leaves of absence, and secondments are all standard and welcome practice.[12]

At a time when 80 percent of employees report being disengaged at their job and the World Health Organization now declares "workplace burnout" a global phenomenon, companies that reduce the logistics and stigmas around taking time off stand to benefit.[13] Consulting firms know this. How else could a sector with notoriously bad work-life balance outperform the tech industry—which itself is known for its perks and creature comforts—in employee tenure?[14]

Making Change

Shortly after his father's passing, Loren's partner received a job offer across the country. Moving would require Loren to abandon his career aspirations at his firm. It wouldn't be impossible to make partner after moving offices, but it would set him back a few years, forcing him to relive a lot of the hard work and late nights since his last promotion.

The move gave Loren an occasion to internalize all that had changed over the past year. He'd sailed halfway around the world and joined his family for their most difficult journey to date. Losing his father forced him to face his own mortality: "I'm at the age my dad was when I was born, which means I could be at the halfway point of my life too. Once I realized this, every future decision about how I lived my life was then assessed against that fact." In the words of Jungian author and therapist Dr. James Hollis, Loren was asking himself, "Who am I, apart from the roles I've played?"

Looking through this lens, Loren realized that he no longer cared about the next step on his current career's ladder. Becoming partner, a pursuit that had consumed him for years, didn't hold the allure it once had. If he wanted to be the kind of father he'd had growing up, he would need a healthier relationship between work and life. And he'd better get started soon.

ooo

When I reconnected with him almost a decade later, Loren's work and personal life were completely unrecognizable to those who knew him as a consultant. Within a year of his father's passing, he and his girlfriend married; they now have two children. Loren splits his time working with his hands, renovating houses, and coaching executives on purpose, meaning, and integrating work and life.

Loren models his current career after the best of consulting: sprints of hard work on something he's passionate about interspersed with breaks to be present for important milestones in life. After the birth of each of his kids, his family spent two months of their parental leave in South Africa and Mexico. On these mini sabbaticals, with the distractions of regular life removed, Loren could be fully present with his family. Above all, he is more comfortable with change, letting go, and preemptively setting out to discover what's next. He's engrossed in his current work but committed to taking a sabbatical every seven years or so to recalibrate.

Loren also looks back on the example of his dad's work life. His father, despite having had an impressive career at the World Bank, routinely chose family over work. He left the office no later than 5:30 each day to pick up his wife at her job so they could drive home together. He exercised for an hour at lunch daily. And he routinely passed up promotions that would have hindered his ability to be the kind of father he wanted to be for his family. This included resisting placements back in his home country of New Zealand in favor of not disturbing his sons' schooling and social lives in America. On top of all that, it was clear that he enjoyed what he did for a living. Loren's happy to report that he's more and more like his dad every day.

ooo

We all feel that magnetic pull to be with loved ones in times of need. It's primal, undeniable, and, as it turns out, backed by rigorous research. The most famous and comprehensive of these studies is the Harvard Grant Study of Adult Development.[15] Starting in 1938, researchers tracked the lives of its eighty participants every two years, collecting data on everything from health to attitudes and personal reflection. Its participants led widely diverging lives, but most experienced periods of significant loss and stress.[16] Despite the differences in life choices, one characteristic of their lives stood out from the others in predicting health and happiness in their eighties. It wasn't the quality of their genes but the quality of their relationships. While everyone knows that relationships are important, how many of us are able to give them the time and attention they deserve? The Grant Study—among many others—reminds us that it could very well be a matter of life and death . . . if you need that kind of incentive.

Loren dedicated his sabbatical to caretaking. While his father's time of need was very clear and acute, Loren's need for self-care was more difficult for him to diagnose in any particular moment. It also wasn't clear to him when he should have begun healing in the first place. In fact, we saw that some choices he made extending back as early as college had impacts on his health more than a decade later. The timing of Loren's midlife awakening is an overwhelmingly common trajectory. It's not that we cast our patterns and perspectives in stone as much as we are unwittingly carried forward by the inertia of our earlier choices. Like tributaries combining to join a larger river, seemingly small decisions—about what internship to take, for example—that may seem benign at the time can have unintentional downstream effects. But what if Loren had made time to recover and get perspective before he chose his career (and working habits) to begin with?

7

Healing and Finding Yourself

Before I can tell my life what I want to do with it,
I must listen to my life telling me who I am.
—Parker Palmer, *Let Your Life Speak*

I first met twenty-year-old Audrey Pe in 2022 on a panel at a conference in Silicon Valley. As a sophomore in high school in the Philippines, she'd started a nonprofit called WiTech (Women in Tech) aimed at empowering women to enter tech fields. Now operating across a dozen countries, WiTech has inspired tens of thousands of budding entrepreneurs and techies through its mission to educate and empower youth to break gender stereotypes.

I felt like a slacker next to Audrey, but when she asked me about my work on sabbaticals, I received an enthusiastic response from the change-maker, who smiled and jumped in with her own story.

"My gap year was . . . is probably the only reason I'm here today," she said.

"The fact that I *didn't* take a gap year was my biggest college regret," I told her, revealing a two-decade-old wound. "What did you do on your year off?" I asked. "Backpack?"

"Actually, I didn't travel much at all," she replied. "It was more a year to recover. I figured out a healthy relationship with work and spent quality time with my parents, mostly. Read a bunch." She continued, "It honestly doesn't sound that cool, but when I got to college, I felt like I started with a full tank. It saved me from burning out, which is the norm at a place like Stanford."

When Audrey told me her gap year was the most important decision of her entire life, I realized I'd gotten a few important things wrong about how I thought about gap years, and sabbaticals more generally. First, I hadn't even included gap year takers in the early interviews for my research. I'd mostly connected with people in the middle of their careers about their time off. What could someone more advanced in their career learn from a teenager's glorified victory lap after high school?

But as I diversified the interview pool for the academic study, I began hearing the need to take off due to burnout from younger and younger folks as well. I initially dismissed their descriptions as no more than an echo of the cultural zeitgeist, like how someone in their teens would repeat their parents' political views. But the more I spoke to gap year alums, students, and young professionals, the clearer it became to me that the path to college, let alone your first job after graduation, was more grueling, accomplishment-focused, and job-like than I'd realized. It was no wonder (and no exaggeration) that young adults were entering the workforce already sorely in need of a break to get back to baseline.

These gap year stories also made it clear to me that there was something deeper connecting young adults at the beginning of their careers to adults in the thick of theirs. As you'll learn in this chapter, conquering burnout isn't simply a matter of getting sufficient rest or finding work-life balance. It requires figuring out who you really are, outside of the influences of your peers, parents, and colleagues, and aligning the way you live your life accordingly. This is one of the most important and challenging tasks of your life, so naturally, the sooner you sort this out the better.

But as I saw from countless older sabbatical alums, figuring out your place in the world isn't a once-in-a-lifetime task for eighteen-year-olds. Living in alignment requires recurring adjustments over the course of your life, informed by who you are, how you've changed since the last time you checked, and clarity about who you want to be. As it turns out, there's both a rich history and a thriving industry enabling gap years with universal lessons for people of all ages. There's a reason many grown-ups call their sabbaticals their "adult gap year."

The Gap Year

Gaps are things you fill or correct, like a gap in your teeth or on your résumé. And gap years are often perceived as the opposite of continuing one's education. By taking a gap year, you're delaying matriculation, entering into a gulf of your own making between where you were and where you're supposed to be. But educators have always played a pivotal role in the existence of gap years. In fact, many schools now encourage students to take them, citing the academic, maturation, and mental health benefits they've observed among gap year alumni.

Audrey's decision to delay matriculation is still relatively rare, more so in the US than in Europe. In 2019, a little more than 3 percent of students in American universities deferred admission, compared to 6 percent in the UK and 9 percent in Australia.[1] But that number is growing, buoyed by the pandemic, which saw an estimated 16 percent of rising college freshmen postpone enrollment, opting against spending a very expensive year on Zoom.

The idea of a gap year can be traced back to a rite of passage among young, upper-class European men undertaken at around twenty-one years of age, purportedly for educational purposes. In the heyday of the so-called Grand Tour—from the seventeenth to the early nineteenth centuries—participants would be expected to learn French, good manners, and sophistication during their travels. Returning tourers could expect fast-tracked careers in diplomacy.

The modern iteration of the gap year can be traced to post–World War II Britain. When the military draft ended in the sixties, campus administrators observed that (at least the male) students performed much better after a few years of growing up. Volunteer opportunities abroad sprouted up to fill the joint interests of students and administrators. The first became the namesake for gap years itself: Gap Activity Projects (GAP) in 1972.* GAP placed close to fifty thousand students in eighteen countries, offering volunteer opportunities such as teaching, community outreach, and conservation.

American gap year organizations initially focused more on college graduates than high school, prioritizing domestic exploration (National Outdoor Leadership School) and domestic and international service (AmeriCorps or Teach for America and the Peace Corps, respectively) before entering the workforce in earnest. However, advocacy for gap years after high school has been increasing in the US, and from a surprising source: universities themselves.

Harvard has recommended taking a gap year to incoming freshmen in its letter of admission since the 1970s.[2] Delaying matriculation for a year is as easy as pressing a button in a newly admitted student's online portal. In an article in *The New York Times* entitled "Time Out or Burn-Out," then-Dean of Admissions William Fitzsimmons explains their rationale:

---

* In a cruel twist of capitalist fate, Gap Activity Projects was forced to rebrand itself in 2008, after clothing retailer Gap Inc. sued a gap year organization called "Gap Sports" for trademark infringement. The newly rebranded Latitude Global Volunteering was liquidated during the pandemic in 2021.

Extraordinary achievements are never based on emulating someone else's achievements . . . burnout is an inevitable result of trying to live up to alien goals. We encourage admitted students to defer enrollment for one year to travel, pursue a special project or activity, work, or spend time in another meaningful way.[3]

Each year, a significant contingent takes Admissions up on this offer: on average, close to 5 percent of the student body is on a leave of absence.[4] According to Harvard's dedicated gap year page—the school also has a gap year society, with elected leadership positions and a house dean advisor—a recent class of gappers spent their time traveling to more than twenty-six countries and engaging in activities as diverse as teaching English in the Coyoacán District of Mexico City and volunteering on political campaigns and with nonprofits.[5]

Harvard quotes returning gap year students describing their year away as "life-altering," a "turning point," the value of which "can never be measured and will pay dividends for the rest of their lives." Not a pause before starting the next chapter of their life but inserting another chapter altogether.

Dozens of American colleges and universities accommodate students' postponing freshman year in one way or another. Participating institutions range from the experimental and nontraditional like the New School and Evergreen State College to private schools like American University to public state schools like Indiana University South Bend. Even the cost of a gap year is a hurdle that universities are beginning to take upon themselves. In 2009, Princeton began offering a free, structured international gap year program, the Novogratz Bridge Program.[6] Other schools, like the University of North Carolina at Chapel Hill, provide stipends, student loans, and college credit for participants in approved gap year programming.

Audrey's Gap Year

Audrey grew up an only child in Manila, the Philippines' megacity capital. After realizing that she would be their first and last kid, her parents went all-in on parenting, quitting their demanding banking jobs in favor of more flexible and less time-intensive careers.

Unlike most of her peers, Audrey was dead set on a STEM education from an early age. She was hooked from the moment she was introduced to basic coding on an assignment to steer a snake through a maze using text-based commands instead of arrows or a mouse. Audrey attended the Multiple Intelligences International School, which trains students to be the protagonists in their own education. So, when Audrey's interests in coding surpassed what the school could offer, she had no trouble motivating herself to self-teach on her own time.

The International School also stressed the importance of role models and mentors, bringing in professionals, mostly doctors and lawyers, to talk about their careers with the students. Because there were no speakers in tech—certainly no women—Audrey set about finding her own mentors. The problem was, without the cover and credibility of the school behind her, she found it impossible to get busy tech leaders to speak to her.

Audrey wasn't easily discouraged. She launched a blog called *Women in Tech—WiTech* for short—delivering instant credibility in her new role as nonprofit founder slash journalist slash tech blogger. True to her tech-native generation, she decided to learn about tech careers in public, and it became her brand. WiTech took off across the Philippines, whisking Audrey to far-flung islands for talks and gatherings with aspiring young techie women.

The more she learned about a career in tech and its prerequisites, the more Audrey became convinced she needed to go to school abroad; only an institution in the US could offer the combination of curriculum and access to the tech epicenter. This decision is very rare among Filipinos, especially women. Although an estimated 10 to 20 percent of its diaspora works abroad, less than 1 percent of Filipinos leave the country for tertiary education. Most of Audrey's new WiTech mentors had gone to (and some had dropped out of) top tier schools in the US. Audrey had her heart set on the Ivy Leagues, with Ivy-adjacent Stanford as first choice, given its location in the birthplace of tech. It also offered convenience for visiting her parents; there's a nonstop flight from San Francisco to Manila.

To improve her chances of getting into an Ivy, Audrey transferred to an international baccalaureate school, where the pressure increased significantly. For the first time in her life, she wasn't even close to the top of her class. Not only that, but the programming classes were also much more difficult than the online lectures she'd been cruising through. WiTech was blossoming, but Audrey was wilting.

"I was only sleeping four hours a night," she told me, "waking up at five a.m., commuting to school, going straight to the library, then speaking on a panel or organizing a get-together before dragging myself home to chug coffee to prepare for the next day. It was the roughest year of my life."

Then Audrey got the bad news: she'd been rejected from all the Ivies and waitlisted at Stanford. She was heartbroken. After she peeled herself off the couch, where she'd spent that weekend mourning, and spoke with her parents, another path surfaced. She would take a year off to focus on WiTech and reapply the next year. As Audrey saw it, WiTech was hitting its stride, expanding outside the Philippines. Another year of growth could strengthen her application. Plus, she enjoyed the work much more than school.

A week later, she found out she got into Stanford.

That week between disappointment and acceptance was crucial. Audrey had become so excited about her year-off plans that she decided to delay matriculating. Taking a year off before attending Stanford was easy; a request for a leave of absence for an academic year could be submitted online. She didn't even need to talk to anyone.

After the buzz of graduation faded, Audrey noticed she was enjoying the weekends more. The *Sunday scaries*—what she called the feeling of panic that set in when the weekend was drawing to a close—had disappeared entirely. Armed with the cover story of growing her nonprofit but without her day job as an overachieving high school senior, Audrey was able to embark on "a completely different life."

First up was sleep. The week following the madness of graduation, Audrey hardly left her room, her parents delivering meals to her door.

Once her sleep debt was repaid, she focused on fitness, hanging up her competitive tennis racket and taking up indoor cycling with her mom. The syncopated drumbeats of work and school slowed to a more enjoyable tempo, including new weekly rituals. Saturday mornings were for curling into a window seat with her mom at the Corner Tree Cafe after their workout. Audrey bonded with her dad over trips to the grocery store and in the kitchen each night, where she learned to cook. Practicing mise en place and sushi construction became her worldly substitute for the international travel to speaking gigs that were canceled on account of the newly raging pandemic. And she joined a Goodreads challenge, devouring one hundred books over the course of the year. Without the weight of a backpack full of textbooks, Audrey rediscovered her love for sci-fi and other lighter reads.

WiTech thrived with Audrey's focus and energy. Membership grew fivefold, and the nonprofit expanded to twenty-five chapters in ten countries, including one near Stanford in the heart of Silicon Valley. Keen to preserve her healthier relationship to busyness and stress, Audrey hired leaders for WiTech who could take over the day-to-day operations and keep her workload manageable. When the time came to move to Palo Alto, Audrey was confident she could fold schoolwork back into her schedule without her life going off the rails. Personally, she felt strong, confident, well fed, and happy. Her relationship with her parents had never been stronger.

The Impact of a Gap Year

You'd be hard-pressed to find a gap year alum who looks back on their time before school as a defect. But do breaks from our normal life, like gap years, "work"? Because a gap year is often a product a student pays for, the impact of gap years has been dissected from a number of angles, many relevant for those of all ages taking a year off.

Still, despite the relatively large number of gap year alumni, *rigorous* data on the impact of a year off before college is scarce. It's easy to see why: measuring something standardized, like a GPA, is simple, while looking at something squishier, like happiness or fulfillment, is much tougher. How do you figure out how someone's life would have progressed if they hadn't taken a year off?

Broadly speaking, there have been two approaches toward understanding the impact of gap years: alumni surveys and college performance upon return. Gap year alumni surveys paint a very clear and consistent picture. Gappers—as they're sometimes called—reliably describe their breaks as pivotal, life-defining points that changed the meaning of education for them forever. Dr. Joe O'Shea, a university administrator and author of *Gap Year: How Delaying College Changes People in Ways the World Needs*, conducted hundreds of interviews with students, family members, and gap year organization staff members before and after gappers' years away. His findings echo the conclusions of so many seemingly biased gap year organization websites: people returned with increased confidence, a better awareness of themselves and the world, and generally more "ready" for the next steps in their lives.[7]

There have also been studies that try to quantify the impact of gap years on gappers' likelihood of success in the future. The most rigorous study in this vein was conducted in 2012 at Middlebury College by then-Dean of Admissions Robert Clagett. Clagett was inspired to study the impact upon hearing another dean say "Every American takes a gap year—it's called freshman year!" to a roomful of prospective students.[8]

Not exactly inspiring to students, let alone parents footing the bill.

Clagett wanted to better understand the impact of gap years on admitted students, so he built a model to predict a student's academic and extracurricular success based on years of historical student applications and transcripts. Using this approach, Clagett discovered that gap year alumni had significantly higher GPAs starting in their freshman year and held a disproportionate number of leadership positions on campus.[9] These results were replicated in another study at the University of North Carolina at Chapel Hill years later, leading to the creation of UNC's gap year scholarship program.

Gap year studies in the UK and Australia eased most parents' number one concern: Will my kid ever even return to college? Gap year alums are more than twice as likely to finish college in four years compared to their peers.[10] Papers in 2007 and 2012 showed no negative impact in matriculation or graduation rates between gap year takers and their peers and instead indicated an *increase* in academic performance among gap year alums.[11] Australian psychologist Andrew Martin found that students at the *lower* end of the grade distribution benefit most from a gap year, because time away from their environment increased their intrinsic motivation to learn.[12]

This is a universal lesson: we perform better, whether it's at school or work, when we are driven by personal interest, as opposed to extrinsic factors like peers, supervisors, or parents. Nationwide, only 41 percent of college students finish their degrees in four years; the leading reason for failing to do so is realizing midway through their degree that they want to do something else. If that number feels high, think about the inverse: What are the odds that almost 60 percent of students truly know their career direction well enough to bet a year or two's tuition on it at age eighteen?

I heard echoes of this finding from sabbatical alums of all ages during my research. Similar to parents' chief concerns about whether their kids would want to return to school, many prospective sabbatical takers worry about whether they'll ever want to return to work again. I've found this fear to be overblown. Think of sabbaticals more like psychedelics than opioids: they expand awareness, but as far as I know, they aren't addictive . . . though they are quite contagious.

○○○

The studies clearly justify taking a year away from school from a return on investment (ROI) perspective, but nevertheless, I wanted more insights as to what was driving these more transformational changes, and whether they could apply to people of all ages taking a year away. Dr. O'Shea went one layer deeper than GPA and extracurriculars to measure a student's broader progress on all the life skills that college is supposed to help students develop outside the classroom, like emotional, social, personal, and—ideally—moral maturity.

Using the lens of college student development theory, O'Shea came to view gap years as more than a fun time away from college. He considers them a tool to develop the exact skills that college is supposed to impart: figuring out what you gravitate toward, what you're good at, and what's out there in the world. In other words, how to make sense of the many changes in your life, choose one path over another, and begin crafting a life for yourself. If you're anything like I was at the start of my sabbatical, you might feel like the jury is still out on these dimensions in your life. You're not alone.

In academic parlance, how we develop our beliefs and perspectives during our formative development years is called "meaning-making."[13] As we experience challenges to our existing mental models—say, meeting people from another part of the world for the first time in college—our understanding of what's possible expands to include this new information. When our previously lived experience and our new observations conflict, we're forced to deal with this cognitive dissonance and grow as a result.

Meaning-making occurs at a fast clip early on in our lives, then slows down as we gather more evidence about the world. Think back to your most naïve teenage or college beliefs—where did they come from? Some people absorb their parents' views of the world, while others revolt against them. Growing up is about constructing an internal identity separate from external influences. You increasingly become a separate self as you develop your own beliefs, preferences, and taste for your life.

A growing chorus of voices believes that colleges and society have failed students in the realm of personal formation. Perhaps the most popular critic is author and former professor William Deresiewicz, who viewed this as a uniquely modern phenomenon in an essay in *The New Republic*, which spawned his book *Excellent Sheep*:

> *Our system of elite education manufactures young people who are smart and talented and driven, yes, but also anxious, timid, and lost, with little intellectual curiosity and a stunted sense of purpose: trapped in a bubble of privilege, heading meekly in the same direction, great at what they're doing but with no idea why they're doing it.*[14]

At its best, college provides a training ground for young adults encountering this transition to adulthood, but Dr. Marcia Baxter-Magolda's studies suggest that "universities too readily supply students with formulas for success, so students do not have to develop self-authored ways of knowing."[15] It's not entirely their fault: parents and students alike want to leave college prepared for what's next; otherwise, what are you paying for? But in practice, instead of equipping students with the ingredients for self-discovery, college can feel like a gentle funnel that deposits them onto a lifelong treadmill from the SATs to Social Security. How many graduating seniors feel like they are the primary authors of their own story?*

My interviews with aspiring sabbatical takers and alums revealed the long-term consequences of inauthentic choices at the outset of one's career. At the risk of sounding dramatic, many folks see a sabbatical as one of the few opportunities in their lives to spend their time in a way they choose. So much of the dissatisfaction that catalyzes sabbaticals later in life can be traced back to the rushed, socially conditioned, and otherwise externally shaped decisions made in high school and college. This insight will come as no surprise to a psychologist, of course. As we grow older, these influences remain, while our perceived ability to change tack reduces drastically. This is why having a socially acceptable break from the life path on which we've found ourselves is so valuable, no matter how far along the journey we are.

Doing Less Going Forward

A couple of years after we first met, I went to visit Audrey to see how her time at Stanford had treated her since her gap year. It was an unseasonably chilly spring afternoon, windy and rain-swollen. I had on two jackets, while Audrey wore shorts. "I just came back from a run, so my body's warm," she explained. "I'm training for the San Francisco marathon—I picked up running on my gap year as well!"

We met on a Wednesday during finals week, at Stanford's almost stereotypically Californian campus: sprawling and forested (it's an actual arboretum), buzzing with students in sandals and sunglasses crisscrossing its intersections on bikes.

---

* Given that an estimated 85 percent of American parents pay for at least some of their children's college costs—and one-third cover the full bill—it's no surprise they exert significant influence over their kids' choices there.

Audrey ordered a triple Americano at the outdoor cafe in the library quad. When she saw the look on my face—it was almost 5:00 p.m.—she bashfully offered that she'd been addicted to coffee since she was fourteen, the year she started her nonprofit.

Classes had gone great, and she'd landed her dream internship at a venture capital firm for the summer. Since I last saw her, she'd transitioned leadership of her nonprofit to a new executive director. This thing that had given her so much, and taken so much of her sleep, was more or less in her rearview mirror. She was pointed in a new direction entirely. As far as I could tell, she seemed happy. But as we returned to her gap year, a darker expression came over her face, as if a cloud had passed in front of the sun.

"I wasn't okay during the time leading up to my graduation from high school," she admitted. "I wasn't sleeping. I felt this endless pressure comparing myself to others with no end in sight. I went to sleep every night thinking I should be doing more, both on the academic front and with WiTech. I'm not going to say it was joyless, because I enjoyed what I was doing most of the time. Looking back, I feel like I was in an accomplishment trance."

She continued: "I can point to the conferences, speaking gigs, and the expansion of WiTech over the course of the gap year, but my time off was really a way to say goodbye to the place I grew up in and the people who raised me. I rarely made time for my parents in my normal life. Over my gap year, I learned to care a little less about career and more about loved ones."

Audrey credits her gap year for helping remind her how much she enjoyed parts of school before the competition increased and school became solely about achievement. Her reinvigorated reading during her year off carried over into her studies at Stanford; Audrey realized that she'd taken enough English classes to qualify for a minor on top of her technology major. And she credits the time in the kitchen with her father for her fastidious meal planning regimen at Stanford. As a junior, she's off the meal plan, saving money and eating healthier than her classmates, she reckoned. Audrey believes that, compared to her high school friends, she's significantly less burned out and, on average, happier.

As Audrey walked me back to the parking lot, she pivoted the conversation to me and asked for my advice on her summer internship. It turned out it was only a part-time offer—and her classmates had been pressuring her to take another part-time offer with a start-up so she could get two unique experiences over the summer.

"Should I do it?"

"What would gap year Audrey tell you to do?" I asked.

She smiled. "I'd rather spend more time running in the mountains with my boyfriend."

A Tool in the Fight Against Burnout

The lens through which we tend to evaluate something like gap years or sabbaticals in general is whether taking one is "productive." Does taking time off between high school and college help you choose the right major, finish faster, or get a better job? Or, later in adulthood, will a sabbatical accelerate your career or otherwise add value? My conversation with Audrey in Palo Alto got me thinking about when taking a gap year could come in handy, through the lens of my own university experience.

My first semester teaching at the graduate level had shown me that the problems that gap years address don't disappear with age. More than half of my office-hour meetings were about stress and anxiety instead of homework. Though my students were well past high school, mostly in their late twenties and early thirties, many expressed feeling like they were living someone else's life. Their biggest fear was remaining stuck in careers they'd chosen for the wrong reason. Others had felt confident about their career aspirations until coming into contact with their super-achieving classmates in jobs they had never even heard of prior to graduate school. Thinking back to what Audrey said gave me another lens through which to view gap years, one that is even more relevant to those in all stages of their career: as an effective tool to combat burnout.

Recent research on increasing trends of mental illness among college freshmen reinforces my observations. A 2018 study found that more than one-third of incoming freshmen suffered from mental health problems, a trend that skyrocketed during the remote school years of 2020 and 2021.[16] The same study also found that mental health issues were directly associated with lower academic performance and higher dropout rates.* This is precisely why Dean Fitzsimmons's letter to new college admits encouraged them to "pause from their demanding lives . . . before burnout becomes the hallmark of their generation."[17]

Nearly twenty years later, Anne Helen Peterson made this same case in her viral 2019 piece "How Millennials Became the Burnout Generation." Peterson traced the origins of youth burnout back to overscheduled and hypervigilant child-rearing, up through the "productization" of our lives through social media. Burnout, she argues, "isn't an affliction experienced by relatively few . . . but, increasingly, and particularly among millennials, the contemporary condition."

Peterson wasn't exaggerating. If anything, she'd understated how widespread burnout had become. The World Health Organization proclaimed burnout an occupational phenomenon across the world that had become more norm than exception for all workers, not just millennials.[18] Next came a somewhat predictable onslaught of products and services offering solutions to burnout, from meditation apps to bespoke weekend getaways. The term "burnout" seemed to be everywhere. In the words of author on (and victim of) burnout Jona-

---

* More than 80 percent of gap year alumni agree, citing a break from the stress leading up to college as the reason for their time off, with more than a third explicitly feeling burned out, according to the largest study of gap year participants.

than Malesic: "Everyone is burned out, but no one knows what that means."[19]

The term "burnout" was first coined in Christina Maslach's research on people in caregiving professions, like nurses, teachers, and social workers. In response to chronic stressors on the job, those in her study exhibited three dimensions that define burnout: emotional exhaustion, cynicism, and a feeling of ineffectiveness, or reduced personal accomplishment.[20] The people in Maslach's study cared deeply about the service-focused mission of their work. The reason they burned out was structural—no matter how hard they worked, they struggled to feel like they made a difference. As convenient as it may sound, you can't solve structural problems about your life and work in five minutes a day, via an app or other small tweaks in your life. A more dramatic approach is needed.

I'm extremely hesitant to join the chorus offering another solution to burnout. To be clear, I don't think sabbaticals, or their gap year cousins, are a cure-all. But I've heard a growing chorus of sabbatical takers who believe that their time off was one of the first times they felt free of the conditions Maslach described in her research. I've also witnessed people returning from their sabbaticals feeling refreshed and burnout-free, only to slip back before long into the same state from which they left. I believe there are two reasons for this.

First, the extended nature of the time off allows for healing and restoration in ways that shortcuts cannot. Plenty of academic research, spanning from physiological work on cortisol (a stress hormone) to psychological theories on how we spend and replenish our emotional, physical, and mental resources, explains the need for extended time to heal.[21] Sabbatical takers in our study routinely expressed that it took much longer, typically six to eight weeks, to even begin feeling healthy and normal again. As much as we want a long weekend or a weighted blanket to reverse the ills inflicted by years of hard work, it's not realistic. More drastic measures are needed to alleviate the symptoms in the moment, and maintaining this feeling over time is even more difficult.

The reason that most people—even many sabbatical takers—struggle to alleviate burnout in the long term is because it's a structural problem. It's about *how* we return to what we do once we're back, whether that's school, work, or attending to family. Burnout blossoms when we feel ineffective in our roles and lack the personal resources to accomplish what needs to be done. This is where the impact of sabbaticals comes into play.

Two of the most cited changes among sabbatical takers were increases in perspective and confidence. For those who left their jobs to take a sabbatical, their newly restored resources emboldened them to realign their work with their personal values, skills, and vision for their future. Sabbatical takers who returned to their jobs used their reentry as an inflection point to better align their current skill set and interests so that their job could work for them again.

Reprieve alone is necessary but not sufficient to dislodge burnout. Quitting your job isn't a guaranteed fix either. You must use the observations from your sabbatical to craft a more sustainable relationship between work and life. It might be as simple as doing less work that you've outgrown, inherited, or that otherwise makes you miserable. Or it could require switching teams or sectors to better align who you're becoming with what you're doing. For some sabbatical alumni, simply knowing that another sabbatical is on the horizon is enough of a light at the end of the tunnel to infuse their work with meaning. Returning from a sabbatical better off in the long run requires pairing your observations and experiences during your time off with commensurate changes and actions upon returning home.

ooo

Audrey was able to avoid the path that leads so many mission-oriented people, like those in Maslach's study, to burnout. It certainly describes my experience with burnout—never feeling like the job was done, sacrificing my own health and personal relationships to make the business work because so many of our customers and employees depended on its success. As for Audrey, even though she cared deeply about the mission of her nonprofit, she realized in her gap year that it was impossible to both run the organization and also excel in school, find a job, and handle all the other things that awaited her in college. Armed with this perspective, she transitioned out of the organization she founded. She reordered the priorities of her life in service to her health and relationships.

Audrey helped me to see sabbaticals—gap years now included—as a crucial tool against burnout. Not just because of the reprieve sabbaticals offer from work but also because they enable self-authorship for the next phase of life for those who embark at any age. Audrey isn't exceptional just because she's brilliant or privileged or lucky. She's exceptional because she listened to herself when her body and mind were telling her to slow down. And she represents a generation no longer willing to accept burnout as the price of success.

Most of us can't go back and take a gap year after high school or college. But the lessons from gap year experiences remain valuable at any stage of life. These stories have made it clear to me why so many sabbatical takers called their time off their "adult gap year": the journey of self-authorship, growth, and understanding may begin in your teens, but it certainly doesn't end there. Those of us on the other side of graduation understand that once you swap school for work, the pace of personal growth and the lines between your job and your identity begin to blur. But if you know where to look, you can find pockets of the working world that make it easy, even mandatory, to step away and get perspective on who you are outside your role at work.

8

Seeking Permission

Withdrawal can be the very best way of stepping forward.

—David Whyte, *Consolations*

Scott Mann oozes ex-military. Tall and imposing, with a haircut not quite regulation (but still a buzz cut's faint relative), Scott is the type of guy whose posture you find yourself matching, as I did at a workshop in Nashville in February 2020. He's also the type of guy I fear talking to about my work on time off.

Normally, broaching the subject of sabbaticals engenders one of two reactions: intense interest or bemused dismissal. Telling someone of Scott's background that I'm dedicating my productive earning years to studying time off always feels like a risk. If anyone would perceive sabbaticals as self-indulgent, wouldn't it be someone whose job involves life-and-death decisions? But as often happens, my assumptions were proven wrong. Moments after I introduced myself and my work, Scott dropped his Southern aw-shucks persona and declared: "Without a doubt, my sabbatical with the Air Force War College saved my life, and the lives of my men in Afghanistan."

"Wait; I thought you were in the army," I said, confused and a bit embarrassed at my lack of military knowledge.

"Yessir—well, the Green Berets, to be accurate," Scott gently corrected. "Every branch of the military sends their officers away from the field to their war colleges on a regular clip. It's part education, part relationship building, but also a lot of rest, relaxation, and time with family. It's certainly not all sand volleyball, but it's a world away from combat zones and war preparation."

I was surprised that someone so clearly dedicated to his military career would appreciate time off. But mostly I was thrilled that a long-standing, enormous, and competent organization like the US military would offer a sabbatical at all, let alone in a time of active war. It would be like an NBA team routinely benching a star player during every finals. But some of the world's most demanding, high-stakes organizations don't just tolerate these breaks from routine work, they support them, provide them, and sometimes mandate them. The US military intentionally sequesters its leaders for extended stretches of time because time *away* from the fight is an essential part of the fight. This is surely good news for those of us who report to an office and not to military operations, because it means that sabbaticals don't have to be an either/or proposition, either good for you or good for your career. When done strategically, they can be both.

The only thing is that many of these organizations don't refer to them as sabbaticals at all. While this may be bad news for those of us trying to normalize extended leave (me), it's good news for those out there (maybe you) who are hoping to get the benefits of a sabbatical while appearing to stay on the straight and narrow in your career.

ooo

So far in this book we've covered people who've taken a sabbatical because their company offered one and those who had to break free without the comfort of returning to their jobs. But a third path exists, one that offers many of the same benefits of a proper sabbatical while allowing the organization and the individual to each couch the break from routine as part of business as usual. I call these "sabbaticals hidden in plain sight." These strategically placed breaks-by-another-name are a key component to the longevity and success of some of the oldest and most successful firms. They are also a way that both individuals and companies can experience extended breaks in ways that work within their own context and constraints.

Apart from the US military, some of the world's most exclusive organizations—elite management consulting firms, investment banks, and venture capital firms—pay their employees to take extended time away from their routine job. These departures go by different names, like temporary secondments outside the company, sponsored graduate school, or a flexible position "in residence" at an investment firm.

From surveying the many individual and institutional sabbaticals over the course of my research, I've identified three paths for taking a sabbatical when neither you nor your company calls it such. There are the employer-mandated breaks, like Scott's in the US military, which occur within the organization itself but operate completely differently from their routine business. Second, there are externship-like breaks, which occur outside the organization and can either be sponsored by companies or embarked upon individually, like the MBA and other external mid-career transitionary programs. Finally, there are more self-guided and less structured opportunities that provide credibility through a job title and association while expecting little in return, like the entrepreneur in residence. Understanding how these opportunities can serve you personally can help you carve out an important experience within an industry you wish to stay in, and also create a guilt-free sabbatical on your own.

Scott: Active Duty Refreshment

The US military has long recognized that sustained professional growth requires deliberate pauses for reflection and skill-building, which they provide in the mandated program away from the front lines that Scott participated in called Active Duty Refreshment (ADR). Active Duty Refreshment is standard procedure for more than a quarter of a million officers across all branches of the US military. According to military historian Dr. Bill Williams, these breaks are used to spur "intellectual growth and professional development" among military leadership, and are actually required for promotion. Initially, the programs can take the form of six-week online remote learning courses, but officers singled out for high command must attend in-person residencies for nine months or longer every five years or so.[1]

Though Scott complained about the timing of his ADR—he missed out on joining his fellow troops deploying to Afghanistan immediately following 9/11—he later realized that his studies with the air force were important in ways he could only appreciate in retrospect. As he reflected: "Despite the frustration of being back in school while my colleagues deployed, understanding the structure and workings of another branch we're collaborating with gave me skills my army colleagues lacked. Not to mention the relationships I made with my new peers. When I deployed to Afghanistan at the end of that year, I found myself radioing in to many of the commanders I'd studied with in North Carolina for air support. I came away with insight into how they work and their incentives, which helped me garner their attention in crucial moments in combat. There's no doubt that the time we spent together also gave them a unique look at my soldiers' realities on the ground as well."

Make no mistake about it, Active Duty Refreshment is not like any other sabbatical described in this book. Most sabbaticals involve stepping away from your routine job in all senses to pursue personal growth, creative projects, or simply to rest and recharge. Scott's refreshment leave is mandated by his employer and is technically classroom-based training. He didn't have to negotiate for it, worry about financing it, or justify it to skeptical colleagues.

But graduates from these programs overwhelmingly describe an environment where learning is almost secondary to their experience. On ADR, Scott was able to step back from the intensity of his work, reconnect with what mattered most to him, and return with fresh energy and clarity. These are human milestones, not standardized grades. It's a practical policy that acknowledges human beings need extended rest periodically to perform at their best. And that giving people substantial time away isn't a cost to be minimized but an investment in long-term performance and retention.*

Scott's glimpse into the inner workings of a different branch of the military gave him the ability to do his job better. Not only did this translate into lives saved but both military branches also experienced increased efficiency as a result. In addition, Scott built a handful of personal relationships during those twelve months that he would maintain for the rest of his career.

Every military officer I've spoken to has echoed these sentiments. Dr. Williams describes his own experience in the Air Force Squadron Officer School glowingly: "By being away from my regular job for a while, I expanded my horizons, learned new things about myself, and better understood how my job fit into the Air Force mission."

And if you're able to get below the surface a bit, their sabbatical story becomes more personal and human. For many soldiers, it's one of the few times they are in the same place with their family for an extended time without the stresses of impending deployments or

---

* Militaries in general have had a significant impact on how civilians work: one of the roots of our forty-hour workweek can be traced to wartime Britain, where studies on productivity and morale in munitions factories led to the capping of work shifts at eight hours per day.[2]

recovering from being on one. Williams reflects, "There has recently been some criticism of the military's professional military education programs related to academic vigor, but to be honest, the value of the program wasn't the academics—you could complete that coursework online relatively quickly—but the personal development. After six weeks, let alone six months, I knew more about myself and was therefore a better officer than when I arrived."

Active Duty Refreshment programs offer real, important knowledge for military officers and enlisted troops. But the military also knows that the soft skills like relationships across branches, team-building, and sufficient time for rest and family bonding are crucial to high performance over the medium and long term. When an organization whose very survival depends on peak performance builds sabbaticals into its operating model, it sends a clear message about their necessity more broadly.

Graduate School

For us civilians, moving up the ranks in our careers can also require a graduate degree. But getting one is a completely different endeavor, requiring us to leave our jobs (and salary) behind and to spend our own money to pursue a degree. Many of these general master's degree programs, like those in public policy, health, and mid-career executive education, mirror the components of a successful sabbatical. They offer a prolonged absence from the workforce, the opportunity to learn in a self-directed way, and generally open individuals up to possibilities they never before considered. The reprieve from direct work lends institutional legitimacy to the extended breaks, correctly framing time away as an investment in human capital, not an indulgence—which is exactly how we should be thinking about sabbaticals as a broader society.

The most popular approach for early- to mid-career transformation is society's most acceptable sabbatical: the MBA. Like the military's

ADR, companies have been using the MBA to outsource their business and personal skill training for more than a century. Business schools were first tailored to the needs of corporations, arming employees with sharper analytical skills and fluency in the business-specific skills of accounting, bookkeeping, and finance. Your company would hold your slot at work while you acquired the skills necessary to move up within the ranks upon your return. And like the military's programs, the MBA also served dual purposes an organization struggles to deliver on a day-to-day basis: developing crucial professional skills while providing the extended break that employees need in order to recharge and perform at a high level over the course of their careers.

It doesn't come cheap. MBA students enrolled in top institutions pay the highest tuition among all graduate degrees, costing as much as $85,000. But they also return to higher pay than their non-MBA peers. On average, the person who graduates from a top tier school can expect to see an $80,000 pay bump after returning to the workforce a mere eighteen months later.[3] This makes for a potentially quick payoff for those students footing the bill themselves and demonstrates that firms consider it a worthy investment in their future employees. Apart from just a pay bump, MBAs graduate with higher self-confidence, self-esteem, and self-efficacy.[4] These traits not only sound good in brochures, they're also proven ingredients to career success in the self-directed protean career era, as we saw in chapter 5.[5]

The MBA is most commonly used by management consulting and investment banking firms, where it's standard practice to send their strongest junior employees to attend business school—footing the bill for their tuition as long as the employee returns to the firm after graduation. In management consulting specifically, most junior staff won't ever make it to the ranks of senior management (up), so they end up leaving (out). Junior employees feel pressured to show growth and improvement, and the external seal of approval of professional certifications and degrees is a big part of this system. Business school flips the script of career progression from "up or out" to "out to go up." It's a corporate version of the same story I've heard over and over from sabbatical alumni—sometimes the best way to move forward in life is to take a step to the side, off your current trajectory. While it may seem orthogonal or counterproductive to our growth, it's actually providing a better angle of attack for the next leg of the journey. And as with the military's ADR, some of the most valuable ingredients of an MBA aren't exactly advertised in the recruiting brochures.

James and the Business of Self

James Allworth went to business school for the same reason many people do: he'd been a good student in college and ended up a consultant after graduation. The consulting-to-business-school pipeline is to the twenty-first century what law school was to the twentieth century—a great cover for twentysomethings who don't yet know what to do with their lives.

Over the next two years, instead of just equipping him to move to the next rung of the career ladder, business school took James on a journey of self-discovery, a major career detour, and a dramatic change in his personal life.

I first met James before he started business school at Harvard, and he charmed me right away. Seemingly out of central casting for an athletic and affable Australian, he was tall and messy-haired, with a booming voice, killer accent, and big laugh. Physically, James had a triangle-shaped torso and wingspan befitting his childhood as a nationally ranked swimmer, but his personality was more friendly (Australian) shepherd than competitive greyhound.

James was fresh off a four-year stint living out of a suitcase, following in the footsteps of his father, who worked in management consulting. James had always dreamed of working in tech in Silicon Valley, and business school seemed like a good way to get there. His competitive drive hadn't waned since he'd graduated at the top of his class at the Australian National University. Nevertheless, he viewed b-school as a chance to slow down a bit. He didn't expect it to be easy, but he welcomed the legitimate excuse to unplug from the frenetic pace of the international consulting lifestyle. It's not clear that anyone puts in fewer hours at business school than in consulting, but the blend of activities—socializing, clubs, and special interest groups—and the relative autonomy provide a distinct change of pace.

James's personal journey took a turn after he enrolled in one of HBS's most popular classes in his second year: Authentic Leadership Development, or ALD. Taught by former Medtronic CEO and *True North* author Bill George, students of this class—which has been oversubscribed since its launch in 2004—affectionately refer to it as "therapy class." Graduates recall regular tears as they learned to plumb their own emotional depths and to make space for others to do the same. Courses like this abound at the top MBA programs; Stanford's most popular is known as "touchy-feely" class. James described ALD as an introduction to vulnerability, which taught him to lower his walls, reflect deeply, and use this self-knowledge to build more authentic relationships. It was this experience that challenged him to think about his lack of a romantic life. Was something going on beneath the surface that prevented James from opening up to another person?

James's experience might sound like an outlier in a degree that is more known for producing Fortune 100 executives than executive coaches. But the business school curriculum has evolved to meet the needs and desires of its students, whose career success requires more than just analytical techniques and frameworks.

Social science power couple Gianpiero and Jennifer Louise Petriglieri describe the importance of the two-year container an MBA provides in their paper "Identity Workspaces: The Case of Business Schools."[6] The Petriglieris believe that the MBA has an outsize impact on students because it gives the time, space, and permission to develop as a human, not just a businessperson. This self-work is crucial to increasing your personal agency and self-esteem, which are the preconditions to making changes in your life or restoring confidence in your current path.[7]

Our identity is constantly evolving over the course of our lives, but it changes most intensely during specific inflection points and transitions in our lives. This is why people feel like they grow most during times of extreme discomfort, either professionally or personally—say, after a breakup, health scare, or death of a loved one. You're not just experiencing hardship, you're forever changing how you view the world and what's possible as a person in it.

Business school becomes this crucible experience for many graduates. It's an extended period when you're set apart from your routine life, which has become a ritual for many people in the professional class. It's a protected space to experiment, change, or simply recover. Stop me if this sounds familiar.

MBA programs have two other qualities the Petriglieris describe as key to updating your identity while you're in school: social defenses and rites of passage.[8]

Rites of passage contain three stages: separation, liminality, and reincorporation.[9] To attend an MBA program, you separate from the normal path of a nine-to-five job—often geographically as well. You exist in a liminal state, having set that identity aside for a while in service of learning and transformation. Finally, you are reincorporated back into society. Many graduates reemerge into leadership roles or in different careers entirely. Going off to college has a similar effect; it's an honored transition to adulthood in our society. Rites of passage work best when they are widely recognized and supported by the community you belong to.

Social defenses give us permission to do something we might otherwise fear or feel unsafe doing. For most, the MBA's widely accepted credentials offer a much more socially acceptable reason to take a year or two off than a self-guided sabbatical would. According to the Petriglieris, social defenses give people the room to make sense of a transition to a new identity without having to face the judgment or censure of their peers. It's the difference between someone thinking that taking time off means you're not serious about your career and viewing you as elite for completing a two-year graduate degree, no matter to what extent you've actually changed on the inside.

Society generally agrees that mid-career schooling is valuable and worth stepping off the straight and narrow career path to pursue. This should be our aspiration for sabbaticals, whether they happen inside an institution or on our own.

James in B-School

Once James got a taste of applying the business school curriculum to his life, he took full advantage, leading him to the larger-than-life figure of Clay Christensen (and at six foot eight, he was also large *in* life), who famously coined the term "disruption." Though Christensen's class had historically focused solely on business dilemmas, the professor had changed tack after receiving a terminal cancer diagnosis during the semester. Christensen transformed his final lecture into a strategy for how to live a good life. Why, he asked, did so many of his fellow HBS classmates, now decades out from graduation and with significant financial and personal resources, regret the way their lives had turned out?

James had impressed Christensen in class, and in turn he offered him a job as a postgraduate fellow, to work with Christensen directly on turning his ideas into a book on the subject. Approaching graduation, James found himself in the unexpected position of having three attractive job offers. He could live out his pre-MBA dream of working in tech and return to Apple, where he had worked during his summer internship. He could return to Booz Allen, where a promotion, pay raise, and the prospect of wiping out about a hundred thousand dollars in school debt awaited him. Or he could go with Christensen.

The decision would have been a no-brainer for pre-MBA James: a job at the hottest company in tech, based in the birthplace of start-ups. But this choice left James dissatisfied. There was something about Christensen's emerging strategy-of-life project that was increasingly difficult to rule out. James had felt his priorities shift during those eighteen months in business school. Instead of viewing his choice as sacrificing salary, prestige, and promotions, James began to see it as getting paid for gaining the space and techniques to live a more satisfying life. When viewed through Clay's lens of how to correctly allocate time to what's important in his life, the prospect of acquiring industry experience at the expense of continuing personal introspection felt wrong.

So James turned down his other offers and began his work with Christensen. Over the next year, he turned Christensen's final lecture into a *Harvard Business Review* article that became an instant classic. Shortly afterward, together with writer Karen Dillon, James and Christensen expanded the article into a *New York Times* bestselling book called *How Will You Measure Your Life?*

Alongside all this external progress, James realized he'd invested far too little in his personal life prior to taking time off for school. Ironically, business school—ostensibly focused on career advancement—helped him imagine an existence that wasn't defined by professional achievement. Through deep conversations and observing the life experiences of his peers, James also came to understand that he was gay and came out to friends and family.

"You think you're going to learn about ROI [return on investment] and demystify business terminology, and there is a lot of that," he remembers. "But what stood out to me the most was developing empathy for my classmates—not only through their vastly diverging points of view in class but also through witnessing how different their life experiences were. . . . There's an incredible amount of diversity across so many spectrums in a place like that." If James's career suffered because of his choice to extract himself from the worlds of consulting and tech, it's hard to figure out how. After the book was released, he moved to the West Coast to work at one of tech's most attractive unicorns.

Stories of profound personal transformation are becoming more and more common in business schools and other similar programs as they respond to student demands for personal development–focused coursework. In so doing, business school has gradually become an ideal catalyst for broader personal transformation, providing the space to explore, experiment, and reflect, while at the same time honing the academic skills that are valued by the outside world.

Full-time MBA programs aren't alone in providing this dual benefit. There are a lot of other options that provide the same socially acceptable cover as the MBA for learning, personal growth, and transformation. Mid-career executive business certificates and other graduate programs have steadily risen in popularity in the twenty-first century.[10] They are shorter than the traditional MBA, and almost always paid for by employers. In addition, volunteering organizations like the Peace Corps and fellowships like Fullbright offer credentials to explain your absence from the workforce, as well as community and learning befitting a rite of passage. It's up to you whether to find a program that works for you (if you need a cover story) or strike out on your own and design one.

The Entrepreneurial Career

On the other side of the spectrum from being able to take leave from within an organization is the self-directed career of an entrepreneur. For founders, there is no company to foot the bill for your personal development, nor is there a certification to pursue that would make you more attractive to future employers or investors.

Entrepreneurs embody that self-directed, protean career approach to work where individuals must take charge of, well, everything. Few jobs embody uncertainty like entrepreneurship, but significant breaks from the front lines, no matter how intimidating and uncertain, have long played a role in start-up land as well.

Some of the most successful entrepreneurs have hatched their business ideas on sabbatical, such as Salesforce's Marc Benioff and Impossible Foods' Dr. Patrick Brown. Steve Jobs famously took a forced sabbatical after being fired by the board of Apple, during which he practiced calligraphy, which helped cement the importance of design in his products for decades to come. Armed with either a supportive company policy (Benioff worked for long-standing sabbatical policy stalwart Oracle) or enough confidence and resources to strike out on their own (Brown sought more positive impact with his work), these trailblazers understood that innovative ideas need time and space to be discovered. Smart investors have taken notice of this trend. Eager to tap into—and reap the rewards from—these creative breaks, many venture capital firms host in-house programs for founders in between ideas called entrepreneurs in residence (EIR).

The EIR's job description is pretty sparse. You get an email address, a desk, and the option to work from the investor's office. Most EIRs are part-timers who are paid a modest salary—a small fraction of what they would make as founders—but the job title offers something more difficult to quantify but still incredibly valuable: validation. This is particularly important when the chances of starting your next company hinge on being able to sell a possible funder on your potential.

Having an email address at a venture capital firm opens these doors. It also helps people understand what you're doing in between more easily explainable roles at work. Jenny Elizabeth, an entrepreneur and sabbatical alum who took an EIR position between leaving a medical tech company and founding an electrification company, described the interim role to me as providing an "easy, one-sentence description for yourself, which is especially important in a world where an elevator pitch might be all the time you get with someone."

The first entrepreneur-in-residence program started in Silicon Valley in the 1990s. Foundation Capital, the original investor behind Netflix, considers its EIR program to have been crucial to its ongoing success and to have played an important role in office dynamics.[11] There are a few reasons for this. First, EIRs often join in for crucial meetings where investment decisions are made and start-up founders pitch their company ideas. For as much money as they oversee, venture capital firms are notoriously small operations. Foundation, for example, has just three general partners responsible for its latest $350 million fund, and fewer than thirty employees total. EIRs are also well-connected (and relatively cheap) members of the team who help find and evaluate potential investments. Adding one or two EIRs for this purpose can mean the difference between your firm finding the next Amazon or one of your many competitors getting there first.

Performance data at VC firms is private and tightly held, but the proliferation of EIRs in the industry indicates their value. Some firms estimate that as much as 40 percent of their deal flow comes through the EIR program, and a 2010 study of leading venture capital firms in the US and Israel showed that companies led by former EIRs provide a greater return for investors.[12] Organizations with EIRs benefit from new ideas and outside perspectives without the commitment of a full-time hire. Entrepreneurs get structured time away from their routine to explore what's next. But the EIR program also adds value to entrepreneurs on a less quantifiable, more human basis by bridging a gap on a résumé and, for many, allowing them time and space to recover from the pressure-laden role of an executive.

Nick Soman, CEO of Decent Healthcare, credits his time as an EIR at Foundation not only as the catalyst for his new company but also for saving his marriage.

"If you get yourself into a relationship hole due to how you work, it's hard to imagine getting out of it by doing things the same way," Nick reflected. "If I was going to be an entrepreneur again, I needed to do it differently."

As an entrepreneur in residence, Nick's company-creation process was *very* different from what he'd done in the past. He'd started his last company at home after long days at a demanding job. As an EIR, he had a more flexible schedule for the first time in years. This enabled him to take on more work at home, so his wife could fulfill her dream of returning to school.

From a work perspective, Nick learned valuable lessons about how Foundation evaluated deals. He was able to be in the room where brilliant founders tried to convince investors, and in the other room where investors explained the logic behind their decisions. For him to start another company, he'd have to succeed in the same arenas. His EIR role encouraged him to think bigger, and the exposure helped sharpen his aim. Within months, he'd raised $8 million for a new health insurance company idea. And Foundation Capital, which didn't typically invest in the healthcare sector, led the round.

For those of us who don't aspire to be venture-backed entrepreneurs, the EIR concept has spread throughout other industries. Universities, Fortune 500 companies, nonprofits, and even governments now post EIR-like positions (so-called experts in residence) to attract outsiders with skills and experiences vastly different from their regular staff. These experts typically aren't fully employed or compensated, but neither are they just "between jobs" or "taking time off." Their résumé suddenly tells a story of being sought out for expertise rather than stepping away from the grind. What was once a career gap is now a prestigious-sounding appointment, befitting perhaps the broader impact this break can have on the rest of one's life at the same time.

ooo

Most of us want to take a sabbatical but seek permission in order to feel confident doing so. There are legitimate fears and constraints around taking extended leave. But instead of missing your chance in life by holding off in hope of finding the perfect opportunity, look more closely at some of our society's preexisting breaks from routine. For example, sabbaticals hidden in plain sight offer something tangible to show for your time off, a cover story to act as a social defense. Proof you did something "worthwhile," while also giving yourself space to explore, heal, and learn.

The very fact that many of us feel like we need evidence shows we're still operating under outdated assumptions about what constitutes legitimate professional behavior. We're working toward a world where cover stories are no longer needed. One where it's okay that military war colleges are as much for restoration as they are for education. Where MBA programs recognize that their competitive advantage over employers isn't just delivering business skills but also providing much-needed space, and a rite of passage, for the holistic development of human beings. Where entrepreneur-in-residence programs are recognized for delivering both business and personal returns to founders and investors. These examples reveal something important: when we stop treating extended time away as something that requires justification and start recognizing it as strategic human capital development, the need for elaborate explanations disappears.

But make no mistake about it: The reason these elite organizations and sectors have embraced sabbaticals is less about generosity and more about the recognition of a new reality. The days of climbing a single corporate ladder for forty years are over. These organizations understand that in an economy where the average person will have more than a dozen jobs over their life, time for reflection, recovery, skill-building, and strategic planning isn't optional, it's essential for staying competitive. Consulting firms that give their employees a two-year paid break from work employ more than 30 percent of MBA graduates each year, who return to their ranks reenergized for the next leg of their career.

For the rest of us, we can try to use these examples to create our own sabbatical. There are options that offer creative opportunities like externships or paid personal development to lend professional legitimacy to very human needs for recovery, exploration, and professional growth. Or borrow a title from a short-term gig to give yourself the psychological permission you need to focus on your career holistically, yourself included. However you choose to step away, the next section will explore how to make the most of your time off.

THE FIELD GUIDE

9

First Principles

The experience itself is the curriculum.

—Will Kabat-Zinn

You've arrived at the "practical" section of the book, the part where you learn what you should do and what to avoid. The part some of you flipped to pretty early in your reading journey, maybe first thing.

I get it.

You want this book to be a productive experience, so why not fast-forward to the part where someone tells you how to do it?

I promise I will do that. But first, I need to tell you that in my professional opinion, while a prescriptive manual may be what you *want*, it's not really what you *need*.

The most transformative sabbaticals are not merely destinations rife with accomplishments but journeys of self-understanding. A vacation is about doing, whereas a sabbatical is more about *being*. To paraphrase Proust, the real voyage of discovery consists not in seeking new landscapes but in seeing yourself anew upon your return. The biggest risk you'll face won't be from doing the wrong things but from not admitting you're wrong and trying something else instead.

There's a limit to how much you can prepare for a sabbatical. There's also a limit to how much you *should* prepare. You must make room for the unexpected opportunities that arise precisely from the *lack* of a plan, and the emotional discomfort that may accompany that. I get that this sounds like the worst-case scenario for the type As among us, but exploration enables growth, and growth requires discomfort. That's the threshold you must cross on any journey of transformation, and the gooey insides of Sabbatical Land.

The advice you'll appreciate the most from me won't be a concrete recommendation for a beautiful beach or secluded retreat. Rather, it will be what helps you create the initial conditions for success: your sabbatical should be long enough, it must contain the right components, and these pieces must be in the right order. These three guiding principles—setting, ingredients, and order—kick off the Field Guide.

I call this section a field guide because it's meant to be consulted on the journey, as a reference to better understand what you're experiencing, instead of a rigid how-to manual. Therefore, this will *not* be a *do this, don't do that* checklist but rather scaffolding to frame the journey in front of you. You'll learn best practices, how to approach planning your sabbatical, and common pitfalls. Additionally, at the end of each chapter I will distill the lessons into reflection prompts you can return to at your own pace.

In the next chapter, we'll dive a little deeper to help you apply these macro principles across the three phases of a sabbatical: preparation, the messy middle, and the integration that comes toward the end of your time off. After that comes a sampling of more modest, bite-size sabbaticals, followed by a chapter examining a sabbatical from the perspective of the "work self" we all return to, what's in it for you and your employer, and how to bridge the gap between personal desires and work responsibilities. Then comes a final chapter on common difficulties sabbatical takers face on their journeys. Then I'll wish you well on your way.

Three Guiding Principles

Setting: Duration and Disconnection

DURATION: *BIG* TIME OFF (MORE THAN YOU'RE COMFORTABLE WITH)

In our time-scarce society, carving out enough uninterruptable time for your sabbatical is undoubtedly the most difficult step you'll face. Is it any wonder that the most common question I receive is "How much time is sufficient for a sabbatical?"

I believe the sweet spot for sabbaticals is between six and twelve months.* It's not easy to take such a big chunk of time off, which is why most people take an abbreviated break of a month or six weeks, kicking the can down the road for a longer break when things open up in the future. While you'll still undoubtedly get some benefits from an extended vacation, which we'll discuss further in chapter 11, don't mistake a shorter break for a sabbatical. Not taking enough time off puts you at risk of ending up just short of the sought-after experience. It often takes six to eight weeks to *begin* to feel like you're truly disconnected from routine life.

We've all experienced that moment toward the end of a vacation when we finally feel like we're sinking in and enjoying ourselves, only to realize it's time to head back to reality. It's like that with sabbaticals. The most transformative aspects of sabbaticals often don't start until

* That may sound like an extraordinarily long time, but it's also minuscule in the scale of our careers: a half year out of the forty most of us work is only 1.25 percent of our total time on the job.

at least two months in, after we've had a chance to heal and sufficiently leave our former life behind.

While there is ample evidence to suggest that anything under two months is too short, there's less clarity on how long is too long. A small chunk of people I've interviewed felt as though being out of the workforce for more than a year felt right, and it worked for them. That said, I've witnessed significantly more folks who kept moving their return dates further and further into the future, getting caught in a cycle of self-doubt and guilt the longer they stayed outside of routine life. This makes sense: sabbatical takers feel enormous pressure to make their hard-won time off "worth it." If their problems haven't been resolved or their lives completely changed, can they really return to regular life satisfied?

Stressing yourself psychologically and financially while waiting for the perfect job is almost always worse than taking a modest next step *toward* your ultimate goals. So plan for sufficient time in Sabbatical Land, but consider setting a deadline for returning to work, even if—especially if—you haven't yet landed on your dream job.

DISCONNECT: SET IMPENETRABLE BOUNDARIES

Once you create the right container, you need to protect it by setting boundaries. This is more difficult than ever. Some thirty years ago, going abroad meant untethering. Your boss couldn't reach you. Getting in touch with the folks at home meant an expensive long-distance call. As for the news, *The New York Times* didn't go online until 1996, and you'd need to be in a cybercafe to read it. Now, a flick of the thumb could reveal a crisis at work, a salacious news story, or a pressing issue closer to home, and in the process spoil your serenity for the rest of the day.

I'm a purist when it comes to not working while on sabbatical, particularly when it comes in the form of consulting gigs related to your routine job. No matter how attractive the opportunity seems—no matter how little time it claims to take up—these projects tend to expand to fill the time available. A two-hour call once per week has a surprising amount of disruptive force, preventing spontaneity, requiring connectivity, and psychologically tying you to a past version of yourself. So set an away message and create a mail rule to auto-delete all inbound emails. Make sure your colleagues understand what constitutes a sufficient "break the glass" moment to interrupt your time off.

Money might be able to buy you incrementally more time off, but it can *never* replace the large swaths of uninterrupted time off it destroys. No matter how tempting it may seem, you will regret porous boundaries between your old life and your time off.

Ingredients: Embodiment and Play

GET OUT OF YOUR HEAD AND INTO YOUR BODY (AND SOUL)

Most of us spend the majority of our days in our heads. We use our bodies over the course of our workdays, sure, but typically we're crammed into tight, angular workspaces—like our cars and our cubicles—performing familiar motions, such as typing while sitting at a ninety-degree angle. It has gotten so bad that many of us rely on our devices to remind us to move around during our waking hours. If your job requires physical labor, it probably doesn't allow for much creative expression. Instead, your actions have been edited for efficiency.

Even outside work, we spend most of our time in our head, not our bodies. We plan, we socialize, we watch movies, we learn, we teach others. The little time we spend engaging with our physical bodies is usually reserved for "productive" purposes like working out.

So it's no surprise that when faced with the opportunity of a sabbatical, many folks' first instinct is to be more mental than physical. We hope to master a new language, tackle an overflowing bookshelf, or take a class for self-improvement. But while intellectual self-improvement can and should be part of your sabbatical, a whole host of mental, creative, and physical benefits are derived from returning to the corporeal and tactile instead. Getting back to your body, you might say.

Engaging in creative hobbies—such as arts and crafts, experimenting in the kitchen, and woodworking—is associated with reduced depressive and anxiety symptoms, as well as enhanced life satisfaction.[1] Throw pottery clay, take dance lessons, get your hands dirty gardening, or spend time upside down in yoga class. Give your mind a break for a bit. Physical work creates the psychological distance we need from our old lives to conceive a new chapter.

COMMIT TO PLAY

Play is an essential aspect of a transformative sabbatical. Unlike achievement-oriented tasks like writing a book or training for a marathon, play has no ultimate goal other than joy. Enjoying an activity for its own sake is not something most of us prioritize in our normal lives. How often do we wander around a museum with no timeline or ditch our well-crafted plans to follow an unproven hunch? As we saw in Winston from chapter 1, even the least "productive" acts of play can have enormous effects on the rest of your life.

As a rule of thumb, your sabbatical is long enough if you have enough time to pivot. When we vacation, especially an American-size one—two weeks max—there's little room for error, change, or a new direction. A delayed plane can have a domino effect that disrupts the entire trip. Getting it all done within the allotted window of time is more accomplishment than exploration.

On the other hand, when we have enough time and space to play, there's less pressure throughout. We can lose track of time and take detours that lead us in entirely new directions. For example, a travel companion's last-minute cancellation could force you to embark on a leg of your trip alone. On my sabbatical, when a last-minute injury derailed plans with a friend to scale a difficult mountain on New Year's

Eve, it took us on an entirely different (and, in retrospect, much more relaxing and enjoyable) vacation scuba diving in the Komodo Islands.

Chip Conley from chapter 5 encourages attendees at the Modern Elder Academy to follow a "scent of possibility." You don't need a master plan—for some folks, it's better to test out life specifically without one—but once you figure out which track you want to follow, be prepared to adjust accordingly as the direction changes over time.

Order: Put Everything in Its Place

DETOX FIRST

Once you've created the right setting and planned the type of activities you'd like to pursue, you need to think about the order in which to do them. The first step is surprisingly difficult.

If you're like most people, when you arrive in Sabbatical Land, you'll want to run off and attack your to-do list straightaway. But one of the biggest regrets I hear from sabbatical alumni is not taking a beat at the beginning to detox and heal. Yes, *heal*. Aarti from chapter 3 is a perfect example. As soon as she broke free from work, she rushed off to New York to interview people for her book. Soon she was fully immersed in the writing process. She was about two months in when she realized she'd been running on adrenaline. Only after she began to listen to her body, which was completely burned out from the prior decade of hard work, did she invest in some limited recovery. The thought that her burnout could persist underneath the surface even after she escaped work had never occurred to her. Aarti is hardly alone. The functional workaholism with which we operate at work is deeply engrained and impairs our ability to even sense that we need recovery.

Avoid this common mistake by decompressing first at the start of your sabbatical. This can take many shapes, from an organized retreat to an extended stretch off the grid in the wilderness. Escaping your everyday surroundings by treating yourself to a long weekend away can fit the bill. But for the best results, get as far away as possible geographically from your routine life and do absolutely nothing for a little while. The combination of new surroundings and a gaping time zone change removes possibilities for productivity and disrupts your normal patterns enough to reset your experience of daily life. Whatever you do, make sure to give yourself gratitude for the hard leg of your journey before setting off immediately on all the exciting (and well-deserved) plans you'll cook up.

EXPLORE AND EXPERIMENT LATER

Who you are by the end of your sabbatical may look nothing like who you were when you started. You'll view your initial choices—for your sabbatical and possibly your life—through a completely new lens. But how much you transform depends on how widely you've expanded the aperture for what's possible.

Exploration can take many forms. It doesn't have to mean traveling far from home, though I'd highly recommend it. Think about exploration in two ways: inward and outward. Outward exploration is usually what first comes to mind: traveling to that place you've always wanted to see. Being there in person offers more than a first-person view of something breathtaking. It shows you other ways a life can be lived. How do other people work? How do they interact with nature and loved ones? Americans—and anyone too busy to get out of their bubble—can especially benefit from seeing different ways of existing and working up close.

Inward exploration requires no travel, and those who pursue it might more accurately be called seekers than explorers. As you'll recall from the archetypes chapter, seeking means using your time to explore different parts of yourself with your time off. This might mean reaching back into your personal history to stoke old passions. Remember that art competition you won in middle school? Or seeking might entail making space to attend to interests or lingering questions you've had about yourself but never given time and energy to.

As we explore, we'll often want to try some of the feelings, places, and urges on for size, which turns exploration into experimentation. This shift is crucial for a transformative sabbatical, compared to simply a restorative one. Our research found that while most sabbatical takers returned with greater well-being and enhanced perspective on their lives, those who spent a significant portion of their sabbatical trying something new changed their trajectories the most. As long as you experiment without expectation or the need for it to get you somewhere you're not, it can be a productive tool in your sabbatical arsenal.

Whatever you choose, spending enough time in this middle stage of exploration and experimentation—between healing and synthesizing—is critical for significant change. Just don't rush into it.

In Practice

Duration

- **Align your sabbatical with work, personal, and destination calendars.** For example, overlap with your kids' summer break or outside the "busy season" at your job (or during, so you miss it altogether . . .).
- **Seek out personal references as exemplars.** Interview five people in your life who have taken sabbaticals to help you build confidence that it is possible for you.
- **Journal.** What's the longest break you've ever taken? The longest amount of time off you can imagine taking? List your fears about being away for so long to help combat them.

Disconnection

- **Minimize distractions.** What are the channels through which work colleagues, friends, and family members contact you? What strategies can you implement before your sabbatical to test reducing the flow—for example, an auto-away email response?
- **Plan for personal emergencies.** Develop a plan of action for emergencies, such as urgent health issues while you're away or a crisis at home. Recruit a friend or family member to handle things without your input.
- **Set work boundaries.** Meet with coworkers before your departure to set expectations around responsiveness. Enlist two trusted people—one inside the organization and one who knows you professionally but is not at your job—to screen if something should be escalated to you.

Embodiment

- **Engage with nature.** Spend extended time outdoors, preferably doing something requiring physical exertion, toward the beginning of your time off.
- **Do something tactile.** Opt for activities that take you out of your head and into your hands or the rest of your body.
- **Prioritize restoration.** Put yourself in a place for true rest and recovery; you've earned it. Whatever feels restorative to you, make sure it is nourishing and low-effort.

Play

- **Reconnect with your people.** Spend time with people you miss or are inspired by.
- **Ask your inner child what to do.** What hobbies or interests once occupied your time and imagination?
- **Be fearless.** Identify a handful of outlandish, irresponsible, unimpressive things you'd do if no one was watching. Take acting, improv, or singing lessons. Don't worry, everyone else you know is busy working!

Order

- **Map out your plans.** First, how will you detox? Then, what is your anchor exploration activity? Lastly, dedicate at least 10 percent of the length of your sabbatical *prior* to your return to synthesizing and reacclimating.

10

Preparing, Departing, and Coming Back

We aren't seeking the meaning of life but
the experience of being alive.

—Joseph Campbell

Now that we've identified the guiding principles of a proper sabbatical, let's dive into the nitty-gritty. For planning purposes, I divide a sabbatical into three phases: before, during, and ending. The before stage is the pre-departure planning and prep required once you've decided to take a sabbatical. It's where you lay out your hopes and dreams for your sabbatical and wrestle with the logistical hurdles that can prevent you from getting out the door to begin with. The during stage is what happens when you're on sabbatical—a few tweaks and warnings can help you avoid the most common pitfalls among sabbatical takers and ensure that your sabbatical provides you with what you need. (Which may not be what you wanted.) The ending is the last few weeks or so of your sabbatical, when you're shifting from exploration mode into contemplating next steps. Let's visit each chronologically.

Preparation

The preparation stage is the lead-up up to your sabbatical. In the best circumstances, you'll have months or years to plan your extended leave. While this is seldom the case, you will find that however long you have to prepare, a considerable amount of the up-front work will consist of financial planning to make your sabbatical a reality. That part of your *before* may take years. It may take months. Then there is the logistical overhead. The organization and preparation that goes into subletting your apartment or finding new schools for the kids. Not to mention canceling any recurring payments and responsibilities (read: the gym membership you rarely use) to help symbolize a new chapter.

Sabbatical preparations will be different for everyone, which is why you'll want to put together a spreadsheet or a good old-fashioned checklist to figure out next steps for your individual situation. Take heart: This isn't the dry admin required when figuring out a new insurance carrier or renewing your driver's license. Sure, the details may be a little annoying, but when you think of the adventure that is your sabbatical, you'll approach the project with the enthusiasm of a child cooking up their Christmas list. During the preparation phase, I suggest you get your finances in order, keep a journal, and resist publicizing your time off.

Understand Your Finances

Affordability is an aspiring sabbatical taker's primary concern, and it is a valid one. There's no right answer about how much you should accumulate in savings, how big your rainy-day fund should be, or what unexpected outlays are on the horizon. This will always be true, sabbatical or not. Taking a sabbatical is a leap of faith that time spent without earnings can be an investment instead of just an outlay. If the examples in this book are moving you along this spectrum from fear to confidence, wrapping your mind around your finances can provide some ease.

The money question comes in two timescales: short-term feasibility (can I actually afford to do all the things I want to do?) and long-term financial impact (how will taking off from a steady income impact my eventual retirement?). Each person has a unique financial picture and hangups around money. Your parents' experience with financial instability, or their discomfort with temporary unemployment, can still hold power over your relationship with working and spur guilt around taking time off. But their beliefs are usually out of step with your lived experience and context. Your mission on sabbatical is to reexamine your relationship to money. It's a chance to wipe the slate clean and actively choose how you want to spend your hard-earned money going forward.

IDENTIFY YOUR CURRENT EXPENSES

If you've never thought in depth about your spending, a financial planner can help translate and guide you through constructing a budget for your time off. Increasingly, financial planners who specialize in career breaks have sprung up.

While hiring a professional can relieve a fair amount of pressure, spending the necessary time preparing your finances for a sabbatical yourself can help catalyze a larger transformation. For example, many sabbatical alums, like Winston and Kristin from chapter 1, return from their time away realizing it's easier to decrease their spending going forward than to increase their salary.

The first step is to figure out roughly how much money you've been spending for the last few years. This provides a baseline of historical spending in regular life so you can make a sabbatical budget. Once you've done that, you can dissect the main components of this spending.

Begin with a cash flow analysis. Start by identifying which expenses are fixed and which are variable. Fixed costs are things you can't easily change, like an auto loan, rent, utilities, or a mortgage payment. Variable costs are everything else: how much you spend on entertainment, food, etc. Variable costs won't disappear during your sabbatical, but you'll have more control over what you spend, and depending on where you go—Scandinavia, where the cost of living is high, or Thailand, where the cost of living is low—you may actually be able to lower them.

Your next step is to figure out how you can temporarily turn off your fixed expenses. Or better yet, convert them into a net positive cash flow to help fund your sabbatical. The most common method is by subletting property (rental or owned) such that you break even, or potentially even make money while you're away. Move in with a friend temporarily while your apartment is sublet or give up your lease altogether and put your belongings in storage for a year. It may feel uncomfortable, but you'll gain valuable perspective about which costs are choices versus inevitabilities. You might be surprised. By the end of my sabbatical, I'd survived on a fraction of the amount of clothes that populated my prior closet. To this day, my wardrobe remains (relatively) svelte.

Beware: sometimes the monetary savings aren't worth the logistical hassle. For example, you *could* do a long-term rental of your car to a trusted friend or family member, but that's usually more trouble than it's worth. Try to balance potential savings with the incremental hassle and distraction during your time off.

TAKE A BALANCE SHEET PERSPECTIVE

After you've determined your fixed and variable expenses, it's time to dissect your finances from a balance sheet perspective. If cash flow is the pace at which you spend, the balance sheet is the amount of money you have in total. By dividing your total savings and liquid assets (things like stocks or other investments you can sell easily for cash) by your burn rate (how much you spend on a monthly basis, assuming no income), you'll get a rough idea of how long you can take off before you completely run out of money. Obviously, you won't want to spend down your entire bank balance, and it's better to cut your sabbatical short than to have money concerns lingering in the background throughout. You will likely want to set a boundary of cash reserves you're comfortable with, depending on your relationship with uncertainty, whether that's three months, six months, or two years. Knowing this number in advance will remove the worry from the back of your mind during your sabbatical and allow for ample job search time at the end.

For example, if you have $100,000 saved up and you normally spend $7,000 per month, you can take off more than a year before running out of cash. If you can offset half of that spend by reducing your housing costs through subletting, then you have twice the runway. Another way to think about spending on your sabbatical is that you're swapping out your fixed living costs at home for lodging while you're away. We don't often think about a $3,000 mortgage as the equivalent of spending $100 per night on a hotel, but it is. And you might be delighted by the wondrous types of places you can live in the world for a modest premium (or savings!) on your rent or mortgage.

SET FINANCIAL CHECKPOINTS

Plan for whatever amount of time you are financially and logistically comfortable with and then reevaluate at preset points during your sabbatical. For example, if you feel like you can comfortably take nine months off, don't check your bank account balance every month. No matter how rock-solid your financial planning, seeing money only come *out* of your account is extremely uncomfortable. Obsessing over it will lead to second-guessing your decisions and erode your hard-won sense of disconnection.

Once you've made your budget, set a calendar invite for the

planned midpoint of your sabbatical to ask yourself if anything has changed that impacts your ability to stay the course financially, or if you feel comfortable extending your runway further to accommodate more time off. You'd be surprised how often your prediction for what you'll prefer six months from now will differ from what you think when you get there. You may also be surprised at how little you spend during your time off, or at least how much you're enjoying spending it.

Track Your Progress: Keep a Journal, Starting Early

One of my most treasured possessions is the journal covering the lead-up to my sabbatical through to its conclusion. My pre-sabbatical self felt stuck at work and let down in my relationships. I was also constantly beating myself up over failing to take a sabbatical sooner and for not having the energy to properly plan the one that was rapidly approaching. Rereading these entries remains helpful to this day, because they remind me how difficult it is to be conscious of longer-term negative modes of being. Left uncorrected, these spells fester into a general dissatisfaction with life that begins to feel normal and inescapable.

But in my journal, I also expressed wild dreams and aspirations for what I wanted to do on my sabbatical. Journaling is an opportunity to lay bare your most audacious plans for life on the heels of one of the most promising chances to bring them to bear. The entries could be visionary blueprints for the future, or just snapshots of what once seemed critical in your life.

For you non-journalers, trust me: even you will appreciate the value of having kept a psychological record while on sabbatical. Journaling is one of the *only* concrete prescriptions I'll make in this book. You'll appreciate how, over the course of your sabbatical, so many of your previously burdensome concerns melted away. I know I did. I know too that over time, my entries became more whimsical and less dramatic and existential. It felt like my prior concerns had been exfoliated to reveal my better self. I've never written so much in my entire life—and I've hardly journaled since, to be honest—but when I happen to crack it open, my sabbatical journal transports me directly to the most memory-dense period of my life.

I know, I know. Keeping a journal is like meditating; you know it's good for you, but when it comes down to it, it's far easier said than done. I'm asking you to start a journal before you go on sabbatical for a reason. Sure, keeping a travelogue will help you remember the small details and delights of your time off. But a journal is more intimate and introspective. By writing down your thoughts, you stay with them longer than you might normally be comfortable with. This sort of exploration leads to the self-awareness that is the hallmark of a sabbatical. Recording your evolving thoughts and feelings before you take time off will help you understand who you were pre-sabbatical and will be an invaluable tool for your post-sabbatical growth.

Our research interviewees consistently expressed that their sabbatical gave them enhanced perspective on their lives. This perspective doesn't come from geographic distance alone but from the psychological distance that allows us to see how much of our emotional state is shaped by circumstance. In other words, much more of how we feel about our lives is within our control to change, but we must fully disconnect from it to believe it.

The best way to appreciate the changes that your sabbatical has brought about is to go back and review your mental state in the pages of your journal. Reading how you felt about your life in the lead-up to your sabbatical helps you decide how closely you'd like to return to that life. Recording what moves you during your time off also gives you new information about other directions to head toward. You'll see what you wanted to accomplish, and what you thought was important, and how that has changed.

If you're struggling to fill the blank pages of your journal, consider these three reflective framings. First, look back on the prior year. What are the accomplishments, difficulties, and people or moments you feel most grateful for? Next, zoom out further, considering the last five to ten years of your life. What are the things you're most proud of, the difficulties and failures, and how do you aspire to live in the next decade of your life? Finally, zoom in to the span of your sabbatical. What do you hope to explore, how do you aspire to feel by the end of your sabbatical, and what are the barriers you believe will get in your way?

Should these prompts intimidate you, start more slowly, by simply writing down two or three thoughts or observations you had on that day. There's no real right or wrong way to record your pre-sabbatical experience.* But please, get a journal—your future self will thank you.

Resist the Urge to Publicize Your Time Off

One of the biggest threats to a successful sabbatical isn't costs or logistics; it's announcing to the world that you're going on sabbatical. I'm serious.

It's a completely natural instinct to want to publicize your time off. You're doing something that's out of the ordinary, so it makes sense that you'd want validation from others. You might also want to own the narrative of your career break to make sure people know it was your choice (read: you didn't get fired). Or perhaps you want to thank your employer for giving you the break.

While you may encounter nothing but support (and jealousy) after this announcement, there's a danger here. Publicizing your sabbatical opens the door for people to—at the risk of sounding dramatic—

* If it means the difference between recording your thoughts and not, then yes, you may use a voice recorder and transcription service. There is ample research specifically about the power of writing for well-being, but getting your thoughts out via voice memo is better than nothing and can be fun to relisten to down the line.

destroy your sabbatical. Even when you're incredibly explicit about how and why you're taking time off, folks in your network will want to help by getting you gainfully employed again. They also tend to feel better as a result of coming to your aid. There are many names for this phenomenon, from the Aladdin Principle to the Ben Franklin Effect to the Helper's High.[1]

The problem is, the next step in your life is *not* to search for a job but rather to escape the impulse to do so for a little bit. You're best off quietly slipping from the shores of normal life, saving the announcement of your departure counterintuitively until you're plotting your return. Don't spend your precious time off worrying about what people will think of your absence; they're too busy with their lives to notice.

If you feel like you must tell the broader world about your departure, be very specific about your intentions to disconnect from the working world. Don't go into detail about what you're doing, and stick to the facts that can help you avoid feeling guilty about your unresponsiveness during your time off. For example, "I'm taking off from work to spend more time with family and to cross some items off my bucket list. I won't be checking email, or [insert platform here], until [month]—thanks for helping me make the most of my first major break from work in X years, and I'll talk to you on the other side!"

Once you've determined a date upon which you will be reengaging with the working world, set an auto-response. This should let the sender know their email will be deleted before a specified date of return and invite them to email again after that date if necessary. If you're returning to your job, identify who to get in touch with in your absence, and when to reach back out.

It's far better to broadcast your sabbatical to the public in retrospect, toward the end of your time off, as you contemplate your return. At that point, you'll have more confidence about your next steps and clarity about what you're seeking from your network in the first place.

During

Don't Create New Bosses

At the start of my pilgrimage, I was brimming with excitement about what I was about to do. Every day my mind and journal were full of thoughts, realizations, dreams, heartbreak, and setbacks. This was it: after years of anticipation, I was finally embarking on a long-awaited journey of spiritual and physical exploration. I felt electric and alive. I was also incredibly lonely. So I figured I'd share my thoughts with my friends and family in an email.

The island of Shikoku, where my pilgrimage took place, is divided into four sections, each with its own significance: awakening, ascetic training, enlightenment, and nirvana. I figured I'd send an email after each one. One email every two weeks. Not a big deal.

From that point on, the email gained an outsize level of importance. I found myself writing drafts in my head and then hunched over my phone composing and editing long screeds about my trip. I stressed out when I'd crossed over a prefecture border without sending my newsletter, and I fretted over the recipient list, a laborious process made even tougher without a laptop. Upon my return, many people told me they'd enjoyed following along. Some admitted they rarely got through the entirety of my multi-thousand-word messages. Looking back, those emails seem a bit over the top.

When we step away from our routine work, a vacuum is left in its place—one that we instinctively try to fill. This can result in some pretty bizarre cravings and behaviors, which are probably best reserved for journal entries rather than public-facing sabbatical manifestos. For me, it was a report that I hoped would encapsulate my experiences to the world back home. And help to communicate (read: justify) my time away. But I had, in effect, given myself an unintentional assignment. It was a Trojan horse containing my underlying achiever mindset. Writing the email took me away from being present in my own experience and, frankly, stressed me out a little bit. Your mileage may vary, but beware of creating new bosses, obligations, or restrictions during your sabbatical. This time away can and should be a relatively selfish period in your life, when you set your normal commitments down for a while. Only by truly putting them aside can you determine which things you'd like to pick back up—which patterns and habits still serve you, and which sap your time and energy.

Not sure if you're creating a new boss? Ask yourself whether the activity resembles work. Is there a deadline or a concrete outcome? Many hope to finish a book during their sabbatical. To de-workify this intention, experiment with writing; see how it feels before committing to an enormous project. Another sabbatical taker was hell-bent on hand-making an entire dining set for their friend's wedding instead of simply experimenting with passion for clay. Having a goal can be rewarding; just beware of our deeply engrained tendency to be productive.

Another test for whether your activity can unintentionally detract from your sabbatical is whether it recurs endlessly (like those meetings at your job you were so eager to escape from). Be vigilant when committing to a recurring practice, like weekly dance lessons or a multi-week certification program like yoga. Structure can be helpful for your mental health, but try to avoid making commitments for your future self on sabbatical. Otherwise, even the lowest-stakes obligations can feel like a boss and prevent you from pivoting toward what's calling you in the moment.

Challenge Yourself (to Do Something Very Uncomfortable, Unproductive, and Uncharacteristic)

By the time you've managed to get yourself on sabbatical, you've likely achieved some sort of ease, if not mastery, in your current career and life. While expertise feels comfortable, a sabbatical requires a different approach for maximum growth: what I call productive discomfort. To achieve this, identify ways to break out of your comfort zone. Pursue activities that are either new or so far in the past that you will approach them like a beginner again.

For a lot of office-bound folks, breaking free from your comfort zone can mean getting back into shape, or perhaps pursuing an intimidating physical challenge. For example, take sabbatical alum Catalina. She had spent eight years leading a much more sedentary office job existence than she would have liked. Approaching her sabbatical, she feared that she would never be able to accomplish some of the trekking goals she'd dreamed of, including a multi-week hike in the Himalayan mountains called the Annapurna Circuit.

So the first thing she did on her sabbatical was get back into shape in the lead-up to her trek. It was her way of detoxing after years of being deskbound. Years after her sabbatical, Catalina recalled the feeling of joy and pride she felt upon persevering through the highest mountain pass along the trek, at almost eighteen thousand feet above sea level. Not only does it remain one of her most treasured memories but it also gave her the psychological courage to uproot herself and move to Europe after building a decade-long career in Kenya.

While physical challenges help you clear your mind and strengthen your body, I'd encourage you to think beyond physical discomfort. Yes, finally running that marathon or summiting that peak is a great objective. But why not broaden your imagination to things you once liked about yourself, things that you stopped because you "weren't good enough," or that you grew out of. For me, that was singing and songwriting.

I'd sung in choirs growing up but always felt intimidated by the talented soloists around me. So I resigned myself to being a support singer and solidified my identity as a "good blender." As I approached my sabbatical, however, I found myself drawn to learning a new instrument—the ukulele—and writing my first songs. I even performed at desolate open mics on my solo journey in New Zealand, an experience that was uncomfortable enough to feel like I'd overcome some important barrier inside me. It may have only been a few songs, but the experience reacquainted me with something long buried inside.

Traveling to a foreign country is a great way to ensure productive discomfort. Studying and working abroad, for example, enhances self-understanding, increases creativity, and leads to greater professional success.[2] Because everything is new, even the most mundane situations, like crossing the street in a country that drives on the opposite side of the road, require a moment of reflection and presence. This beginner's-mindset benefit deepens over time as you shift from tourist to traveler.

As a reminder, you don't have to venture around the world to put yourself in a growth-spurring environment. Volunteering with a new population in your community or joining an improv, acting, or dancing class can cultivate the same catalysts for growth at a fraction of the cost and logistical hurdles. More inspiration for those approaching their sabbatical with limited means—either time or money or both—can be found in chapter 11.

Spend Time Alone

Some of my fondest sabbatical memories stem from those times when I was traveling alone. I hitchhiked for the first time, was invited to join random tables at restaurants, and even accepted a few strangers' kindness to sleep on their couches along the way. I struck up conversations I wouldn't have if I'd had a companion and became surprisingly comfortable on my own. I learned how to convert loneliness into solitude.

If you've never traveled alone, I urge you to do so. It's sometimes uncomfortable and lonely, but it creates the otherwise impossible opportunity to learn about who you are and what you do when the support of another person—especially one who knows you in routine life—is removed. One sabbatical interviewee, an attorney, remarked that her time backpacking and volunteering in Patagonia gave her the chance to consider who she had become over the years, "apart from the positions and responsibilities" she'd been holding.

This advice holds especially true if you are partnered and/or have children. Intertwining your life with another soul or two has numerous benefits but doesn't allow for many independent choices on how to spend your time, let alone extended introspection.

Spending time alone doesn't mean you need to be alone for a long time. Consider building in retreats—a weekend or a week or more if possible—to investigate yourself anew. In the same way that you're likely to forget how much of your life is informed and impacted by work, you may forget how few of your choices are yours alone. Give yourself the gift of exploring something deeply important to you, whether it's a creative retreat, a long weekend exploring a new city, or volunteering for a cause that's important to you.

Spend Time with and for Others

Potentially lost in all this focus on serious topics like self-discovery and personal transformation is the importance of levity and joy. I encourage you to carve out a meaningful amount of time cultivating these lighter feelings *with* and *for* other people. Spending time with others not only forces you to get out of your own head but also opens up new possibilities for the rest of your sabbatical: Who knows where a new relationship or fresh ideas from old friends could lead?

Invite friends to join you on portions of your sabbatical. Use your newfound flexibility to slot into the schedules of busy friends and loved ones you've been unable to see for far too long. Or just link up with fellow travelers along the way. You may bristle at the idea of joining organized treks or tours (I know I do), but they can be a great way to connect with new people, especially if you tend to be introverted when traveling alone.

As to spending time *for* people, the research on this is clear: spending time helping others results in increased happiness, reduced stress, improved self-esteem, a stronger sense of purpose, and even potential health benefits like lower blood pressure.[3] Some of my fondest memories of my six-week pilgrimage include the few days I spent volunteering at the beginning of the trek, handing out care packages to those embarking on the journey.

Spending time for others doesn't have to mean volunteering per se; our sabbatical interviewees count the times they spent visiting friends and family with whom they'd fallen out of touch as some of the most meaningful parts of their time off. These investments in time not only make for fun memories on sabbatical, they start a ripple effect for the relationship, launching new traditions and reasons to get together going forward.

Ending

The further away from the beginning of your sabbatical you get, the greater the pressure you'll feel to get back to work and your "regular" life. Thoughts about things like jobs, finances, and your future start to push in from the outside. Left unchecked, these anxieties about next steps will seep into your sabbatical, interfering with the rare experience that is your extended time off. This is why the last phase of your sabbatical should be regarded as a distinct part of that time off.

When does the "ending" of your sabbatical begin? In broad terms, it's the time when you begin thinking of winding down your sabbatical and approaching reentry into regular life. For some people, that might be days before their scheduled return time. For others, thoughts about reentering the "real world" may creep in a month or two ahead of their end date, especially if they'll need to find a new job. And for those who feel reentry anxiety *throughout* their sabbatical, we'll talk about how to let go of those feelings and simply be present for the amazing journey that is your time off.

Rather than let these anxieties rush the ramparts at times of their own choosing, be intentional about what you do and how you treat this last portion of your sabbatical by establishing structure, codifying reflection, and adjusting expectations.

Schedule Reflection Check-Ins

You must plan for reintegration to regular life ahead of time. If you don't, the concerns about your future will likely intrude on the carefree first parts of your sabbatical. Start by scheduling concrete on-ramps: points where you allow yourself to delve back into practicalities like jobs, finances, and logistics about your future. Set actual appointments on your calendar for these reflections.

You can think about these inflection points as physical spaces over the course of your journey. For example, Himalayan treks have "teahouses" where hikers rest and refuel before tackling the next segment of their journey. The teahouses serve not only as places to rest but also as critical "waypoints" that break the trek into navigable subsegments. Waypoints are critical because often the more adventurous the journey, the longer and more ambiguous the route; you can't just walk directly to the finish line. You can steer toward the next point on the map, which provides you with an opportunity to reflect, reorient, and change course. Finding your way along your life is more akin to how ancient seafarers and modern backpackers find their way: by way-finding. A way-finding approach calls for navigating to the next obvious landmark, as opposed to heading straight for the destination. It's great for avoiding obstacles and has the added benefit of chunking seemingly impossible tasks or journeys into manageable segments.

Your sabbatical also requires waypoints—spaces for reprieve, reflection, and recalibration. A waypoint doesn't have to be a separate geographic destination on your sabbatical, but it does need to be an intentional block of time—say, a few hours alone with your journal. If the journaling at the beginning of your sabbatical is solely forward-looking and the entries over the course of your time off are primarily backward-looking, reflecting on the most recent days and weeks, waypoint journaling must stitch these two perspectives together. How have the choices you've made to date felt, and how would you like to change tack to more closely pursue your curiosities and instincts?

I suggest scheduling at least three check-ins. The first should be approximately at the halfway point of your sabbatical. The purpose of this waypoint is to reflect on the length of your time off. Do you feel that the amount of time you've budgeted is sufficient to accomplish the things you set out to do? If not, is it possible to adjust, or otherwise shift priorities within the constraints you face? Use this check-in to reflect on what you've experienced so far compared to your expectations.

The second and third check-ins should come toward the end of your sabbatical. The purpose of these reflections is to determine what the last portion of your break should entail. Probe your experience so far: Are you finding yourself drawn toward something you've experimented with during your time off, or are you feeling anxious about your next career steps? If the former, you might want to push your sabbatical end date out further. If the latter, you might need to wind your pure sabbatical time down and bring your job search forward.

Networking and interviewing require a completely different mindset from sabbatical mode. It's better to either fully immerse yourself in your time off or fully commit to a job search—not straddle both. That's why the concluding third of your sabbatical should still be work-free. Your last check-in should happen toward the very end of your time—say, less than a month prior to returning. Use this to determine whether to extend your time or transition into job search mode. If you find yourself going back and forth on this decision, extend! It's easier to leave Sabbatical Land ahead of schedule than to try to win back the mindset from a break you've already left.

Synthesize Your Learnings

After you've made the decision to return to work, carve out time to synthesize your sabbatical learnings before beginning the job search. Otherwise, you'll find yourself back at a job without having sufficiently considered what your sabbatical means for you going forward. You've got to give yourself time and space to chart your next steps.

Get out your journal and first consider all the things you've done, seen, and felt while on sabbatical. Compare your experiences and feelings while on sabbatical to your expectations. Out of all the things you could have chosen to do with your time off, why did you make the choices you did? Reflect on how you felt doing those things, compared to how you wanted to feel. Pay particularly close attention to those things you felt like you "should" do versus those you truly wanted to do. This is a great time to refer back to your pre- (and early-) sabbatical journal entries to help you notice the differences.

Next, use any and all objective measurements and experiments to complement your qualitative observations. I took a host of personality and aptitude tests during my sabbatical to see whether I'd missed anything when thinking about my career fit. Johnson O'Connor runs a multiday test that analyzes everything from pitch recognition to color differentiation to finger dexterity skills in order to provide very specific career path recommendations. A career coach can steer you toward other assessments like the Needs and Values framework or something like the Enneagram. Take each individual assessment with a grain of salt but consider trends across multiple tests as a signal among a portfolio of perspectives.

Finally, reach out to friends, family, colleagues, and supervisors to get their perspective on you. One of our research participants, Danyil, sent out a survey to ask his friends questions like "When do you recall me at my happiest?" He used the answers to help fill in blind spots for things to do on sabbatical—such as spend time visiting friends with children as opposed to more solo travel—but also to inform the types of jobs he wanted to end up in on the other side. Remember, you can often tell what type of advice someone is going to give before they open their mouth—everyone wants to validate their own choices, after all—but combined with your existing data points about yourself, you should be able to triangulate the truth.

Settle for Less

One of the most surprising findings from my work on sabbaticals came three years after our paper was already published in a peer-reviewed journal. As I continued to follow up with the participants in the study, I noticed that most of them had already moved on from their post-sabbatical jobs. Going into the study, I assumed that given enough time, space, and perspective, people would do a pretty good job at landing their ideal next steps. For the most part, this seemed to be the case; people typically ended their interviews with me by talking about how they ended up making a switch to a new job, getting promoted, or moving positions in their existing company. Some realized they were happy enough all along.

However, upon circling back with these people seven years later, many reflected that what they'd thought was their dream job actually turned out to be just another step in their search for meaning in work. Some overcorrected toward what had given them pleasure during their sabbatical. One such alum, James, was so significantly impacted by his time spent in meditation retreats and yoga teacher training that he felt pulled to a start-up that helped yoga studios book and manage their programming calendars. However, in order to fit the needs of the organization, he had to bend over backward, so to speak, to manage tasks that didn't align with his natural skill set and interests. James took the wrong position in order to try to carry over some of his best memories from Sabbatical Land. His next career stop was far removed, mission-wise, but fulfilling perhaps because of the stark lines it helped him draw between his work and his personal identity.

Compare this to Paul, who spent a chunk of his sabbatical testing his hypothesis that he'd like to someday own an eco-retreat. Paul spent two months working at various retreat centers in Hawaii and Costa Rica. He did most jobs, from back-of-the-house kitchen to shadowing the owners to get a better sense of what their work actually entailed. His takeaway was that sometimes your personal interests and professional work should stay separate. This won't hold true for everyone; the "experimentation" step during your sabbatical helps make sure your dream job works in reality as well.

The other common mistake among sabbatical alums is extending a watered-down version of their sabbatical by searching indefinitely for the perfect gig. An extended job search is an extended job search, not a sabbatical. Prolonged unemployment leads to job search fatigue, which creates a vicious cycle of poor mental health, motivation, and overall well-being.[4]

Avoid this fate by setting clear boundaries around where your sabbatical ends and where your job search begins. But also, set a reasonably tight timeline. Like dating, a successful job search depends not just on finding the right opportunity but on finding your counterpart at the right time. Perhaps *unlike* dating, it's better to accept a less-than-ideal gig while you continue your dream job search over the medium term. A so-called stepping stone job satisfies our psychological needs for time structure, social connection, and purpose while also helping recover the financial investment of our sabbatical.[5]

And You're Off

I try my hardest to avoid giving people any concrete recommendations for their sabbatical for two reasons. Recommending a course of action on sabbatical is like recommending a vacation, music, or a movie; individual taste just isn't objective. Plus, many times what folks think they want isn't really it anyway. What excited me when I was thirty-two, with few responsibilities holding me back and hungry for exploration, didn't appeal to many other thirty-two-year-olds (and, frankly, to my present self either).

The second reason is no matter what activities you choose to fill your sabbatical with, they'll tend to deliver the experience you needed to have. Most of us need to watch how our best-laid plans play out when all our constraints—and excuses—no longer apply. Our friends and family can insist we have trouble relaxing until they're blue in the face, but until we witness how our own restlessness erodes our time off, we won't understand it—let alone be able to change it.

My hope is that these recommendations lend you the confidence needed to do something difficult and unpredictable. Even if you can't create the ideal conditions for a sabbatical, there's ample value in doing your best with what you have to work with. In the next chapter, we'll explore the strategies and results from more modest sabbaticals.

In Practice

Preparation

Finances

- **Find your burn rate.** Conduct a twelve- to twenty-four-month retrospective on your finances. But don't let the perfect be the enemy of the good. You can take monthly checking account balances and credit card statements as a proxy.
- **Identify and reduce your variable expenses.** These are expenses for things you don't *have* to buy. Separate other expenses into categories like food (non-optional) and things you buy or do that are somewhat optional. Which can you reduce or eliminate depending on your plans?
- **Identify and mitigate your fixed expenses.** These expenses are unavoidable, such as a mortgage, rent, car payment, and utilities. Determine how to reduce or eliminate as much of these costs as possible, through subletting or moving things into storage temporarily.
- **Evaluate your balance sheet.** This is the total amount of money you have. Determine the smallest amount of liquid assets (cash) you'd feel comfortable ending up with on the other side of your sabbatical. Budget in three to six months to find a job upon your return.
- **Identify your flame-out date and check-in dates.** Figure out when you would completely run out of money and work backward to figure out how much time off you *could* comfortably take. Now set calendar reminders to review your spending during your sabbatical so that it's not lingering in the back of your head during your time off.

Journal

- **Before your sabbatical.** Keep a list of the activities you're aspiring to do, and which ones you're committed to.
- **During your sabbatical.** Write a bulleted list of memories, experiences, and places you stayed on a daily or weekly basis. Recording them will help transport you back into the sabbatical mindset on later reflection.
- **Toward the end of your sabbatical.** How have your pre-sabbatical expectations changed, and what aspects of your sabbatical would you like to carry forward?

Publicizing

- **Announcing leaving.** Be succinct, share few details, mention only when you are returning, and decide how you will address emails sent during your absence. Be clear that you will not receive or reply to any emails during your sabbatical.
- **Announcing returning.** This is your opportunity to talk about what you did and what your intentions are for the future, and, crucially, to help normalize time off for people in your network who are considering taking a sabbatical themselves.

During

New Bosses

- **Be wary of expectations.** Goals for your time off that are more work-like, such as those with concrete deadlines, recurring commitments, and strict measures of success can be hazardous to your happiness on sabbatical.

Challenge

- **Overcome fear.** Identify activities you've always wanted to do but were afraid you wouldn't be able to do. Remember that you don't need to succeed at everything. Set aside perfectionism and do something purely for enjoyment.

Alone and With Others

- **Prioritize time alone.** How much time can you spend alone, and how much time do you want to? If traveling alone sounds scary and you've never done it, I would encourage you to do so.
- **Find companions.** Identify people from different phases of life who give you energy. Where are they, what types of activities do they like doing, and how could you intersect?

Ending

Checking In

- **Set calendar reminders for check-in points.** These aren't assignments but invitations to reflect and course-correct by reviewing finances and evaluating what gives you energy. Don't be afraid to pivot!

Synthesizing

- **Journal.** Collect your reflections about ending your sabbatical. What does your experience mean for changes you can make to routine life going forward?
- **Ask for advice.** Create a list of friends whose advice you trust and craft an email soliciting their input to inform your next steps. There could be some signals that you can integrate into your personal reflections to guide your next steps.
- **Experiment with personality or career tests.** Consider taking a few third-party assessments—not as verdicts but as additional data points about what you're good at, what drains you, and what you want more of.

Settling for Less

- **Journal.** Many sabbaticals end with more questions than answers. This is okay! Ask yourself the following journal prompt questions during your final sabbatical check-in:
    - What have I left undone on my sabbatical?
    - What are my goals for the next time?
    - What about my routine life am I excited to return to, and what am I dreading?

11

On Modest Sabbaticals

The search is what anyone would undertake if he were not sunk in the everydayness of his own life. To become aware of the possibility of the search is to be onto something.

—Walker Percy, *The Moviegoer*

I know, I know.

Most of the protagonists in this book accomplished superhuman feats on sabbatical. They wrote books, sailed across the ocean, and created companies from scratch. They traveled abroad, shirked responsibilities for a while, or moved logistical mountains to bring their responsibilities along with them. And all had the good fortune (and finances) to finagle a trip of epic proportions. Together, we are working toward a world where paid and predictable sabbaticals are as common and institutionally supported as parental leave. But we also can't afford to delay our dreams indefinitely until the optimal window arrives.

If your constraints are more constraining, fear not: this chapter is for you. The scope of these sabbaticals may be more modest, but the outcomes are still meaningful. And by the way, if you've got "grander" ambitions for your sabbatical, this chapter is especially for you—an impressive-sounding itinerary isn't a prerequisite for extraordinary results. Sometimes the opposite is true. Prioritizing the exotic puts you at risk of overlooking the wonder in your own backyard, hiding beneath the crust of your routine life.

Shorter, cheaper, closer-to-home sabbaticals still offer an opportunity for a shift in perspective, as well as a chance for a mental and emotional reset. They provide time to rediscover creativity and purpose—and, perhaps most importantly, to reconnect with the people who are important to you. This chapter introduces you to several people who weren't able to empty their bucket lists completely, but even with limited time and resources, came away transformed.

Doug: Returning to His Roots and His Marriage

Doug Bozick grew up as one of four boys on a farm in Western Pennsylvania. His parents were homesteaders; his mother devoted her energies to tending the garden while raising Doug and his brothers. Doug loved theater but was discouraged from pursuing it by his parents, who made it clear that hobbies were nice, but work was about making a living—not doing what you love.

After graduating from college with a "practical degree" in accounting, Doug got his CPA as a sort of insurance policy for his career. Once he met his wife, Jennifer, they decided to travel before having children, so they set off around the world for six months. When Jennifer became pregnant, they moved back to Oakland, where Doug settled into another job at a large conglomerate he took out of a sense of responsibility instead of passion or even interest.

The job quickly became intolerable. Doug's role required extensive international travel, which led to Jennifer leaving the workforce and staying at home to raise their two children. Then Doug became unemployed. At the time, it seemed more like a blow than a blessing, but with a year's severance after his division downsized, Doug decided to take over primary caregiving responsibilities so that his wife could shift back into career mode and build up her own law practice.

Initially Doug found the transition difficult. Although his work responsibilities no longer ruled his daily agenda, he found himself waking up stressed about what needed to be done. A detox was in order. Doug had enough examples from earlier in his life to know how best to break free from work concerns: an epic international trip, like the one he and his wife had taken before settling down. But at this stage of his life, he knew he had to find a way to create the same wonder and separation within his geographic and family constraints. So he turned inward toward his childhood interests.

Almost thirty years since his last theater performance, Doug joined a local acting troupe where he got to shake off the dust onstage, in public. He also planted a garden, which stretched him in new ways completely unrelated to work and reconnected him with memories of his mother. One day during yoga, he found himself crying during shavasana; his body and mind were so grateful for the new life he'd been living. The reduction in stress had peeled off excess pounds, and his days gardening added a deep tan for the first time in years.

But the most important change from his sabbatical was a transformation in his empathy for his wife. Doug firmly believes that the sabbatical saved his marriage. He doesn't consider himself in any way a traditionalist about gender roles in relationships, but he admits that until he took the time to spend his days with their children, he had trouble fully comprehending the scope of his wife's role as primary caregiver, particularly with a child who requires special attention. While he saw himself as a supportive parent, it took being on the "front lines" to realize how little time and energy caregiving left for anything else. When deciding where and how to return to work, Doug prioritized jobs that would either give him the flexibility to spend more time at home or the financial capability to hire a nanny so that both he and Jennifer could focus their efforts on building their careers.

When it came time to return to work, Doug looked for roles that aligned with both his values and his family's needs. He now believes he's arrived at the sweet spot—he works for a company with a sabbatical policy. His work is mission-aligned and also offers flexibility to dedicate time to himself and his family every three years. By slowing down and stepping into the rhythms of caregiving, gardening, and theater on his sabbatical, Doug gained empathy, clarity, and a more sustainable vision for the life he wanted to lead, which ultimately helped him show up differently at home. Doug's story illustrates how a sabbatical, even one close to home, can be a turning point toward a more intentional, balanced life.

Monisha: A Kid-Sized Sabbatical

Monisha Kapila grew up the daughter of hardworking Indian immigrants—her mother was a bank teller and her father an engineer. She had always been curious about the possibility of working for a nonprofit but had ruled it out after college because it didn't pay well enough to please her parents. But Monisha's time spent working in a microfinance organization and the financial inclusion arm of Capital One convinced her to leave the for-profit world for good to start her own nonprofit, ProInspire.

Monisha never looked back from her transition into a nonprofit leader. But growing her own organization took a toll on her personal life—when she had her first child a year after starting, she took less than a month's leave. Two years later, she took no break for the birth of her second child. It's not surprising, then, that eight years into ProInspire, Monisha began to run out of steam. Luckily, a board member knew other nonprofits gave their leadership sabbaticals in order to prevent founder burnout. He gave Monisha permission to design her own policy, which she modeled after the organization's parental leave policy (a policy unused by Monisha but available to her employees). Monisha decided to take two months' leave, timed to align with her children's summer break.

Her goals for her time off were modest. They'd planned a trip abroad to London and an annual road trip to Michigan and Chicago to see family and friends. But there were weekends here and there with no plans, and Monisha could spend her weekdays supervising a minor home renovation that had never gotten off the ground between her and her husband's normally busy schedules. Monisha had three goals for her sabbatical: to not *have* to do anything related to work, to spend quality time with her two kids, and for ProInspire to realize that it would be okay without her.

Monisha's sabbatical got off to a slow start. She struggled to disconnect because her time "off" was Swiss-cheesed with preexisting work-like commitments. For example, she'd agreed to sit in on an important meeting with funders two weeks into her eight weeks off. This meant that the first couple of weeks felt compromised, and her thoughts still raced about work two weeks after the meeting was finished.

Monisha used a sabbatical coach to focus herself on what was possible during her time off and made plans to spend a long weekend with each child individually, doing whatever they chose. These weekend trips were two of the highlights of her time off—one child wanted to visit a hotel with a water park a few hours away, while the other requested to spend a weekend visiting presidential libraries. Monisha realized that these were some of the only times she'd spent focused alone time with her children one-on-one outside of routine caretaking; her kids bragged about their mommy weekends for years afterward.

Monisha also carved out time for herself, the highlight of which was a yoga retreat at the Kripalu center in western Massachusetts' Berkshires. Though her retreat was less than a week, she developed a daily journaling practice there and first swapped out her prodigious coffee consumption for tea; both of these habits remain to this day, almost fifteen years later. Monisha also remembers the small moments, the feeling of space, and the enjoyment of daily rituals that had never fit into routine work. For example, she'd stop at a cafe next to her yoga studio to read a book for thirty minutes on a weekday.

Upon returning to ProInspire, Monisha rolled out the sabbatical policy to all her employees after five years of tenure. She also committed to hiring her replacement, with a goal of enabling her transition out of the organization before qualifying for her next sabbatical. Seven years later, Monisha successfully transitioned out, taking a nine-month sabbatical to explore her next steps, in advance of her kids entering high school.

A relatively short sabbatical closer to home helped Monisha rediscover the parts of herself that she'd pushed aside and lost connection to, as work priorities that always felt urgent elbowed their way into her life. Monisha's story reminds us that sabbaticals are about more than stepping away from work—they're about stepping into parts of life that often get sidelined. While Monisha may not have entirely transformed her life like Winston from chapter 1, taking even a modest amount of time was enough to reconnect with her children, reestablish personal rituals, and ultimately reimagine her role as a leader. In the space she carved out, both she and her organization grew stronger, proving that making room for rest can be one of the most strategic decisions a founder makes. A modest sabbatical can give you the push and perspective shift you need to make smaller but meaningful changes that ripple forward in your life with the opportunities available to you.

Lily: Finding and Serving Community in Her Own Backyard

After working for various early-stage start-ups in the Bay Area for seven years, Lily Chandrasekher felt as if her whole existence had been spent peering into a computer screen. She worked in user experience (UX), a role that serves to help companies better understand their customers, but her days—and, increasingly, her life—seemed mostly reactive, responding to Slack messages or emails or the urgent requests of her colleagues and clients. Weekends seemed more oriented toward recovery from work than joyous respites brimming with possibility. She became convinced that a change was in order, and upon the recommendation of a friend, Lily began working with Alice Chen, a life coach who happened to have a growing career-break practice on the side. After saving up enough money to feel comfortable without a paycheck for six months, Lily quit her job and took a sabbatical.

For the first segment of her time off, Lily hoped to do a complete digital detox. To fill the empty space of scrolling and consuming, she mined for joyful habits and practices from her past. Lily had loved playing piano, but retreading her classical training felt joyless, so she took jazz piano lessons instead. She wanted to get out of her head, so she pushed herself out of her comfort zone by taking various movement classes, including the one in which she felt the least confident: West African dance. Long convinced that her bookshelf was "taunting her," Lily set upon a reading journey, focusing on fiction and moving on to the next book quickly if the first one didn't catch her imagination. Lily felt overwhelmed with gratitude for the gifts of these books and wrote a handwritten thank-you note to each of the authors after reading them. (Some of them actually wrote back!)

Lily also wanted to explore her adopted hometown of San Francisco. Though she'd moved there from the East Coast almost a decade prior, she felt as if she hardly knew people outside her professional network and from the neighborhoods outside her commute. She knew a couple of nonprofits working in ocean conservation by reputation and became a regular presence at various nonprofits during what would have been the workday. Lily volunteered varnishing and restoring boats and kayaking next to swimmers navigating from beneath the

Golden Gate Bridge to Alcatraz. She also plumbed an interest in growing her own food by volunteering at a community garden for formerly incarcerated people in nearby El Sobrante, California.

Lily's original plan was to take six months off, three to focus on herself and three to plot her reentry into the workforce. But as she approached the three-month mark, she felt like she'd just begun to shed her work mindset and deepen into a fulfilling routine. So she pushed out her internal date to begin searching for a job by another three months. Along the way, Lily noticed that she felt less reactive and restless. She'd lost the nagging feeling that she should be checking her inbox or hustling from one place to another. She'd gained enough perspective to understand that San Francisco had truly become her home. The process of stopping it all had given her permission to stay put rather than upend her life.

Lily did make some changes, though. She realized that the pace and uncertainty of working for start-ups was not doing her nervous system a favor. She wanted something stable, with no travel, so that she could continue her volunteer work and the routine that had brought so much meaning. So she went to a conference on career change and planned a series of informal coffee chats with her network. Instead of returning to the hustle of start-up life, Lily ultimately decided to prioritize her newfound pleasures by taking a less demanding job in Big Tech.

Her other life changes were more subtle, but equally important. She returned to the working world feeling more confident that she could leave any job or way of living that didn't feel authentic to her. Six years after her sabbatical, Lily works for a large company with a greater work-life balance and continues to carve out time to continue her volunteering on top of work and family. Lily's sabbatical didn't result in a new direction but in a new way of being: grounded in her community, more confident in her life choices, and with a little bit more room for things outside of work. Her story shows that while you don't need to completely blow up your life to make important changes, buying yourself more time than you've historically been willing to give, even close to home, can still spur big changes.

Derek: Big Meaning from Small Moments

Derek Aguirre grew up in Northern Michigan, the son of a first-generation immigrant who spent his entire career as a tool and die maker at General Motors. Derek went to school at the University of Michigan and joined a nonprofit in Boston called SquashBusters after graduation. SquashBusters offered after-school tutoring and instruction in the racquet sport of squash to low-income teens and tied together two of Derek's passions, sports and education.

After working his way up in the organization over six years, Derek started planning his return to his home state. He collaborated with the founder of SquashBusters to export the program model and its impact to Detroit, founding Racquet Up in 2010. The organization would engage neighborhood public school students and support them with tutoring and mentorship to help them succeed in high school and beyond. The squash component helped them master a challenging sport that, for some, could open the door to colleges that might not otherwise seem within reach.

Over the next thirteen years, Derek grew the organization from just himself to more than twenty staff members and a dedicated nineteen-thousand-square-foot facility. The program has a 100 percent high school graduation and college admission rate and five national squash championship title holders among its graduates. In what we can now regard as a familiar story, Derek was generally satisfied with his career, but also ready for a break. It was at this point, in 2022, after a successful capital campaign, that he seriously began considering a local foundation's paid sabbatical program.

McGregor's Miller Fellows, as its sabbatical-grantees are called, are given six months off and a $25,000 grant to fund their sabbatical. This is on top of their existing salary, which the organization continues paying to truly make the act of taking time off possible for nonprofit leaders of all financial capabilities. McGregor also awards another $25,000 to the organization itself, to be used at its discretion. Racquet Up used these funds to award performance incentives to key staff, provide coaching to those stepping up into leadership roles, and to fund any outside consulting needed in Derek's absence.

Derek split his sabbatical into three chunks over the course of eighteen months, interspersed with work and on a tight budget. He took his first span of time off during the summer of 2023, essentially detoxing from the pressures of work. It was the first time he'd taken more than a couple of weeks off consecutively since college, and the small things stood out to him. For example, he never thought that a midday empty checkout line at the grocery store or a lazy cup of coffee in an empty cafe after the morning rush could provide so much joy. Derek recalled playing guitar every day and taking four dead watches to have their batteries replaced. When, two months later, his family went on vacation together, Derek was able to truly savor the experience instead of feeling like he was sandwiching his time between stresses at work, checking email on the sly.

After the first few months of his leave, Derek returned to what he jokingly referred to as "a shrug" from his staff. The organization he'd brought into existence could operate without him; his absence represented an important inflection point along its progression from fledgling start-up to sustainable nonprofit. Little things marked this passage, like how Derek's colleagues became official signers on the bank account and managed a high-visibility project alongside a key donor. Instead of wilting in his absence, Racquet Up had proven that it could thrive on its own.

For the second portion of his sabbatical, Derek took a couple of trips to the coasts to visit friends, but his most significant journey was closer to home. Derek's father had built a cabin near Lake Huron, a few hours' drive north of his childhood home, which had served as the family vacation spot for many years. Since his father's passing from cancer eight years prior, Derek hadn't returned to the cabin. With the time and headspace afforded him by his sabbatical, he decided to spend a few days at the cabin by himself—which also happened to be one of his first solo trips since getting married and having kids seven years earlier. Though his trip up north lasted only a few days, it offered something he hadn't realized he'd needed: closure. Reconnecting with his childhood memories of the cabin and honoring his father helped Derek find peace with letting go of the past and appreciating his current life.

Derek also returned from sabbatical with a new perspective: while the biggest moments in life—his marriage, the birth of his children, his dad's passing—were the ones that had the power to wrest him from routine, the small ones—like visiting the cabin, running errands close to home, and spending time alone—enabled overdue reflection, recovery, and synthesis. Without them, life galloped by, leaving no opportunity to process and enjoy some of the most impactful moments of all. Sometimes a sabbatical must be molded to fit the contours of our lives. Even when taken in parts, if we can construct sufficient space, as in Heschel's cathedral of time from chapter 2, we can provide the stillness we need to grieve, grow, and return with a fuller sense of self.

Hitting Close to Home

On one of my last business trips before my sabbatical (and eventual departure from my company), I was in Istanbul, working with Mastercard, FICO, and a collection of Turkish banks. During a celebratory dinner overlooking the Bosphorus Strait, one of our bank partners inquired about my plans for my sabbatical. As I excitedly laid out my grand scheme for a spiritual adventure—a comically ambitious plan that spanned from a six-week walking pilgrimage in Japan to a trip to Lebanon to see author Khalil Gibran's resting place and a return to Turkey for the festival celebrating Sufi mystic Rumi—he interrupted with a mischievous smile: "But didn't Gibran live in the US for almost his entire life? He first emigrated to Boston, where you live. Save your money; surely there's at least a monument there to see."*

A spirited debate engulfed the dinner table, which at this point had been heartily overserved, about the lengths to which we go for self-discovery. Another of his bank colleagues even revealed to me that one of the first and largest Sufi retreat centers was in New England, a shorter drive from my house than Rumi's resting place in the Central Anatolia region of Turkey is from Istanbul.

There are two ways to tell the story of my sabbatical. My travels did take me to far-flung places like rural Japan and New Zealand. Traveling there required months, not weeks, and while I spent very little money, given the nature of my time there, they were two of the most expensive countries on Earth to visit. Memories from this time make for great stories of adventure and do loom large in my mind to this day. But it was my time helping a cousin move, learning how to lay tile with my father, and taking care of my mother during her recovery that truly transformed my life. My sabbatical helped me decide that my previous mode of unlimited travel and exposure to new places was incompatible with the life I wanted to live. I'd aged out of prioritizing only myself, but I hadn't aligned my lifestyle to that new reality.

Sabbaticals don't have to be yearlong global adventures. Yes, there's an aspect to the travel and length of time that enables key components of a successful sabbatical—detox, disconnection, and exploration—which is why I recommend traveling in the first half of your sabbatical, if you can swing it. It's really hard to escape the familiar wagon

* As it turns out, there's not only a statue of Gibran in Boston but an entire trail of sculptures done by the writer and artist sprinkled within walking distance of my apartment. The greatest collection of his works is in Savannah, Georgia, not Lebanon.

rut of routine and everyday existence by just subtracting work from it. But long bouts away from home can also add counterproductive emotional and financial stress. Escaping may not be feasible in your current season of life. That doesn't mean you shouldn't make as much space as possible and just go for it. Remember that there is a fine line between escaping to marshal resources to come back stronger and simply escaping to avoid intentionally crafting a meaningful life.

Those of us with greater constraints shouldn't fear a more modest sabbatical. Take whatever the current season of life offers you. After all, you don't have to travel far to revisit the parts of yourself you miss, whether it's an old hobby gone dormant or an undernourished relationship. There's no such thing as a perfect sabbatical, but missing your chance in the hopes of a better opportunity in the future is also a risky bet. Even some modest time off is time well spent.

In Practice

Spend Time with Others

- **Identify family members or friends who need help.** Be direct and ask them how you can serve them during your time of flexibility.
- **Spend time with your nuclear family.** Ask your kids or partner what special thing they'd want to do if you had four days together. Draw a circle around your geographic area to see what's easily reachable.
- **Get involved in your community.** Identify local organizations you'd like to spend time with. Don't feel obligated to commit to a long-term engagement until you're sure it serves you to serve them.

Clear Out Your Backlog

- **Bring overlooked activities to the top of your to-do list.** Do you have books you'd like to read? Personal or professional advisors in your network that you'd like to learn from? Should these begin to feel like work, save them until the end of your time off.

Carve Out Time for Yourself

- **Pick your "for me" activities.** How would you spend a week or two if you didn't have to explain it to anyone? How can you reconnect with the curiosities of your youth?
- **Solo adventure.** If you can't get away for a meaningful chunk of time alone, consider exploring your surroundings on your own while everyone else is at work or school.
- **Celebration.** What are significant milestones you've missed in life, and what can you do to celebrate and honor them now?

12

The Upside at Work

It is only through imagination that men become aware of what the world might be; without it "progress" would become mechanical and trivial.

—Bertrand Russell

All this sabbatical stuff sure sounds good, in theory. Yet despite the overwhelmingly positive impact that extended leave has on individuals and the companies they work for, it's often a hard sell from management's perspective. It's difficult enough for leaders to manage output over the normal course of vacations, sick days, and parental leave, let alone deliver results with fewer staff over an extended period of time. Worse, what if they go through all the logistics to accommodate someone's temporary absence only to have them quit and never return?

It feels like a big ask.

But over the course of almost a decade of research and interviews with sabbatical alumni at every seniority level from all over the world, it's clear that the benefits of extended leave far outweigh the risks—not only for individuals but also for the organizations they work for.

As a start-up founder, leader, and now entrepreneurship teacher, I am sensitive to the real difficulties of running a business where people take off for long stretches of time. As I accidentally became the Sabbatical Guy, I worried that companies would treat me like a pariah and try to shield their employees from the sabbatical message. But often the opposite has been true. They've sought me out to share their examples to help others. And many employers—especially folks working in HR and Talent—were eager to hear about an opportunity to keep their best employees around . . . and happy.

The truth is that group performance improves when employees are able to take sabbaticals. Now, I'm not suggesting a free-for-all where employees have carte blanche around time off. But when approached thoughtfully in the context of the needs of the business and the individual, the benefits of sabbaticals accrue to employees, managers, and the companies that employ them. Armed with this information, employers can better justify the creation of sabbatical policies, and individuals can position their departure in the most mutually beneficial manner. Let's take a look at how—and why.

Foster Innovation

Our day-to-day lives are packed and reactive, governed by task lists and deadlines, which is hardly the type of environment that fosters creativity. Yet creativity is an essential workplace skill, and one that promotes innovation while boosting productivity and adaptability.[1] As technology continues to expand the frontier of what's possible, we must solve the problems of an unknowable future in real time, as they arrive. How we've always done things in the past usually doesn't work forever. This means creativity isn't a nice-to-have skill for a subset of jobs but a necessary tool across almost all industries and functions.

It's hard to manufacture the ideal preconditions for creativity. It's not something you can schedule. Creativity—and its partner, innovation—requires exploration and play, as we saw with Winston in chapter 1.[2] And it requires ample unstructured time. It's no wonder, then, that an increase in creativity stemming from the surplus of purposeless time is one of the most consistent by-products of a sabbatical.

Fostering creativity in our personal lives has positive spillover effects on work itself.[3] This was certainly the case with Cheryl Johnson, the founder and longtime CEO of a Michigan nonprofit called the Coalition of Temporary Shelter (COTS). After working at COTS for twenty straight years in a "go, go, go!" mentality, Cheryl was offered a paid sabbatical from a local foundation.

Unfortunately, Cheryl wasn't wired to prioritize herself. After a lifetime as a social worker and leader, her instincts prompted her to devote her sabbatical to something that would directly benefit COTS. But after working with a coach during the lead-up to her time off, she realized she wanted to develop *herself* as a coach. This led her to a monthlong meditation retreat in Upstate New York and a three-month coaching certification on the West Coast called New Ventures West.

Cheryl returned to COTS refreshed. She was also full of ideas about how to identify and attack the root problem among her community—multigenerational poverty—instead of providing a temporary reprieve. Armed with her newfound coaching skills, Cheryl redesigned the organization's approach to focus on families using intensive case management and longer-term individual coaching. The new programs Cheryl created after her sabbatical have since spread to dozens of nonprofits across the country. Not only did she transform COTS, but she also launched a life coaching practice outside of her work, which stretches and fulfills her in ways that she realized on her sabbatical she needed.

Many companies benefit from allowing their employees to do a tour of duty outside the organization. Consulting firms and banks alike send their employees off for yearlong externships at start-ups and nonprofits to increase exposure to the market outside their day-to-day work. A Philadelphia-based unicorn tech company called Skylight transformed its marquee product after their first sabbatical taker spent part of her time off learning about new technologies, just for fun.

Managed properly, significant time outside an organization can blend the restorative power of extended leave for your existing employees with the burst of new techniques, experiences, and perspectives that a brand-new employee brings.

Clarify Responsibilities

In many organizations, roles and responsibilities aren't always clearly defined. Job descriptions often fail to capture the full scope of an employee's contributions—especially for those with long tenures who tend to put down less than they pick up once promoted.

Think about it. While an employee's job description may evolve during their employment, it rarely represents the full scope of an individual's full contributions. This ambiguity can result in inefficiencies, overlapping efforts, and employee frustration or burnout.

Take sabbatical alum Justin, for example. Over the course of a decade, Justin rose from working in the kitchen of his family's catering company to becoming its CEO. In the process, he expanded the business from serving a few local schools to working with school districts across the state of California. After embarking on a sabbatical of epic proportions by driving an RV to thirty-three national parks with his wife and four children, Justin returned with a markedly new perspective on his role at the company.

The firm had grown significantly under his leadership but had struggled to break free from its roots providing school lunches. While on sabbatical, Justin had conceived of an entirely new path for his company's expansion, which would breathe new life into the business's growth prospects, as well as reinvigorate his interest in the next decade at the helm. But doing so required letting go of many of the operational controls he once held in order to think and direct the company more strategically. As Justin explained, "I realized that I'd been running the company as a player-coach, responding to the urgent needs of the business instead of zooming out to identify an inspiring vision and directing the organization that way. My sabbatical allowed me to think about the business from a much broader perspective, one that, as CEO, I should have been operating from much sooner."

A sabbatical offers an opportunity to reveal the full breadth of an employee's role and responsibilities in a way that regular, shorter vacations can't, because *all* the duties of the leave-taker must be transferred to other people while they're away. The great length of time away on sabbatical offers valuable insight for both the employee and the employer. As they collaborate to define, transfer, and recalibrate responsibilities before and after the break, unnecessary tasks are often identified and removed, while delegated duties may remain with others. And it helps employees get clear on where they bring the most value and where they should direct the most effort. This process ultimately helps streamline operations, boosting both individual effectiveness and overall organizational performance.

If you're a small business leader or early-stage entrepreneur, you might be thinking that there is no way you could weather a critical person stepping away as an experiment for future gain. Try extending the planning window outward. While you may not be able to afford to part ways with your employee six months from now, you can more easily budget for their absence two years in the future.

Offer Stretch Opportunities to Junior Employees

We tend to think of those left behind as paying the price for those who get to take off. But many companies cite this vacuum as a benefit for junior employees instead of a punishment. This is especially true in more hierarchical organizations, such as professional services firms.

A Colorado-based law firm described the stretch opportunity their junior attorneys received as an unexpected, but now major, benefit of their sabbatical policy. The policy was initially put in place to reduce stress and overwork after the unexpected death of one of its partners left the others devastated and looking for answers.[4] Those remaining realized that a culture of overwork and stress was pervasive at the firm, despite the fact that they alone ultimately controlled their workload. So they decided to make a sabbatical mandatory after ten years at the company, with subsequent full-year sabbaticals every seven years.[5] Even more exceptional in such a hierarchical sector, they extended the practice to support staff.

One of the most difficult parts of implementing the policy was figuring out how to manage the workload that partners left behind while on leave. Customarily, a partner would transfer their responsibilities to another partner if they were going to be out of the office unexpectedly. The firm instead decided to assign leadership to the junior attorneys already on the cases. This provided an unusual stretch experience for the younger lawyers, resulting in rare opportunities, like leading trials, that they would typically need to wait years, or switch firms, to access.

It also gave the firm an insurance policy of sorts against a partner departing to open their own firm. Typically, partners served as the sole point of contact with their clients, putting the firm at risk of losing not only a partner but also an entire book of business through their relationships. A sabbatical policy prevents those clients from walking out the door with the partner, since other attorneys at the firm have also formed a working relationship with them. A similar practice of distributing responsibilities and points of contact is mandated by law in the world of finance. Compliance with the various Anti-Money Laundering Acts (2000) and best practices by Federal Reserve banks require that all executives "in sensitive positions be absent from their duties for a minimum of two weeks" per year, and that "all of their tasks be processed by another employee in their absence."[6] This safeguard was designed to prevent pyramid schemes and other unethical dealings but has turned into a sought-after (and relatively long) reprieve for a notoriously overworked industry.*

Provide a Sorting Mechanism

In his book *Good to Great*, author and teacher Jim Collins discovered that one of the most telling differences between good and great companies wasn't their strategy—it was their people. It may sound obvious, but to Collins, it wasn't as simple as hiring the right people. He likened a company to a bus, with the employees its passengers. One of the greatest challenges for any leader (bus driver) is twofold: figure out who belongs on the bus, and then, in which seat (position at the company) they should be.[7] Adding to the complexity of the situation, everything about the inside of the bus is in flux. The order and size of the seats change as responsibilities grow, people leave, and new ones are brought on.

Research on consulting firms has proven that, though it's inconvenient when some employees leave their positions, it actually has a net *positive* effect on the company. The study looked at a consulting firm's so-called externship program, where junior consultants temporarily leave their routine work at the firm to volunteer at a social enterprise or some other mission-oriented organization.[8] As part of the program, these employees retain their consulting pay and benefits while working for a cause they were perhaps more personally motivated by.

The firm was initially concerned about attrition after their employees finished their externships. While there was indeed turnover, closer analysis helped the firm realize that instead of costing them employees

* Though in the aftermath of COVID, Bank of America, Citigroup, Goldman Sachs, and Wells Fargo all introduced paid sabbatical policies for their employees.

who would have thrived in the long term, the program instead served as a helpful sorting mechanism. It turned out that those employees who cared more about missions outside the firm might have been just as likely to succeed in the short run but would have been less likely to stick around or qualify for future promotions. In other words, their not returning after their externships was *good turnover* for the firm.

Looking back at chapter 3, I'm reminded of Aarti's story, where her sabbatical from NPR ultimately resulted in her departure from the radio station to pursue more writing and personal journalism through a podcast. But within five years, she was collaborating with NPR again—at a different level this time, more as a creator and content leader than a journalist. That seat on the bus worked better for Aarti, and, ultimately, for NPR. What was originally no longer a fit needed to be shaken up, explored, and rediscovered. NPR gained a great employee in a different seat on the bus, and Aarti found a way to continue working for a company that had supported her sabbatical and career to date, but in a way that worked better for her.

Spur Tough (but Important) Conversations

Both as managers and as employees, we tend to avoid difficult conversations at work, such as requesting a raise or promotion, or expressing general dissatisfaction. This leads to a variety of concerns festering over time and contributes to the likelihood of people leaving.

One of the toughest topics that is most often overdue is around compensation. Long-tenured staff are chronically underpaid compared to newer employees and those with similar qualifications at other companies in a phenomenon called pay compression.[9] It's not necessarily management's fault—companies tend to think about employee compensation as a salary plus an annual raise, versus going out to the market to see how much that employee would be worth if they got a job elsewhere with their current skills and experience. A sabbatical forces each party to consider what it would be like without the other, and offers an opportunity to revisit roles and responsibilities in order to right-size compensation upon return. While this may seem like a bad outcome for companies, giving a worthy employee a well-deserved raise is likely preferred to losing them to the uncertainty of hiring someone new at market rate anyway.

One of our research participants, Carson, had this exact experience when she and her husband embarked upon a six-month-long "monster[honey]moon" after their wedding. Carson had been working in various roles at a university-based poverty lab since its founding seven years prior. While she enjoyed her job, her roles and responsibilities had changed significantly since helping start the lab with her academic counterparts, but her autonomy and compensation had lagged. Her honeymoon travels in emerging markets gave Carson the chance to remember why she'd gotten into the sector to begin with and reinvigorated her loyalty to the mission. But it also gave her the confidence that she could take her experience elsewhere if she was unable to command greater recognition from her cofounders.

Upon return, Carson was surprised to be met with a preemptive conversation by the cofounders, who'd realized the magnitude of her work in her absence and wanted to do anything they could to keep her in the organization. In her negotiations, she went from "feeling like a cog in a wheel," in her words, to "feeling like a grown-up with power." She was promoted and, two years later, became the executive director. The organization has thrived since her return: the original cofounders were finally able to free themselves from the day-to-day operations so they could focus on research. With Carson fully focused on operations instead of reporting to them (or off at another job altogether), the organization has doubled its budget and quadrupled its staff members and research affiliates. Though managers won't often initiate salary discussions in routine life, after a sabbatical, they are more likely to welcome—and perhaps initiate—that conversation, so even a tough conversation feels worth having.

Build Organizational Resilience

A charismatic leader can mean the difference between a successful company and an unsuccessful one. And the more successful a company with an incredible leader is, the more vulnerable the company can be if that leader departs. This is especially true with start-ups and nonprofits, where the leader is expected to not only set the vision for the organization but also fundraise for its survival. It's also true with large organizations, where the impact of a charismatic CEO might cover up an underdeveloped tier of management that would fail on its own.

A classic example of this is General Electric, which grew almost forty times its size during CEO Jack Welch's tenure, only to lose almost 50 percent of its value in the two years following his retirement in 2001.[10] Relying on a singular leadership figure can be great for business, but it's a risky strategy, and not a great long-term one. Compare this to Apple, whose pioneering founder CEO Steve Jobs helped the company grow twelve times over from 1997 to 2011 by launching some of the most influential products in the history of consumer technology. Importantly, he also groomed and empowered his successor, Tim Cook, once Jobs's cancer diagnosis became clear. Cook subsequently helped Apple grow to almost twenty times its value after Jobs retired.

An example from our research of using a sabbatical to lessen this key-person risk was education entrepreneur Chris Mitchell. Mitchell cofounded the African Leadership Academy (ALA), a pioneering boarding school in Johannesburg, South Africa. ALA drew elite students from across the continent, competing with the best international schools, at a price any admitted student could afford. Chris was proud of what he accomplished with ALA. With the tenth anniversary of the academy on the horizon, he decided to step back for an entire academic year and take a sabbatical in Europe while his fiancée completed her master's degree there.

After a year spent traveling, relaxing, and learning in Europe,

Chris returned to a few new realities after his extended leave. First, his school's operations had flourished in his absence, potentially running even better than with his involvement. Second, the institution's fundraising efforts had fallen off a cliff without him.

In response, Chris decided not to reassume responsibility for operations, instead promoting the person who'd taken over while he'd been away. He returned to fundraising with a renewed vigor in order to support ALA's upcoming ten-year anniversary gala and set a personal goal to transfer fundraising to someone else within three years. He did this because of his third realization: he no longer wanted to live as an expat, especially since his soon-to-be wife would be starting an academic job back in the States.

Chris has since left for a position at the University of North Carolina, but ALA continues to thrive. It has even spawned an entire university, the African Leadership University.

Though Chris's sabbatical functionally marked the beginning of the end of his time at ALA, from a board and longer-term organizational perspective, this outcome was a great success. Chris's sabbatical—and the insights it prompted—helped the nonprofit avoid a common and devastating fate of falling victim to key-person risk.[11] From a long-term value standpoint, Chris is much closer to Steve Jobs than Jack Welch, because his time away forced the organization to reckon with a world in which their charismatic leader departs. By stress-testing that possibility, Chris proved that he had created something of enduring value for investors, alumni, and generations of aspiring students.

Give Employees Purpose (Outside of Work)

Given the choice, most people would prefer to work for a company whose mission aligns with their personal values, and which gives deeper meaning to the majority of their waking hours.[12] Unfortunately, making meaningful products or having a positive impact on the world isn't exactly a knob you can adjust as a business owner.

Consider 3M, the company that famously created Post-it Notes: How many of their eighty-five thousand employees have a meaningful connection to "adhesives, sealants, and tapes"? It's not management's fault, and it's certainly not within the control of most other companies out there in the world that work in less-than-glamorous industries that make the world turn. So instead of overextending themselves to bring a greater sense of purpose to their employees, many companies are giving their workers more time for what matters to them outside of work.* For example, software giant SAP and consumer goods behemoth Johnson & Johnson both offer one- to two-month paid volunteering programs for their employees; SAP's time off is called a "social sabbatical."[14] And brokerage firm Charles Schwab gives a week of paid time off per year on top of existing paid time off to volunteer.[15] Programs like these result in lower turnover and higher engagement when back in the office.[16]

I'm reminded of my interview with a development economist at the US Treasury named Carol. After spending close to two uninterrupted decades at work, Carol finally decided to ask her boss to take advantage of the Treasury's leave without pay (LWOP) policy once she turned forty. Though unpaid, Carol retained her health benefits while taking six months off to care for an ailing family member and to backpack in Patagonia.

By the end of her time off, Carol didn't exactly miss being in the office, but she appreciated how her job gave her the opportunity to live out the aspects of her life that a normal office job would not. Being able to attend to her family during a crisis and fully immerse herself in another country for the first time since studying abroad in college were two of the most important memories of her working life.

---

* Notably, 3M has allowed its employees to spend 15 percent of their time working on creative projects outside their job description since 1948.[13]

It would be an exaggeration to say that Carol was thrilled to return to work, but knowing that there was a light at the end of the tunnel with a future LWOP was a strong motivator to return to and stay at the organization for many years to come.

Create a Culture of Excitement, Not Resentment

An investment advisory firm was one of the last places I expected to find innovation in paid extended leave. But Brighton Jones founder Jon Jones believes that the firm's so-called YOLO policy has been a key to its successful track record and employee longevity.* Despite the somewhat silly name, he considers the policy a very serious matter: his father's untimely death when Jones was three years old serves as a constant reminder that life is too short to be unintentional. So, after sixteen years building up the business, Jones established an extended-leave policy and took one himself with his family of six.

Brighton Jones offers all its 175 employees a three-month paid sabbatical, on top of which an individual can add up to two months of accrued paid vacation, as well as further unpaid leave. It's more than an executive perk for those at the top—this sabbatical policy is available to everyone at the company, not just investment professionals.

Brighton Jones's sabbatical policy has become vital to both the organization's culture and its business model. Taking a sabbatical is mandatory starting at ten years of service, and is intended to remind employees that their job isn't their life and to help the company learn to operate relatively smoothly in their absence. This extended-leave policy helps employees recover from a demanding job; Jones consistently notices increased performance, energy, and collegiality when they return.

---

* YOLO, as in "you only live once," may have fallen (way) out of favor as a term in recent years, but no matter what you want to call your extended leave—Shelley Paxton called it her soulbbatical, for instance—I'm here for it.

But he also sees significant benefits accruing for the organization as a whole. First, the clients experience better customer service. The traditional financial advisory relationship is one-to-one; customers are assigned an advisor who stays their primary contact indefinitely, which requires both loyalty and longevity among employees. And Brighton Jones has found that its employees who have taken a sabbatical ultimately stay longer than before the policy was enacted. The YOLO policy helps the company stand out when recruiting, and to retain talent among more prestigious and higher-paying competitors in traditional finance hubs.

Second, while someone is on sabbatical, Brighton Jones's clients gain multiple touchpoints at the organization. This opens up options for quicker service in the future—a built-in buffer in case someone's out of the office. This also means that when financial advisors retire or leave the industry altogether, the customer has more reason to stay with Brighton Jones after the departure. And former employees are less likely to successfully poach these clients.

Beyond encouraging the firm's best employees to stay, this generous leave policy encourages a strong company culture that recognizes people as individuals, not just coworkers. By coincidence, the day I interviewed the CEO of Brighton Jones on their company policy, an employee was giving a lunch break presentation about his extended leave.

Over pizza (courtesy of the company), the employee talked about his sabbatical, what he did and what it meant to him. This was much more than a "What I did on my summer vacation" slideshow. It was an incredibly popular and rousing session that focused on the many positive things that can happen when you take a step back from routine. The PowerPoint ended with rousing applause and a round of impromptu questions about where the family stayed on their extended leave, how much it cost, and what they would have done differently. This simply would not happen if the benefit was only available to the elite few—when everyone has access, camaraderie builds, instead of resentment.

We've all seen organizations try to manufacture loyalty with Ping-Pong tables and free snacks, but nothing compares to the feeling of goodwill that policies like this engender. So much more than a gesture, this was proof that Brighton Jones recognized the tremendous toll that the *always on* culture of finance exacts on its employees, and that they were willing to do something about it.

Short-Term versus Long-Term Mindset

Not all your suspicions about how sabbaticals impact companies are unfounded. Some sabbatical takers do end up leaving their companies. But it's much fewer than you'd think. In our study, we found that close to 80 percent of company-sponsored sabbatical takers returned to their employer after extended leave.

But that still means that one in five employees who take off don't return. If that were the case with people setting off on regular vacations or the weekend, we'd surely give pause before letting employees out of our sight to begin with. Right?

When evaluating the trade-offs involved in granting your employees a sabbatical, remember that it's not about ensuring your employees work perfectly productively forever. It's about preventing your best people from working while burned out, building resentment about the job, management, and the company as a whole. A leader at the online shoe behemoth Zappos—famous for its liberal HR policies—viewed this focus solely on short-term productivity as ultimately counterproductive.

As we codesigned a sabbatical policy for his team, he wondered why a company would want to trap their employee into staying at a job. In his words: "I don't want employees to stay because they're handcuffed to the desk. . . . If upon the first sight of daylight they sprint for the exits," he told me, "I wouldn't want them on our team anymore anyway. Despite the cost and logistics around bringing on a new employee, we have no shortage of folks who actually want to be here."[17]

One of Zappos's most trailblazing policies was offering new hires $2,000 to quit before they even started the job.[18] After calculating how much money was wasted by training someone who wouldn't be a good long-term fit, the intention behind the policy was to weed out those who were there for the wrong reasons.

Factoring in the cost and inconvenience for the hiring manager to lose a new hire, Zappos determined it was better to know they were keeping someone who wanted to be there to begin with, despite the short-term costs and disruption. Just over a decade after it was founded, Zappos was acquired by Amazon for $1.2 billion and allowed to retain its innovative HR policies in order to inspire changes at Amazon as a whole.

There's no question that, in the short run, extended leave—whether in the form of a sabbatical, parental leave, or medical disability—is disruptive to a company. It lumps extra work on remaining team members and can create the hassle of training someone new. But there are silver linings in the medium to long term. When extended breaks are a routine part of a company's culture, the organization builds the capacity to handle turnover. It becomes a form of resilience training, like a workout of sorts, as the company is forced to fill the gaps the absent person leaves behind. And because of the restorative impact of the sabbatical on the leave-taker, a sabbatical policy can help a company both prevent *and* prepare for the departure of its key employees.

If you're a manager, ask yourself if you want people on your team who would rather quit—most times without even another job lined up—than continue working with you. Turnover is inconvenient, sure. But it's also a fact of business life that leaders need to prepare for.

Alongside the benefit of having motivated, engaged employees filling your ranks is the real possibility of increased productivity, a better culture fit, new ideas, and a whole host of other positives. Two best-in-class companies, tech giant Adobe and pioneering biotech firm Genentech, have also prioritized medium- to long-term success over short-term inconvenience. Both firms were among the first to offer substantial sabbatical policies across the organization. Each company's policy has had a significant ripple effect in their respective industries. Adobe's policies have become commonplace at old-guard tech giants like Microsoft, PayPal, and Oracle. And Genentech's generous paid sabbatical policy created a time-off arms race among biotech competitors, to the point where competition in the sector, from larger orgs like Biogen to newcomers like Denali Therapeutics, all offer sabbaticals as standard practice.

Since launching their pioneering sabbatical policies, Adobe has grown to a market capitalization of around $180 billion, and Genentech was acquired in 2009 for $46.8 billion by Roche. Roche has kept Genentech's sabbatical policy, which has since become the norm for the entire Swiss pharmaceutical giant's one hundred thousand or so employees. We obviously can't tie these companies' successes to their sabbatical offerings, but the policies have persisted across decades and spread across industries and acquirers.

In an economy obsessed with short-term gains, wise business leaders know what drives long-term success. As legendary value investor Warren Buffett said in his 1989 shareholder letter: "Time is the friend of the wonderful business, the enemy of the mediocre."[19]

Our Collective Call to Action

Many of us have two distinct sets of responsibilities in our lives. On one hand, we are responsible for the success of our organizations. We spend the majority of our waking hours at work, and our personal livelihood depends on it. On the other hand, we are human beings with dreams and limited energy and time to spend on the things that transcend work. To my knowledge, no one on their deathbed laments having worked too little.

On the surface, there is an undeniable tension between these two realities: we don't want to lose our jobs if the company performs worse while we are on leave, but we also yearn to live in a world where work and big personal pursuits can live in harmony. In the face of this tension, we allow our fears and the inertia of how work has been done in the past to triumph over our agency to change things. This despite the fact that business as usual hasn't exactly been working well for quite a while now. On almost every meaningful metric, from burnout and stress to presenteeism (showing up to the office while mentally or physically unwell) and engagement at work, things aren't heading in the right direction in the twenty-first century.[20]

The percentage of US employers with formal policies supporting extended leave has grown substantially over the past decade.[21] But we are nowhere close to a working world where anyone, regardless of socioeconomic status, has access to this opportunity. Accelerating this trend requires the individuals, company leaders, and policymakers (Sweden, for example, offers six-month paid sabbaticals to its citizens to start a business) who practice extended leave to step forward and share their experiences.[22] If they do so, we may be able to retain the many benefits that work provides while also fulfilling our personal dreams and aspirations, building in recovery time, and living a life without regret. Armed with the examples in this book, whether you're in a position to craft policy or simply to set an example to others by publicizing your time off, you can play a crucial role in making sabbaticals from work more prevalent and equitable.

In Practice

Leaving Work

- **Take inventory and reassign.** List *all* the activities you do at work, including meetings. Who are they with and what are they for? Who else in the organization could do them?
- **Identify the best and leave the rest.** Which responsibilities do you not want to return to? These will either inform a conversation with a supervisor upon your return or a wish list for your next position down the road.
- **Have proactive conversations with coworkers.** What can you do to act as a mentor to junior employees getting a stretch experience while you are gone? How can you best equip them to carry your load?
- **Share your plans.** Empower decision-makers to normalize taking time off by sharing your story publicly and encouraging those in positions of leadership to do so as well.
- **Depart with confidence.** Speak with ten people who have either left your company or your industry. How are they doing? Figure out how their careers have gone and what leaving your company is truly like.

Policy Design Principles for Leaders

In order for sabbaticals to become more widespread and successful for employees, three enabling factors must be in place:

- **Equitable.** The sabbatical policy must be made available to everyone inside the organization based on their tenure, not their seniority.
- **Support.** At minimum, sabbatical takers must be guaranteed health insurance and a job upon return. Better is full pay,

partial pay, or a stipend. The more support the organization offers an employee, the more loyalty it engenders in them.

- **Disconnection.** Sabbatical takers should be locked out of access to email and other shared company resources and helped to establish one or two internal contacts who can field inbound communications and establish an escalation plan.

13

Troubleshooting and Returning from Sabbatical

A ship in harbor is safe, but that is not what ships are built for.

—John Shedd, *Salt from My Attic*

The surprising truth about sabbaticals is that they are often very difficult.

It's uncomfortable to be out of routine. No matter how prepared you are—no matter how excited—you're bound to question your decision and chafe at the disruption that you've invited into your life. The vacuum left from all the busyness of day-to-day life will spur negative thoughts like uncertainty, doubt, and fear.

The good news is that as long as you're expecting this dynamic, you can treat it for what it is: an unavoidable part of your sabbatical. Perhaps there's a lesson to learn about yourself from how you feel with fewer responsibilities. I can't help you eliminate the tough parts or protect you from them. Even if I could, I wouldn't.

The three most common difficulties sabbatical takers report are uneven circumstances among travel companions, false starts, and the unease associated with being in the midst of a transition. And it should come as no surprise that returning from one's sabbatical can be the most difficult step of all. In this chapter, we'll also cover ways to carry your sabbatical mindset into your post-sabbatical life. Recognizing these dynamics in advance and having a plan to return to routine well can help you navigate the discomfort and uncertainty that arises during your time away.

Uneven Circumstances

After working hard in San Francisco tech companies for almost a decade, Natalia and Gérard agreed that it was time to put their long-awaited plan into motion: they would quit their jobs and go on a yearlong sabbatical. They felt lucky that, as a young couple, they'd been able to align their schedules to embark on the next journey simultaneously.

They were also seemingly in sync with their plans for their time off. After working his way up the ladder at a fast-growing fintech company, Gérard was hungry for a new challenge. He aimed to use his sabbatical primarily to explore what was next for his career. Natalia had studied education in undergrad and spent her career working for various edtech ventures, but helping design digital products for millions felt far removed from the reason she'd gotten into the space to begin with.

During the experimentation phase of their time off, Gérard would be in Mexico City, Myanmar, and Nairobi, where he'd carved out unpaid internships with various fintech start-ups. He launched a website and newsletter, posting his learnings across social media platforms and in regular updates to friends and family. It was a textbook example of learning in public, and he was loving every minute of it.

Natalia, on the other hand, was struggling. She'd spent her first chunk of the sabbatical volunteering for, and living above, an innovative school in rural India. It was a difficult place to live—she lacked many creature comforts, staying in free accommodations to save money and show solidarity with her students. But she relished the chance to get back to feeling a connection and impact with educators on the front lines. Despite this, the gulf between her experience and Gérard's made her feel like she was doing her sabbatical wrong. Should she instead be more productive and focused on her next opportunity?

When they reunited during the next phase of their sabbatical, they both put work aside and began traveling just for the fun of it, making their way through Rwanda, China, and New Zealand. Upon their return, the couple found themselves in the opposite dynamic than during the first phase of their sabbatical. Natalia won a prestigious fellowship from the Aspen Institute, which began just before their official reentry to regular life. Gérard's fintech experiments, however, hadn't turned into job offers. It would be another few months and require a move across the country to New York before their lives fully began to find their rhythm again.

Natalia still treasures her sabbatical as a key milestone in her life and their relationship. But looking back, she believes that a few tweaks would have vastly improved her experience. Gérard's excitement around exploring work on his sabbatical unwittingly influenced Natalia's plans for her time off. She needed the carefree middle stage, where they explored together, at the beginning of her time off. Though they were on the same page for taking a sabbatical, they'd skipped conversations about what it would look like for each of them individually, and so they'd found themselves having made significant plans for themselves independently. After they reunited, Natalia recalls feeling initially relieved to explore and have fun together. But even then they encountered a bit of social whiplash, a common feeling described by couples on sabbatical due to spending time only with each other during their intense travels.

Pulling off a sabbatical when you're partnered is difficult. Even when you manage to sync your scheduled time off, emotional and intentional misalignment can breed feelings of constraint and resentment. Being together twenty-four-seven, with no breaks from each other, can add tension to any relationship.

This isn't just the case for romantic partners; sharing part of your sabbatical with friends and family can be equally challenging. Each occasion to meet up with someone interrupts whatever mental and emotional roller coaster you're on. This is often a good thing, because a sabbatical is such a personal journey that we tend to retreat into navel-gazing and overly self-serious analysis. But it can also be jarring, because a sabbatical is a time of growth and change, whereas getting together with friends and family can anchor us back in our past identities.

The other reason sharing time with others on your sabbatical can be tough is because sabbaticals can be surprisingly difficult. They can bring out lots of negative emotions, fears, worries about the future, regrets, and all the other wounds you've been carrying around but been too busy to deal with.

On my sabbatical, my two best friends from high school surprised me by flying to Tokyo right before I set off on my pilgrimage. I was just coming off six weeks alone in New Zealand, and unbeknownst to them, I was in the midst of a pretty difficult stretch. I'd spent most of my sabbatical battling demons of regret, struggling with the decision to leave my company, and worrying I'd made the wrong call to break up with a partner.

But they were understandably expecting a fun hang—our first proper adventure together in more than a decade. I was not a fun hang. I was grumpy, impatient, and overly obsessed with optimizing our agenda, since I was the one without a job. I felt like I couldn't discuss the difficulties I had been experiencing along the way. I either felt shut down by their insistence that it couldn't be that bad—"Dude, you're on the trip of a lifetime!"—or unable to connect on the deeper level I craved. Ultimately, I hid my dissatisfaction well enough, and it was probably a healthy break from my head trash. But the identity whiplash of my worlds colliding during that vulnerable time of growth was disorienting.

When planning a sabbatical with a friend or partner, make sure you communicate during the planning stage what you each need independently. Sometimes, even figuring out what you want takes a little time apart—maybe just a day alone or a weekend to think. Many of us drag ourselves across the finish line into Sabbatical Land; making space for discernment about what you need as an individual is essential for a successful collective experience.

False Starts

Looking for a job too soon is one of the biggest mistakes we make during our sabbatical. We just don't feel comfortable occupying that in-between space. William Bridges calls this key phase of a transition the neutral zone. The neutral zone is incredibly important to transformation, but it's also messy and chaotic. According to Bridges, we imagine that "renewal comes through fixing something defective or supplying something that is missing. But it is only by returning for a time to the formlessness of the primal energy that renewal can take place."[1] Formlessness might not be on your performance scorecard at work, but it's an essential precondition for creation and creativity, especially on sabbatical.

But the in-between can be scary. Instead of holding the space between jobs sacred, we'd prefer to kick into what's familiar: job-search mode. Take Darren, for example.

Darren dreamt of taking a sabbatical for more than a decade. His year studying abroad in the Netherlands in college still loomed large in his memory—it helped him decompress from academic stress and realize there were almost infinite career paths beyond those presented at Midwest career fairs.

A decade later, Darren found himself stretched and stressed at a company he no longer believed in. He worked up the courage to step away, with grand plans: multi-week ski trips, road trips with each of his parents, and an extended honeymoon with his wife. But less than a month into his sabbatical, Darren unintentionally executed the cardinal sin of Sabbatical Land: he posted online that he had left his job.

To Darren's credit, he didn't ask for help landing a new job. He merely announced that he had left his company, a vague post about stepping back to determine his next steps. However, what Darren failed to realize is that people feel very uncomfortable with their friends being unemployed. That casual announcement triggered an avalanche of questions: "What are you doing next?" "What kind of job do you want?" "Why did you leave?" "You're taking *how* much time off?"

This made Darren even more self-conscious about being out of work. He hadn't cooked up an alibi that he himself believed in enough to push back on the well-meaning problem-solvers in his network. He hadn't even had time to process what it meant to leave the last company, let alone think about a new one. Having neither skied nor honeymooned, Darren took one pre-interview call. That was all it took. He moved quickly through the process and was soon back to work.

Darren reflects back on his time off with great joy, but wistfully: "I didn't give myself the luxury of saying 'I'm going to have X months off without even thinking about what I'm going to do next.' Once I put my first toe in the water, feelings about paycheck and prestige cascaded in quickly."

Importantly, he was able to squeeze in a one-on-one trip with his father before starting his next job. Within the year, his father became ill and subsequently died. Their short trip together featured prominently in Darren's eulogy.

This pattern is much more common than you'd think. It's difficult to take pleasure casting off lines to uncertain shores. It's human nature to crave certainty, but growth and change require us to first relinquish the stage we're in. Otherwise, our next steps more closely resemble the ones preceding them than any vision for the future we've dreamed up. As we learned about burnout in chapter 7, if we don't give ourselves a chance to make structural changes in a life that isn't working for us, we can't expect escaping alone to be a panacea. Doing so requires living a different way for long enough to realize that your life is distinct from what you do and who you are at work. To get there, you must trudge through a phase that has many names, from formlessness to liminality, even a difficult "dark night of the soul."[2] Do your best, know you're not alone, and take heart trusting in what's on the other side.

When Things Are Just Difficult

These discomforts aren't impediments to your sabbatical. Examined at a distance, they can provide insights into the way you're already living in your routine life. You can't change course until you see the pattern you're stuck in. That realization hit me during my pilgrimage in Japan.

Though I wasn't really embarking on the journey for religious reasons, I still promised myself I wouldn't just pop in headphones each day to pass the time, as I would in normal life. The result: I was racked with boredom. Boredom is almost extinct these days. Why zone out when you have more and more frictionless access to an infinite catalog of more interesting options? But as we saw with Winston in chapter 1, without boredom, we lack the fertile emptiness required for creation. But no one likes being bored, fertile or not. And walking all day for six weeks, often along roads buzzing with traffic instead of serene wilderness, was about as boring as it gets.

Part of the traditional outfit for Henros—what the pilgrims on this route are called—was a walking stick modeled after the one that Kobo

Daishi—the Japanese monk responsible for bringing Buddhism to the nation—carried. The walking sticks all had bells attached to the top, intended to remind pilgrims to stay present, a core tenet of Buddhism. As you can imagine, getting lost in your thoughts is an inevitability during nine-plus hours of daily walking, as I was doing. No headphones meant a lot of boredom and bell listening.

In the absence of a phone to satisfy my urge for distraction, I began to obsess over one of my most treasured possessions: the map book. I thought about how many kilometers I was walking each day, converting it to miles per hour to estimate when I would reach my destination. I'd curse the book when something was inaccurate. It was my very analog addiction.

The result of this tracking and obsessing over ETAs had turned what was a walk into a competition. I'd walked faster than most I'd encountered on the trail, passing people much more often than being passed myself. This was particularly ironic considering that this pilgrimage is a circle, ending unceremoniously where it begins—a literal reminder that it is about the journey, not the destination.

Once I'd completed three-quarters of the pilgrimage, I took my first real break: a weekend trip to Hiroshima. As I looked forward to the end, I reflected back on how it had gone thus far and realized my mistake. Armed with my newfound self-awareness, I promised myself that I would slow down during the last ten-day stretch.

I failed at this pretty quickly, which instead gave me approximately nine days to mull over what it meant that I just couldn't relax. As I approached the final temple, I figured it out. This thing that I'd been beating myself up about—my tendency to make everything a competition, my high pain threshold and inability to quit—wasn't likely to change. Certainly not in the span of a few months.

Even my self-critical voice had something to teach me. Why was I focused on the negatives instead of the fact that I'd just successfully walked an enormously long distance on foot in a foreign country by myself? I'd found another, more generous, side to the story that I typically told about myself. While I couldn't bank on slowing myself down, I could steer my extra energy and productivity complex into something with greater meaning for others.

On my final leg, I committed to spending my extra three days doing something positive. I set up shop outside the second temple, offering help and a homemade goodie bag of energy bars, blister tape, and a traditional greeting card for every pilgrim who passed through. The greeting cards were slips of paper customarily given by Henros at temples along the route to express gratitude to those who offer help or alms. The experience helped me gain clarity about myself: if I couldn't change, I could at least channel my relentless energy toward helping others.

When I returned to my guesthouse that evening, I sent an email to a professor who had started a poverty research lab at my alma mater, asking how I could help. That email led me to the next phase of my sabbatical, volunteering my time in the research lab, where I coincidentally met my academic collaborator for the initial sabbatical research.

Those six weeks of the pilgrimage are still the most formative of my entire life. I am 100 percent positive I did not do it correctly. I was functionally illiterate—unable to communicate verbally for the entirety of my walk because I did not speak the language. I botched the elaborate ritual process at most of the temples. I had significant conversations with fewer than a dozen people over the course of a month and a half.

But it still worked! And in ways that changed my life enough to dedicate the next seven years to researching sabbaticals and writing this book to help enable others to go on similar journeys.

There are some lessons that we simply cannot learn from studying, reflection, or even the best teachers. This type of learning, known as empirical or experiential knowledge, is key to the unique ability our sabbaticals possess to change us. The ancient Greeks referred to it as *metis*, the kind of know-how a sailor or healer might possess. These skills can be acquired and mastered only through navigating the world directly. A sabbatical is a rare chance to experience living in a very different way, which opens the door to a life you may not have even noticed stirring inside you.

Returning to Routine Life

No matter how well you've sabbaticalled, there's the pesky matter of returning to "real life." Which parts of your life should you retain, and from which should you move on? How do you keep the magic alive? These are big questions that require a lot of time and energy to attack.

The common tendency is to start early, plotting your next steps for your new life before you've even gotten into the meat of your sabbatical. But it's difficult to anticipate ahead of time what changes you're going to want to make after your return. For this reason, I strongly recommend that you do not try to make decisions for your future self until the last phase of your sabbatical at the earliest.

When I coach sabbatical takers, I conduct detailed interviews with them at the start and end of their time off. I'm particularly interested in their expectations for their time off: How do you feel now (about work, your relationship, yourself) and how do you want to feel upon returning? What activities do you have planned for your time off, and which do you anticipate giving you the most joy? In what way do you aspire to return to your job, if at all?

There's a lot of juicy fodder for discussion around the differences between expectations and reality, between what someone's pre-sabbatical mindset thinks about themselves and what's important. For example, one woman's bucket-list retreat in Scotland was overshadowed by the meaning she took from caring for her ailing grandmother in her one-bedroom apartment in Paris. A gay man's multi-month trip in Southeast Asia peaked when he was stranded in a small village during a monsoon and was able to offer perspective for a young man too scared to come out of the closet himself. A father of three spent a glorious long summer with his kids and wife but experienced his most impactful change via a spiritual awakening during a four-day water-only fast alone in the woods.

Once you've emerged from the other side of your sabbatical, you can evaluate the prospect of returning to your routines and responsibilities with newfound perspective. My advice here is going to sound a bit zany: I want you to put yourself firmly back in your former life for a few days *before* you officially return. Go to the office, shadow your replacements, take people out for coffee who have been doing your job in your absence. You're not just gathering data about how things went in the interim; your goal is to observe how you *feel* about the prospect of returning to your former life. Think of yourself like a character in Dickens's *A Christmas Carol*: the ghost of post-sabbatical you.

For example, Mike Salguero, the founder and CEO of Butcher Box, the billion-dollar food company he started in his living room, returned from his sabbatical with this strategy. Over the course of his three months with his family, he had determined that he did not want to return to many of the day-to-day tasks he'd left behind. Luckily for Mike, he'd implemented best-in-class preparations at his company prior to his departure. He'd documented all his tasks, distributed them to various team members based on appetite and aptitude, and empowered a more junior director to step up into a position of greater responsibility. He also empowered each of these individuals to make decisions without any approval and designated a single point of contact at the company to be an arbiter for all situations where people felt they needed his guidance before proceeding. Furthermore, he layered on top of this person someone from outside his company who knew the business to be a final firewall before any request made it to his phone during his sabbatical. (None did.)

Mike returned two weeks later than he'd anticipated, and once he got back to the office, he told his entire staff that for the remaining two weeks of the month, he wasn't going to be doing any work. Instead, he asked everyone to treat him as if he'd delayed his return another two weeks. During that time, Mike went on a "listening tour," collecting feedback from employees on how their peers performed during his absence and teasing out where things went better and where they fell flat during his sabbatical. Crucially, Mike took detailed notes after each meeting on his personal experience reengaging with the task in question. Taking on some of the jobs felt heavy, while others felt alive with possibility. The prospect of collaborating with certain people, even if it meant working in an area of the business he didn't love, helped inform his choices as well.

Few of us will have the luxury of choosing which parts of our life and work to return to and which to leave behind. But even if your options are limited in the short term, there's always the next job decision point. Or the next one. You will only have one chance to observe how it feels to reattach the various pieces of your former life one by one. As we learned in chapter 7 with Audrey, you can't expect your life to change drastically after your time off if you resume living in the exact same way as before. Upon return, you must decide which aspects of your life to pick back up and which to leave in your past. The key to returning to routine life well is amassing a new portfolio of roles and responsibilities that you're energized to carry forward into the next leg of your life.

ooo

Alas, most of the things that made your sabbatical special are not possible in routine life. To keep everyday life marbled with some ingredients that made your time off so special, make routine escapes, prioritize others' calendars, and practice habitual exploration.

1. Regularly Remove Yourself from Routine Life

Routines can be extremely important—they allow us to filter out distractions and reduce switching costs. But routines can also lull us into sleepwalking through our days, and, therefore, our lives.

After your sabbatical, build regular breaks from routine into your life. Take tech Sabbaths on weekends, work from new environments, and seek out people who approach work completely differently than you do. Go to extremes to reimmerse yourself in Sabbatical Land. Take a red-eye to somewhere exciting over the weekend, even if your Monday morning self will resent you. The goal is to shake things up enough to remind you that the world outside your bubble is awe-inspiring, and that living your routine existence is a choice, not preordained.

If your constraints prevent you from shaking things up sufficiently on occasion, your job is to turn the everyday into something exceptional. Think of sunsets. When you're on vacation, especially near water, the sunset is a daily spectacle. How often in your workaday existence do you stop to view the sunset? You must snatch the extraordinary from everyday life, whether it's going on a weekend silent retreat every year or watching a sunset by yourself outside your office.

2. Spend Time with People You Care About on *Their* Schedule

One of the unexpected delights from many people's sabbaticals is the ability to reconnect with friends and family. With time constraints removed from my life, I was able to drive a few hours and help my cousin move into a new apartment. I could offer to babysit for a stressed-out friend and his partner, who hadn't had a day off together since the birth of their first child.

Once you're back from sabbatical, familiar constraints return. But when you've seen the value of reconnecting with important people, another avenue opens up with some intentional planning. Don't wait until a blowout trip like a sabbatical to see a friend—plan a joint vacation or make your own vacation near them. Reframe the tendency to "keep score" about who adapts to whose plan or takes the lead more often: do whatever it takes to spend time with the people you care about instead of pushing it off to an uncertain future.

Almost no one has the time to pick up stakes from their life right now. But if we're able to look far enough out into the future, our schedules start to look pretty clear. What are you doing six years from now, from June to August? Suddenly, reconnecting with friends and family becomes much more possible. Similarly, plan a vacation with a friend for a couple of years from now, before their calendar fills up. Or just surrender your preferences, align completely with theirs, and give the friendship the injection of shared experiences it requires.

3. Mandate Time for Exploration Outside Work

Almost everyone knows they should be carving out more time for their interests outside of work and family but still struggles to do so. An essential component of successful sabbaticals is experimentation. Sometimes, this experimentation uncovers that we actually didn't want to do an activity to begin with. Having a lot of time off removes some pressure from how you spend it, but we can bring this exploration mindset back into our routine lives where time is scarce.

It's a practice of holding your strong opinions more lightly. You can—and should—listen to your passions and curiosities around how you'd like to spend your time outside work. But treat them like an exploration instead of a commitment. Move through these activities fluidly, without long-term attachment, from a perspective of experimentation.

Routine life gives us significantly less time to experiment. We're already so busy that mustering up activation energy for new things can be difficult. Given this reality, our goal is to be completely ruthless about how to spend our time experimenting. Pick up books often, but put them down more often. Try something for long enough to realize that you either don't actually want to do it or (hopefully) find out that it's worth spending your precious time doing.

ooo

For many people, returning to reality is inconvenient, but not devastating. Despite how enjoyable a sabbatical can be, most folks reach a point where they are ready to return to the real world. No, these aren't just the type A achiever archetypes. As I've said throughout the book, work is not the enemy.

A sabbatical isn't about escaping forever, shirking responsibilities, or refusing to grow up. It's about pulling back, healing, and doing things that feed a different part of ourselves for a while, and returning with much-needed perspective on ourselves, who we're becoming, and which parts of us are no longer served by the life we've been living. The gift of stepping away is not upheaval but the chance to see our lives clearly, while there's still time to make a change.

In Practice

Uneven Circumstances

- **Identify who will be most affected.** List the people in your life you will feel most misaligned with during your sabbatical. For example, this could be a spouse or partner who will continue working as normal, or friends who can't take a sabbatical.
- **Strategize with your partner or travel companion.** Engage in conversations and planning in advance, acknowledging the potential for difficulties around unevenness. Identify spaces during your sabbatical where you can align, and share the ways in which your newfound time off will ultimately benefit the relationship.
- **Set boundaries with others.** For those you may not wish to align with, or who may judge your sabbatical, set boundaries early. Because you have an enormous amount of "free time" on your sabbatical, people will expect you to slot into their schedules. Maintain ownership of your time.

Neutral Zone

- **Journal.** Write down your intentions for your sabbatical up front, as well as the commitments you're making to yourself. Revisit them when you are experiencing moments of doubt and weakness.
- **Engage with a coach or therapist.** People who are trained around the unique experiences of those struggling with identity issues can help put these swings into context. For camaraderie, seek out sabbatical alumni to hear about the ups and downs of their experience.

Returning to Routine Life

- **Make time for self-isolation.** What activities create mental space between your routine life and who you are underneath? How much time can you carve out for them, and on what cadence?
- **Create a relationship list.** Who did you rekindle a relationship with or who did you meet on your sabbatical—can you create a recurring call or annual visit to honor the relationship?
- **Create an exploration list.** What are interests that pique your curiosity? Identify the types of things you have questions about. Give them a try, and move on to the next one if the first doesn't serve you.

SETTING FORTH

Be patient toward all that is unsolved in your heart and try to love the questions themselves . . . live the questions now. Perhaps you will then gradually, without noticing it, live along some distant day into the answer.

—Rainer Maria Rilke, *Letters to a Young Poet*

As I put the finishing touches on this book, I was asked to speak at reunion events for two different generations of alumni. The contrast was stark.

At the first reunion, my former classmates, in their mid-forties, viewed sabbaticals as something to aspire to. They saw them as opportunities to accomplish something they'd always wanted to do or to recover from charging hard in their first decade out of school. They had time to plan, to dream, to strategize for the next decade of their career.

The following week, I addressed alumni in their fifties and sixties. When I mentioned that two-thirds of sabbaticals are catalyzed by negative events—health crises, work burnouts, relationship breakdowns—the room grew quiet. A man in the back row raised his hand, tears in his eyes.

He told us about his wife, who had died less than a year earlier after a nine-month battle with cancer. His voice broke as he described his guilt for not quitting his job entirely to be by her side during her final stretch. “Had I only known that the end was so soon,” he said, “I’d have just quit rather than try to keep work afloat.”

But then his voice strengthened. They wouldn’t share their retirement dreams after all. But they also hadn’t spent their lives waiting for someday to arrive. Right after they married, they had decided to take six months off before having children. “It was one of the best times of our lives,” he said, “a celebration of the official start of our journey as a married couple, but also preparation for the next chapter: becoming a family. There were many things we still hoped to do, but I have few regrets about the time we had together because of those six months.”

The room sat in reverent silence, absorbing the weight of his words. Here was the answer to every question about timing, about uncertainty, about whether we can afford to step away: *What does it cost us if we never do?*

The Space Between Sabbaticals

This book wasn’t written at a compound in the rice paddies of Bali or at the end of a long walk along the Camino de Santiago. I’m not writing as an enlightened guru dispensing wisdom from on high. On the contrary, I write this functionally at the end of my rope, having just reached—and pushed through—a key inflection point in life without a moment of reflection, rest, or exploration. I desperately need another sabbatical.

I’m finishing this book exactly eight years to the month after I first walked across Japan. In the past two years I’ve started an intense new job, moved across the country, gotten married, moved again, and started a family. My executive function self—the one who goes to work, shows up for his partner, executes some semblance of a weekly routine—is overtaxed. The self I got to know on my sabbatical is threadbare and undernourished. My life rests on the scaffolding of my work identity while much of the rich inner world remains locked away, like an undiscovered Cadbury Creme Egg forgotten until June.

But here's what eight years of research and one transformative sabbatical have taught me: this isn't failure, it's human nature. We don't take one sabbatical and achieve permanent enlightenment. We also don't take one sabbatical and never come back to reality. We cycle through seasons of intensity and seasons of reflection, periods of building and periods of being. The gift of a sabbatical isn't permanent balance; it's the capacity to regain it.

I recognize undernourishment because I've known what it feels like to be well nourished. I've felt the terror of stepping away from a dream job and the joy of returning renewed without it. I know that this current feeling isn't Life—it's just a season of life, and I know that a deep and rich counter-season is necessary to stave off regret and fully inhabit what follows. The need hasn't disappeared; it's just ripening.

My sabbatical list grows longer each day: time to process starting a family, space to explore what creativity looks like in this new chapter, freedom to contemplate the next decade. My next sabbatical will likely be much different—more constraints, less loneliness, perhaps more modest. But I have inspiration now from people across the world who've taken sabbaticals in different phases of life, with small children and careful planning. My heart swells at the prospect.

Your Sabbatical Is Waiting

A sabbatical isn't a rigid prescription—it's an empty container waiting for your hopes, dreams, and deepest needs. It's space for the best memories of your life and fodder for the stories you'll tell your future grandchildren or friends. It's insurance against the regret that comes from always planning to live fully tomorrow.

The research is clear: sabbaticals address burnout, increase creativity, improve relationships, and help people reinvent themselves.

Sabbatical takers return with improved confidence and fresh ideas for what comes next. The magnitude of change adds up to what researchers call "peak life experiences"—moments as significant as the birth of a child or death of a loved one.

But perhaps most importantly, sabbaticals teach us that we are not our jobs. We are complex beings with multiple identities, dreams that extend beyond our job descriptions, and relationships that deserve our full attention. In a culture that often reduces us to our professional output, stepping away is a radical act of self-assertion.

The widower at my reunion understood this. He knew that fulfilling our dreams isn't something we are guaranteed to be able to get to do later, after we've achieved enough or saved enough or accomplished enough. Self-actualization should be our birthright, but it requires time and dedication.

The same is true for every desire gathering dust on your someday list, every curiosity you've pushed aside for more pressing matters, every version of yourself you've been too busy to explore.

Your sabbatical is waiting. Not as a luxury you'll only deserve after a big win, but as a necessary investment in the fullness of your life. The only question is whether you'll find the courage to claim it.

In the words often attributed to William Wordsworth: "To begin, begin."

The time of your life awaits.

Acknowledgments

Writing a book is like a sabbatical. At a distance, it seems imminently manageable. But the closer you get to embarking upon it, the more intimidating and impossible it seems. I could not have completed this book without the help of many people, starting with the sabbatical interviewees who entrusted me with incredibly honest stories about the most vulnerable times in their lives. You profoundly changed the trajectory of my life and will change the lives of many others who hear your stories.

Writing a book is also like starting a company. One of the most challenging parts is the earliest phase, when you alone possess undying confidence in the idea. I was blessed with many people who believed in me and this idea before there was sufficient evidence that anything tangible would ever come of it.

Thank you to the academics who brought rigor to this work: Matt, for your initial research support; Kira Schabram, for getting the project over the finish line; Laura Giurge, for your long-term collaboration; and Bryce Fuemmeler and Ian Rush, for helping synthesize research for the book.

Thanks to those who helped make The Sabbatical Project a reality: Gena Chieco and Russell Woo, for believing in this and for dedicating far too many unpaid hours by my side; Jeanette Mellinger, you too; Jeremiah Chikhwaza, for your indispensable help, company, and cajoling from the very beginning; Juliet Mashiri, you too; Brian Thurber, Justin Ziccardi, Ben Atwood, Dan Parziale, and James Allworth, who gently nudged me off the ledge of "Why isn't this idea in the world?" into "I'm making progress getting this idea into the world!"

Thank you to everyone who helped me translate the project into a book. First and foremost, a deep bow of gratitude to my agent Joy Tutela for your steadfast loyalty, instincts, commitment, and gusto. You remain number one on my list of those to help find a way to get on sabbatical. Thanks as well to Beth Giudicessi, Scott Overdyke, Alex Lazarow, Patrick McGinnis, Abby Falik, Mike Yankoski, Smiley Poswolsky, Nick Soman, Yaw Boateng, Christina Wallace, Aarti Shahani, Zach, Nick and Gayle Grader, and the many, many people who made introductions, shared perspectives on the process, or reviewed materials along the way.

When it came to writing, three communities opened their arms wide and gave me food, shelter, and solace. Chip Conley, Gail DiBerardinis, Teddi Dean, and the rest of the Modern Elder Academy crew in Baja: you stretched my imagination, heart, and stomach. Matt O'Donnell and JB Chaim from Santosha and the Hillholm Writing Residency: thank you for helping me embody my identity as a writer, and for introducing me to so many special authors, like Jenny O'Connell and Tod Lending. Nothing made me feel more sane while writing a book than seeing people who do it for a living struggle almost as much as a newbie like myself. And my local writing community at the Writer's Room of Boston: your presence helped me "stay in the room" and put in the hours necessary to pull this book across the finish line.

Thanks to my editors who became loved ones and loved ones who were sometimes forced into editing. Mom, my first editor, thank you for encoding a passion for books into my DNA. Greg Josiah Larson, thank you for being an editor and collaborator in everything from our high school newspaper to my overwrought sabbatical newsletter to this book (and even my wedding ceremony!). Brenda Copeland, thank you for becoming my writing teacher, along with your furry assistant Edna Munro. You turned the isolating task of writing into a learning experience, and you're number two on my list to help take a sabbatical. Kimberly Meilun, your feedback made the book much better.

Thank you to my early readers, Jon Staff, Natasha Krol, Christina Riechers, Matt Evans, Laurie Santos, Jerry Colonna, and others who provided invaluable feedback.

To the broader Sabbatical Project community, including the coaches, alumni, and everyone working in the space, thank you for making the journey less lonely and more fun.

A final note of gratitude to those who contributed to my own sabbatical: Dad, the Riechers-Baleses, the Kimmellingers, Adam Ziccardi, Rudy Reyes Jr., Jim Sullivan, Bill Evans and the LEO crew, Masako, Makoto, David Gilbert, Anna Fedorova, Matt DiDonna, my exemplar Tim Hobden, Fred Swaniker and the ALU crew in Mauritius, and Yusuf Ahmad, my first-ever interviewee.

Last and indispensably: Kaz. Without your unwavering faith throughout the entire process, this book would not exist. Your support, intellect, and creativity made the ideas in this book, and my life ever since we met, infinitely richer. Looking forward to writing the next chapter together.

Notes

INTRODUCTION

1. Stephen Miller, "Nearly Half of Employees Expect to Leave Vacation Time Unused." SHRM, June 13, 2023, https://www.shrm.org/topics-tools/news/benefits-compensation/nearly-half-of-employees-expect-to-leave-vacation-time-unused--w.

2. John Maynard Keynes, "Economic Possibilities for Our Grandchildren," in *Essays in Persuasion* (London: Macmillan and Co., 1931), 358–73.

3. Derek Thompson, "Workism Is Making Americans Miserable," *Atlantic*, February 24, 2019, https://web.ics.purdue.edu/~drkelly/TheAtlanticThompsonWorkismReligionIdentityAmericansMiserable2019.pdf.

4. Ibid.; MaxWeber, *The Protestant Ethic and the Spirit of Capitalism*, translated by Talcott Parsons (London: George Allen & Unwin, 1930).

5. Deloitte, *2025 Gen Z and Millennial Survey* (New York: Deloitte, 2024), https://www.deloitte.com/content/dam/assets-shared/docs/campaigns/2025/2025-genz-millennial-survey.pdf.

6. "Gen Z Helps Fuel Rise in Sabbaticals," *Axios*, May 3, 2024, https://www.axios.com/2024/05/03/sabbatical-work-meaning-benefits-time-off; Society for Human Resource Management, *June 2023 Insights Forum*, SHRM Executive Network, 2023, https://www.shrm.org/content/dam/en/shrm/executive-network/en-insights-forums/June%202023%20Insights%20Forum.pdf; Roy Maurer, "SHRM Benefits Survey Tracks Least Popular Perks," SHRM, June 27, 2023, https://www.shrm.org/topics-tools/news/benefits-compensation/shrm-benefits-survey-tracks-least-popular-perks.

7. Kim Parker et al., "Majority of Workers Who Quit a Job in 2021 Cite Low Pay, No Opportunities for Advancement, Feeling Disrespected," Pew Research Center, March 9, 2022, https://www.pewresearch.org/short-reads/2022/03/09/majority-of-workers-who-quit-a-job-in-2021-cite-low-pay-no-opportunities-for-advancement-feeling-disrespected/.

8. Kira Schabram et al., "Recover, Explore, Practice: The Transformative Potential of Sabbaticals," *Academy of Management Discoveries* 9, no. 4 (December 2023): 441–68.

CHAPTER 1: SETTING A GOOD EXAMPLE

1. D. H. Schunk and M. K. DiBenedetto, "Motivation and Social Cognitive Theory," *Contemporary Educational Psychology* 60 (2020), Article 101832, https://doi.org/10.1016/j.cedpsych.2019.101832.

2. M. K. Judiesch and K. S. Lyness, "Left Behind? The Impact of Leaves of Absence on Managers' Career Success," *Academy of Management Journal* 42, no. 6 (1999): 641–51.

3. S. Aisenbrey et al., "Is There a Career Penalty for Mothers' Time Out? A Comparison of Germany, Sweden and the United States," *Social Forces* 88, no. 2 (2009): 573–605.

4. International Labour Organization, "Modern Daddy: Norway's Progressive Policy on Paternity Leave," August 1, 2025, https://www.ilo.org/publications/modern-daddy-norways-progressive-policy-paternity-leave.

5. H. Ibarra and O. Obodaru, "Betwixt and Between Identities: Liminal Experience in Contemporary Careers," *Research in Organizational Behavior* 36 (2016): 47–64; W. Bridges, *Transitions: Making Sense of Life's Changes* (Perseus Books, 1980).

6. Ibid.

7. A. Van Gennep, *The Rites of Passage* (University of Chicago Press, 2019; originally published in 1908).

8. S. A. Conroy and A. M. O'Leary-Kelly, "Letting Go and Moving On: Work-Related Identity Loss and Recovery," *Academy of Management Review* 39, no. 1 (2014): 67–87.

9. See, e.g., Ibarra and Obodaru, "Betwixt and Between Identities": 56; W. M. Cohen and D. A. Levinthal, "Absorptive Capacity: A New Perspective on Learning and Innovation," *Administrative Science Quarterly* 35, no. 1 (1990): 128–52; A. D. Brown and K. Starkey, "Organizational Identity and Learning: A Psychodynamic Perspective," *Academy of Management Review* 25, no. 1 (2000): 102–20.

10. Stuart Brown et al., "Seeking Balance in Motion: The Role of Spontaneous Free Play in Promoting Social and Emotional Health in Early Childhood Care and Education," *Frontiers in Psychology* (2016).

11. Herminia Ibarra and Jennifer L. Petriglieri, "Identity Work and Play," *Journal of Organizational Change Management* 23, no. 1 (2010): 10–25, https://doi.org/10.1108/09534811011017180.

12. F. G. Ashby and A. M. Isen, "A Neuropsychological Theory of Positive Affect and Its Influence on Cognition," *Psychological Review* 106, no. 3 (1999): 529.

13. Ibarra and Petriglieri, "Identity Work and Play."

CHAPTER 2: WHAT IS A SABBATICAL?

1. W. C. Eells, "The Origin and Early History of Sabbatical Leave," *AAUP Bulletin* 48, no. 3 (1962): 253–56.

2. A. Linscheid, "In-Service Improvement of the State Teachers College Faculty," doctoral dissertation (Ph.D.) at Teachers College, New York (Bureau of Publications, Teachers College, Columbia University, 1928) ("Leaves of Absence," *Teachers College Contributions to Education*, no. 30: 25–30).

3. Ibid.

4. It's worth noting that academic sabbaticals, though technically the origin of the type of sabbaticals we discuss in this book, are almost always quite different. Most academics take a sabbatical from their teaching and departmental duties, to focus on the responsibilities of their third job—publishing research—which is arguably the most important of the three, because their research record determines whether they are promoted. However, many benefits still accrue not only to the academic, but also to their spouse and children, who often get a year in a different place and mindset.

5. Sabine Sonnentag and Cornelia Niessen, "To Detach or Not to Detach? Two Experimental Studies on the Affective Consequences of Detaching from Work During Non-Work Time," *Frontiers in Psychology* 11 (October 16, 2020), https://doi.org/10.3389/fpsyg.2020.560156.

6. J. E. Marcia, "Development and Validation of Ego-Identity Status," *Journal of Personality and Social Psychology* 3, no. 5 (1966): 551–58, https://doi.org/10.1037/h0023281.

7. F. de Blois, "The Etymology of the Sabbath," UCL Department of Antiquity and Middle Ages, July 15, 2015, https://blogs.ucl.ac.uk/calendars-ancient-medieval-project/2015/07/15/the-etymology-of-sabbath/.

8. Wikipedia contributors, "Sabbatical," Wikipedia, last modified May 31, 2024, https://en.wikipedia.org/wiki/Sabbatical.

9. Philip Sopher, "Where the Five-Day Workweek Came From," *Atlantic*, August 21, 2014, https://www.theatlantic.com/business/archive/2014/08/where-the-five-day-workweek-came-from/378870/.

10. A. J. Heschel, *The Sabbath* (Macmillan, 1951), 8.

11. Ibid.

12. Estimate constructed from National Institute on Aging, "Maintaining Mobility and Preventing Disability Are Key to Living Independently as We Age," National Institute on Aging, February 15, 2023, https://www.nia.nih.gov/news/maintaining-mobility-and-preventing-disability-are-key-living-independently-we-age.

CHAPTER 3: WORKING ON TIME OFF

1. Blake E. Ashforth and Beth S. Schinoff, "Identity Under Construction: How Individuals Come to Define Themselves in Organizations," *Annual Review of Organizational Psychology and Organizational Behavior* 3 (2016): 111–37, https://doi.org/10.1146/annurev-orgpsych-041015-062322.

2. R. J. Schlegel et al., "Feeling Like You Know Who You Are: Perceived True Self-Knowledge and Meaning in Life," *Personality and Social Psychology Bulletin* 37, no. 6 (2011): 745–56, https://doi.org/10.1177/0146167211400424.

3. W. A. Kahn, "Psychological Conditions of Personal Engagement and Disengagement at Work," *Academy of Management Journal* 33, no. 4 (December 1, 1990): 692–724, https://doi.org/10.2307/256287.

4. Hazel Markus and Paula Nurius, "Possible Selves," *American Psychologist* 41, no. 9 (1986): 954–69, https://web.stanford.edu/~hazelm/publications/1986_Markus%20&%20Nurius_PossibleSelves.pdf.

5. Herminia Ibarra, "Provisional Selves: Experimenting with Image and Identity in Professional Adaptation," *Administrative Science Quarterly* 44, no. 4 (1999): 764–91.

6. Sabine Sonnentag and Fritz Ute-Friedriche, "Recovery from Work: The Stressor-Detachment Model as an Integrative Framework," *Journal of Organizational Behavior* 28, no. 7 (2007): 738–62.

7. Sabine Sonnentag and Monika Wiegelmann, "Not Detaching from Work During Leisure Time: A Control-Theory Perspective on Job-Related Cognitions," *Journal of Organizational Behavior* 45 (2024): 1,003–24, https://doi.org/10.1002/job.2792.

8. Stephen Cope, *The Great Work of Your Life: A Guide for the Journey to Your True Calling* (New York: Bantam Books, 2012).

9. Laura J. Kray et al., "From What Might Have Been to What Must Have Been: Counterfactual Thinking Creates Meaning," *Journal of Personality and Social Psychology* 98, no. 1 (2010): 106–18, https://doi.org/10.1037/a0017344.

CHAPTER 4: CATALYSTS, ARCHETYPES, AND BARRIERS

1. See, e.g., Ingrid Boveda and A. J. Metz, "Predicting End-of-Career Transitions for Baby Boomers Nearing Retirement Age," *Career Development Quarterly* 64, no. 2 (2016): 153–68; Carsten Wrosch et al., "The Importance of Goal Disengagement in Adaptive Self-Regulation: When Giving Up Is Beneficial," *Self and Identity* 2, no. 1 (2003): 1–20; Jungmeen E. Kim and Phyllis Moen, "Retirement Transitions, Gender, and Psychological Well-Being: A Life-Course, Ecological Model," *Journals of Gerontology Series B: Psychological Sciences and Social Sciences* 57, no. 3 (2002): P212–P222.

2. Mike Tyson, *Undisputed Truth* (New York: Blue Rider Press, 2013).

3. William Samuelson and Richard Zeckhauser, "Status Quo Bias in Decision Making," *Journal of Risk and Uncertainty* 1 (1988): 7–59.

4. H. Patrick et al., "The Role of Need Fulfillment in Relationship Functioning and Well-Being: A Self-Determination Theory Perspective," *Journal of Personality and Social Psychology* 92, no. 3 (2007): 434–57.

5. George A. Bonanno, "Loss, Trauma, and Human Resilience: Have We Underestimated the Human Capacity to Thrive After Extremely Aversive Events?" *American Psychologist* 59, no. 1 (2004): 20–28, https://doi.org/10.1037/0003-066X.59.1.20; S. Filep and J. Laing, "What Is Positive Tourism? Why Do We Need It?" in S. Filep, J. Laing, and M. Csikszentmihalyi, eds., *Positive Tourism* (Routledge, 2017), 3–15; and Mihaly Csikszentmihalyi and Jeanne Nakamura, "The Dynamics of Intrinsic Motivation: A Study of Adolescents," *Motivation and Emotion* 18, no. 1 (1994): 9–22, https://doi.org/10.1007/BF02249374.

6. Robert Eisenberger and Rebecca Huntington, "Perceived Organizational Support," *Journal of Applied Psychology* 71, no. 5 (1986): 500–507, https://doi.org/10.1037/0021-9010.71.5.500.

7. Karsten I. Paul and Klaus Moser, "Unemployment Impairs Mental Health: Meta-Analyses," *Journal of Vocational Behavior* 74, no. 3 (2009): 264–82.

8. Erin A. Cech and Mary Blair-Loy, "The Ideal Worker Norm and Workplace Social Support Among U.S. Workers," *Sociological Perspectives* 64, no. 1 (2021): 5–26, https://doi.org/10.1177/0731121421991432.

9. "Unlimited Vacation Plans May Lead to Fewer Days Off," *Namely Blog*, 2018, https://www.hr-brew.com/stories/2023/06/08/unlimited-versus-traditional-pto.

10. Sarah M. Grubbs, "Work-Life Balance and Parental Leave: Challenges and Benefits for Working Parents," master's thesis, Indiana University–Purdue University, Indianapolis, 2019, https://scholarworks.indianapolis.iu.edu/server/api/core

/bitstreams/06c3f1af-6f4f-40ac-96ca-571f3cb9af0e/content; David Matthews, "Sweden: Where It's Taboo for Dads to Skip Parental Leave," *BBC Worklife*, January 30, 2024, https://www.bbc.com/worklife/article/20240130-sweden-where-its-taboo-for-dads-to-skip-parental-leave; Richard J. Petts, "Stay-at-Home Fathers: Do Gender Role Attitudes and Household Labor Matter?" *Journal of Marriage and Family* 69, no. 3 (2007): 516–31, https://doi.org/10.1111/j.1741-3737.2006.00258.x; Seeta Bhardwa, "Paternity Leave: The Hidden Barriers Keeping Men at Work," *BBC Worklife*, July 12, 2021, https://www.bbc.com/worklife/article/20210712-paternity-leave-the-hidden-barriers-keeping-men-at-work.

11. Chartered Management Institute, *The Flexible Future: Managers' Attitudes Toward Sabbaticals and Time Off* (London: CMI, 2024), https://www.managers.org.uk/knowledge-and-insights/news/time-off-and-sabbaticals-report-2024/.

12. "Workers Are Taking More Sabbatical Time," Gusto, June 6, 2023, https://gusto.com/company-news/workers-are-taking-more-sabbatical-time.

13. Jayne O'Donnell, "Career Breaks Are Common—So Why Are We Still Hiding Them on Resumes?" *CNBC Make It*, November 6, 2023, https://www.cnbc.com/2023/11/07/career-breaks-are-common-so-why-are-we-still-hiding-them-on-resumes.html.

14. Sangheon Lee et al., *Working Time Around the World: Trends in Working Hours, Laws and Policies in a Global Comparative Perspective* (Geneva: International Labour Office, 2013), https://www.ilo.org/sites/default/files/wcmsp5/groups/public/@dgreports/@dcomm/@publ/documents/publication/wcms_242615.pdf; International Labour Organization, *Care Work and Care Jobs for the Future of Decent Work* (Geneva: International Labour Office, 2018), https://www.ilo.org/sites/default/files/wcmsp5/groups/public/@dgreports/@dcomm/@publ/documents/publication/wcms_604882.pdf.

15. Holly Elser, Connor Williams, William H. Dow, and Julia M. Goodman, "Inequities in Paid Parental Leave Across Industry and Occupational Class: Drivers and Simulated Policy Remedies," *SSM—Population Health* 18 (June 2022): 101045, https://doi.org/10.1016/j.ssmph.2022.101045.

16. Harris Cooper, Barbara Nye, Kelly Charlton, James Lindsay, and Scott Greathouse, "The Effects of Summer Vacation on Achievement Test Scores: A Narrative and Meta-Analytic Review," *Review of Educational Research* 66, no. 3 (1996): 227–68.

CHAPTER 5: INFLECTION POINTS

1. Ariella S. Kristal et al., "Reducing Discrimination Against Job Seekers with and without Employment Gaps," *Nature Human Behaviour* 7, no. 2 (2023): 211–18, https://doi.org/10.1038/s41562-022-01485-6.

2. Robert Chess and Jocelyn H. Hornblower, "iRelaunch: From Career Break to Career Re-entry," Stanford Graduate School of Business Case No. SM325 (2020), 6.

3. Katharine Zaleski, "Diversity in the Workplace Benefits: 5 Studies to Take to Your Boss," iRelaunch, March 9, 2022, https://www.irelaunch.com/blog/diversity-in-the-workplace-benefits-5-studies-to-take-to-your-boss.

4. Myra M. Hart et al., "Carol Fishman Cohen: Professional Career Reentry (A) and (B)," Harvard Business School Case 803-185, May 2003 (revised March 2006) and https://www.irelaunch.com/; "The 40-Year-Old Intern," *Harvard Business Review*, November 2012, https://hbr.org/2012/11/the-40-year-old-intern; Carol Fishman Cohen, "Return-to-Work Programs Come of Age," *Harvard Business Review*, September 2021, https://hbr.org/2021/09/return-to-work-programs-come-of-age.

5. US Bureau of Labor Statistics, *Number of Jobs, Labor Market Experience, Marital Status, and Health for Those Born 1957–1964* (Washington, DC: U.S. Department of Labor, August 22, 2023), https://www.bls.gov/news.release/nlsoy.nr0.htm.

6. D. T. Hall, *Careers in Organizations* (Glenview, IL: Scott Foresman and Co., 1976).

7. Anne Herrmann et al., "The Protean Career Orientation as Predictor of Career Outcomes: Evaluation of Incremental Validity and Mediation Effects," *Journal of Vocational Behavior* 88 (June 1, 2015): 205–14, https://doi.org/10.1016/j.jvb.2015.03.008.

CHAPTER 6: FEELING HUMAN AGAIN

1. B. W. Smit et al., "Out of Sight, Out of Mind? How and When Cognitive Role Transition Episodes Influence Employee Performance," *Human Relations* 69, no. 11 (2016): 2,141–68, https://doi.org/10.1177/0018726716636204.

2. J. Fisher, "Workforce Burnout Survey," Deloitte, 2015, https://www2.deloitte.com/us/en/pages/about-deloitte/articles/burnout-survey.html.

3. Cassie Mogilner West and Sanford E. DeVoe, *How Vacation Increases Happiness: A Developmental Perspective* (UCLA Anderson School of Management, 2019), https://www.anderson.ucla.edu/documents/sites/faculty/review%20publications/research/West-Mogilner-DeVoe2019_How_Vacation_Increases_Happiness.pdf.

4. Jessica de Bloom et al., "Vacation (after-) Effects on Employee Health and Well-Being, and the Role of Vacation Activities, Experiences and Sleep," *Journal of Happiness Studies* 14, no. 2 (May 12, 2012): 613–33, https://doi.org/10.1007/s10902-012-9345-3.

5. Jessica de Bloom et al., "Do We Recover from Vacation? Meta-analysis of Vacation Effects on Health and Well-Being," *Journal of Occupational Health* 51, no. 1 (January 1, 2009): 13–25, https://doi.org/10.1539/joh.k8004.

6. S. E. Hobfoll, "The Influence of Culture, Community, and the Nested-Self in the Stress Process: Advancing Conservation of Resources Theory," *Applied Psychology: An International Review* 50, no. 3 (2001): 337–70.

7. O. B. Davidson et al., "Sabbatical Leave: Who Gains and How Much?" *Journal of Applied Psychology* 95, no. 5 (2010): 953.

8. Philip Brickman and Donald T. Campbell, "Hedonic Relativism and Planning the Good Society," in Mortimer H. Appley, ed., *Adaptation-Level Theory: A Symposium* (Academic Press, 1971), 287–305.

9. Annie Dillard, *The Writing Life* (New York: Harper & Row, 1989), 32.

10. Conversation with the author, June 16, 2020.

11. Stéfanie André et al., "Fathers, Families, and Society: A Two-Decade Systematic Literature Review on the Contexts and Consequences of Paternity and Parental Leave for Fathers," *Social Sciences* 14, no. 3 (March 10, 2025): 168, https://doi.org/10.3390/socsci14030168; Linda Haas, *Policy Is Not Enough: The Influence of the Gendered Workplace on Fathers' Use of Parental Leave in Sweden* (Stockholm: Jämlikhetskommissionen, 2019), https://jamstalltstockholm.se/app/uploads/2024/01/Haas_2019_policy-is-not-enough.pdf.

12. M. Nisen, "How McKinsey Does Work-Life Balance," *Quartz*, September 21, 2014, https://qz.com/267489/how-mckinsey-does-work-life-balance/.

13. A. Wynn and Aliya Haimid Rao, "The Stigma That Keeps Consultants from Using Flex Time," *Harvard Business Review*, May 2, 2019, https://hbr.org/2019/05/the-stigma-that-keeps-consultants-from-using-flex-time.

14. G. Lewis and Joseph Sorongon, "Industries with the Highest (and Lowest) Turnover Rates," *LinkedIn Talent Blog*, August 11, 2022, https://business.linkedin.com/talent-solutions/blog/trends-and-research/2018/the-3-industries-with-the-highest-turnover-rates.

15. Harvard Study of Adult Development, *Adult Development Study*, accessed June 23, 2025, https://www.adultdevelopmentstudy.org/.

16. Dilip V. Jeste and Maja Gawronska, "Triumphs of Experience: The Men of the Harvard Grant Study," *American Journal of Psychiatry* 171, no. 2 (February 1, 2014): 230–31, https://doi.org/10.1176/appi.ajp.2013.13111502. Note: Not an incredible diversity of participants, who were mostly white men (including one John F. Kennedy Jr.) at an elite Ivy League university. However, the study

was later expanded to include a more representative sample from the Boston area, now tracking their children and spouses as well.

CHAPTER 7: HEALING AND FINDING YOURSELF

1. "Still Only 2–3% of US Students Take Gap Year," *Gap Year Solutions* (blog), December 21, 2023, accessed October 6, 2025, https://gapyearsolutions.com/blog/still-only-2-3-of-us-students-take-gap-year/.

2. Dennis Cauchon, "Time Out or Burn-Out for the Next Generation?" *New York Times*, December 6, 2000, https://www.nytimes.com/2000/12/06/national/time-out-or-burn-out-for-the-next-generation.html; William Fitzsimmons et al., "Time Out or Burn Out for the Next Generation," Harvard College (Admissions), 2000, PDF, https://explorientation.com/wp-content/uploads/2014/05/Time_out_or_burn_out_Harvard_Admissions.pdf.

3. Ibid.

4. FAS Student Services, *How to Take a Leave of Absence*, Harvard University, accessed October 9, 2025, https://studentservices.fas.harvard.edu/how-take-leave-absence.

5. Harvard College, "Considering a Gap Year," Harvard College Admissions, accessed June 23, 2025, https://college.harvard.edu/admissions/apply/first-year-applicants/considering-gap-year.

6. Office of International Programs, Princeton University, "Novogratz Bridge Year Program," Princeton University, accessed October 10, 2024, https://oip.princeton.edu/our-programs/novogratz-bridge-year.

7. Gap Year Association, *Gap Year Alumni Survey 2020 Supplemented with 2015 AmeriCorps National Civilian Community Corps Survey Data*, 2020, https://www.gapyearassociation.org/gap-year-research/.

8. Anna Nickerson, "The Search for Data on Gap Year Effectiveness: An Interview with Bob Clagett," *Gap Year Solutions* (blog), August 24, 2020, https://gapyearsolutions.com/blog/the-search-for-data-on-gap-year-effectiveness-an-interview-with-bob-clagett/.

9. Gap Year Research Consortium at Colorado College, *Gap Year Research Outcomes: Academic Outcomes*, 2012, https://sites.coloradocollege.edu/gapyearresearchconsortium/gap-year-research-outcomes/academic-outcomes/.

10. Ibid.

11. E. Rose Birch and P. W. Miller, "The Characteristics of 'Gap-Year' Students and Their Tertiary Academic Outcomes," *Economic Record* 83, no. 262 (2007): 329–44.

12. A. J. Martin, "Should Students Have a Gap Year? Motivation and Performance Factors Relevant to Time Out After Completing School," *Journal of Educational Psychology* 102, no. 3 (2010): 561–76, https://doi.org/10.1037/a0019321.

13. Robert Kegan, *The Evolving Self: Problem and Process in Human Development* (Cambridge, MA: Harvard University Press, 1982).

14. W. Deresiewicz, "Don't Send Your Kid to the Ivy League: The Nation's Top Colleges Are Turning Our Kids into Zombies," *New Republic*, July 21, 2014, https://newrepublic.com/article/118747/william-deresiewicz-ivy-league-elite-education-waste.

15. Marcia B. Baxter-Magolda, "Self-Authorship: The Foundation for Twenty-First-Century Education," *New Directions for Teaching and Learning* 109 (2007): 69–83, https://doi.org/10.1002/tl.266.

16. WHO World Mental Health Surveys International College Student Project: Prevalence and Distribution of Mental Disorders, *Journal of Abnormal Psychology* 127, no. 7: 623–38, https://doi.org/10.1037/abn0000362.

17. Dennis Cauchon, "Time Out or Burn-Out for the Next Generation?" *New York Times*, December 6, 2000, https://www.nytimes.com/2000/12/06/national/time-out-or-burn-out-for-the-next-generation.html.

18. World Health Organization, *Burn-Out an "Occupational Phenomenon": International Classification of Diseases* (Geneva: World Health Organization, 2019), https://www.who.int/news/item/28-05-2019-burn-out-an-occupational-phenomenon-international-classification-of-diseases.

19. Jonathan Malesic, *The End of Burnout: Why Work Drains Us and How to Build Better Lives* (Berkeley: University of California Press, 2022).

20. C. Maslach and S. E. Jackson, "The Measurement of Experienced Burnout," *Journal of Occupational Behaviour* 2, no. 2 (1981): 99–113, https://doi.org/10.1002/job.4030020205.

21. Stevan E. Hobfoll, "Conservation of Resources: A New Attempt at Conceptualizing Stress," *American Psychologist* 44, no. 3 (1989): 513–524, https://doi.org/10.1037/0003-066X.44.3.513.

CHAPTER 8: SEEKING PERMISSION

1. Email correspondence with Bill Williams from July 2019 to June 2024.

2. Health of Munition Workers Committee, *Memoranda on Industrial Fatigue and Hours of Labour* (London: Ministry of Munitions, 1917); Royal Economic Society, "The Health of Munition Workers Committee," *Economic*

Journal 27, no. 105 (March 1917): 86–90; and International Labour Organization, Hours of Work (Industry) Convention, 1919 (No. 1), adopted November 28, 1919.

3. John A. Byrne, "The MBA Bump: MBA Grads Now Get an $85K Bump Over Pre-MBA Pay," *Poets & Quants*, March 10, 2023, https://poetsandquants.com/2023/03/10/mba-pay-increase/.

4. Yehuda Baruch and Maury Peiperl, "The Impact of an MBA on Graduate Careers," *Human Resource Management Journal* 10, no. 2 (2000): 69–90.

5. Ibid.

6. G. Petriglieri and J. L. Petriglieri, "Identity Workspaces: The Case of Business Schools," *Academy of Management Learning & Education* 9, no. 1 (2010): 44–60.

7. G. E. Kreiner et al., "Where Is the 'Me' Among the 'We'? Identity Work and the Search for Optimal Balance," *Academy of Management Journal* 49 (2006): 1,031–57.

8. Petriglieri and Petriglieri, "Identity Workspaces."

9. A. Van Gennep, *Les Rites de Passage* (Paris: Émile Nourry, 1909).

10. National Center for Education Statistics, "Graduate Degree Fields," *Condition of Education*, U.S. Department of Education, accessed June 12, 2025, https://nces.ed.gov/programs/coe/indicator/ctb/graduate-degree-fields.

11. Ashlee Vance and Claire Cain Miller, "6 Months, $90,000 and (Maybe) a Great Idea," *New York Times*, February 27, 2010, https://www.nytimes.com/2010/02/28/technology/start-ups/28eir.html.

12. D. M. Rosenblatt and A. J. Thelen, "Entrepreneur-in-Residence Programs: A Survey and Analysis," *Journal of Private Equity* (1997): 37–47; J. Schwarzkopf et al., "How Entrepreneurs-in-Residence Increase Seed Investment Rates," *Venture Capital* 12, no. 1 (2010): 65–81.

CHAPTER 9: FIRST PRINCIPLES

1. Jessica K. Bone et al., "Creative Leisure Activities, Mental Health and Well-Being During 5 Months of the COVID-19 Pandemic: A Fixed Effects Analysis of Data from 3725 US Adults," *Journal of Epidemiology and Community Health* 77, no. 5 (May 2023): 293–97.

CHAPTER 10: PREPARING, DEPARTING, AND COMING BACK

1. Eric Weiner, "Why We Like People Who Ask Us for Favors," *Time*, June 11, 2024, https://time.com/6987094/doing-favors-benjamin-franklin-effect-essay/;

L. Dossey, "The Helper's High," *Explore (NY)* 14, no. 6 (November 14, 2018): 393–99, doi: 10.1016/j.explore.2018.10.003, epub October 23, 2018.

2. William Maddux and Adam Galinsky, "Cultural Borders and Mental Barriers: The Relationship Between Living Abroad and Creativity," *Journal of Personality and Social Psychology* 96, no. 5 (May 2009): 1,047–61; D. S. DeRue et al., "Learning Agility: In Search of Conceptual Clarity and Theoretical Grounding," *Academy of Management Journal* 55, no. 6 (2012): 1,316–37; J. D. Campbell et al., "Self-Concept Clarity: Measurement, Personality Correlates, and Cultural Boundaries," *Journal of Personality and Social Psychology* 70, no. 1 (1996): 141–56.

3. M. J. Poulin et al., "Giving to Others and the Association Between Stress and Mortality," *American Journal of Public Health* 103, no. 9 (September 2013):1,649–55.

4. K. I. Paul and K. Moser, "Unemployment Impairs Mental Health: Meta-Analyses," *Journal of Vocational Behavior* 74, no. 3 (2009): 264–82, https://doi.org/10.1016/j.jvb.2009.01.001; C. R. Wanberg, "The Individual Experience of Unemployment," *Annual Review of Psychology* 63 (2012): 369–96, https://doi.org/10.1146/annurev-psych-120710-100500.

5. Marie Jahoda, *Employment and Unemployment: A Social-Psychological Analysis* (Cambridge University Press, 1982).

CHAPTER 12: THE UPSIDE AT WORK

1. Michael Boyles, "The Importance of Creativity in Business," *Business Insights* (blog), Harvard Business School, last modified July 20, 2023, https://online.hbs.edu/blog/post/importance-of-creativity-in-business.

2. Gregory Bateson and Paul Martin, "Play, Playfulness, Creativity and Innovation," *Animal Behavior and Cognition* 1, no. 2 (2014): 99–112.

3. Fekadu Beyene Tessema and Fikremariam Abebe Tebeje, "Family-Work Resource Spillover Effects on Employee Creativity: The Mediating Role of Organizational Innovation Climate," *Journal of Business Research* 145 (2022): 113468, https://doi.org/10.1016/j.jbusres.2022.113468.

4. Chris Ford, interview with author, June 12, 2018.

5. HBC Boulder, "Recruiting," accessed June 12, 2025, https://www.hbcboulder.com/recruiting.

6. Board of Governors of the Federal Reserve System, "Supervisory Guidance on Required Absences from Sensitive Positions," SR 96-37 (December 20, 1996), PDF, 1, https://www.federalreserve.gov/supervisionreg/srletters/SR9637.pdf.

7. Jim Collins, "In the Right Seats," JimCollins.com, accessed June 12, 2025, https://www.jimcollins.com/media_topics/inTheRightSeats.html.

8. Alison Wynn and Aliya Hamid Rao, "The Stigma That Keeps Consultants from Using Flex Time," *Harvard Business Review*, May 2, 2019, https://hbr.org/2019/05/the-stigma-that-keeps-consultants-from-using-flex-time.

9. Syndio, "Loyalty No Longer Pays: New Employees Make the Same or More Than Tenured in 83% of High-Paying Jobs," April 20, 2023, https://synd.io/press-release/tenure-and-pay/; and Michael J. O'Brien, "Study: Employee Longevity Often Doesn't Pay," *Workspan Daily*, April 28, 2023, WorldatWork, https://worldatwork.org/publications/workspan-daily/study-employee-longevity-often-doesn-t-pay.

10. Pier A. Abetti, "Case Study: Jack Welch's Creative Revolutionary Transformation of General Electric and the Thermidorean Reaction (1981–2004)," *Creativity and Innovation Management* 15, no. 1 (2006): 74–84, https://onlinelibrary.wiley.com/doi/pdf/10.1111/j.1467-8691.2006.00370.x.

11. Deborah Linnell and Tim Wolfred, *Creative Disruption: Sabbaticals for Capacity Building and Leadership Development in the Nonprofit Sector*, CompassPoint Nonprofit Services & Third Sector New England, April 2009.

12. "Employees Who Feel Aligned with Company Values Are More Likely to Stay," Qualtrics, April 25, 2022, accessed October 6, 2025, https://www.qualtrics.com/articles/employee-experience/company-values-employee-retention/.

13. Google modeled their program after the one started in 1948 by 3M. See, e.g., "Life with 3M," 3M, 2024, https://www.3m.com/3M/en_US/careers-us/workingat3m/life-with-3m/.

14. SAP News Center, "SAP Social Sabbatical in Action," December 2022, SAP, https://news.sap.com/2022/12/sap-social-sabbatical-resiliency-and-impact-in-action; and Johnson & Johnson, "A Johnson & Johnson Program Lets Employees Take Paid Time Off to Volunteer," *J&J News*, April 23, 2017, https://www.jnj.com/caring-and-giving/johnson-and-johnson-program-lets-employees-take-paid-time-off-work-to-do-good-national-volunteer-week.

15. Charles Schwab, "Schwab's Time to Volunteer," Schwab Jobs, https://www.schwabjobs.com/time-to-volunteer-at-schwab.

16. Eva Boštjančič et al., "Corporate Volunteering: Relationship to Job Resources and Work Engagement," *Frontiers in Psychology* 9 (October 3, 2018): 1,884.

17. Tyler Williams, interview with the author, Las Vegas, May 10, 2022.

18. Adam Robinson, "Zappos Pays Employees $2,000 to Quit. This Superstar CEO Has a Different Approach," *Inc.*, January 12, 2018, https://www.inc.com

/adam-robinson/zappos-pays-employees-2000-to-quit-this-superstar-ceo-has-a-different-approach.html.

19. Warren E. Buffett, "1989 Letter to Shareholders," Berkshire Hathaway Inc., March 2, 1990, https://www.berkshirehathaway.com/letters/1989.html.

20. Tania Gaspar et al., "Burnout as a Multidimensional Phenomenon: How Can Workplaces Be Healthy Environments?" *Zeitschrift für Gesundheitswissenschaften* (*Journal of Public Health*) (2024), https://doi.org/10.1007/s10389-024-02223-0; Z. Zhao et al., "The Mediating Effect of Job Burnout on Perceived Stress and Presenteeism Among Geriatric Caregivers in Long-Term Care Facilities," *Journal of Geriatric Oncology* (forthcoming), https://www.sciencedirect.com/science/article/pii/S0197457224004452; Ana Catarina Vaz et al., "Presenteeism and Burnout in Nurses: A Review of the Literature," *Encyclopedia* 5, no. 3 (2025): 93, https://doi.org/10.3390/encyclopedia5030093; and Gallup, "Employee Burnout: Causes and Cures," Gallup Workplace Report, 2020, https://www.vanede.nl/media/2669/gallup-iii-employee-burnout.pdf.

21. *Leave Management and HR Trends Report 2024* (New York: NFP, 2024), https://www.nfp.com/insights/leave-management-and-hr-trends-report-2024; "Gen Z Helps Fuel Rise in Sabbaticals," *Axios*, May 3, 2024, https://www.axios.com/2024/05/03/sabbatical-work-meaning-benefits-time-off; and Society for Human Resource Management, *June 2023 Insights Forum*, SHRM Executive Network, https://www.shrm.org/content/dam/en/shrm/executive-network/en-insights-forums/June%202023%20Insights%20Forum.pdf.

22. Sean Fleming, "Sweden Gives All Employees Time Off to Be Entrepreneurs," World Economic Forum, February 11, 2019, https://www.weforum.org/stories/2019/02/sweden-gives-all-employees-time-off-to-be-entrepreneurs/.

CHAPTER 13: TROUBLESHOOTING AND RETURNING FROM SABBATICAL

1. William Bridges, *Transitions: Making Sense of Life's Changes*, rev. ed. (Da Capo Press, 2004), 141–42.

2. Joseph Campbell, *The Hero with a Thousand Faces* (Princeton University Press, 1949), 109–10.

Index

Index

Index

Index

Index

Index

Index

Index

Index

Index

Index

Index

About the Author

DJ DiDonna is a senior lecturer of business administration at Harvard Business School, where he teaches MBA courses on entrepreneurship and building meaningful professional and personal lives. He has spent his career translating social science research into real-world tools for positive change.

In 2019, DiDonna founded The Sabbatical Project to define, explore, and research the role of sabbaticals in modern life. He has helped organizations around the world—from nonprofits to Fortune 50 companies—design and implement sabbatical policies. His work has been featured in *The Atlantic*, *Harvard Business Review*, *Time*, *Fast Company*, *The Wall Street Journal*, and *The New York Times*. Previously, DiDonna cofounded EFL Global, a fintech company that made more than $2 billion in capital available to underbanked businesses and individuals across twenty countries before its acquisition in 2018. DiDonna earned his MBA from Harvard Business School.

On his sabbatical, DiDonna walked nine hundred miles on a pilgrimage in Shikoku, Japan; helped lead the Wilson Sheehan Lab for Economic Opportunities at his undergraduate alma mater, Notre Dame; and unskillfully remodeled his kitchen. Outside work, you can find him plotting how to be in the Big Outdoors.

Learn more at www.thesabbaticalproject.org.